I0188711

Access Your Online Resources

Don't miss out on the Online Resources included with your purchase!

Your purchase of this product unlocks access to our Online Resources page. Elevate your study experience with our **interactive practice test interface**, along with all of the additional resources that we couldn't include in this book.

Flip to the Online Resources section at the end of this book to find the link and a QR code to get started!

Mechanical Aptitude Test

Secrets

Study Guide

Your Key to Exam Success

Written and edited by the Mometrix Workplace Aptitude Test Team

Mometrix offers volume discount pricing to institutions. For more information or a price quote, please contact our sales department at sales@mometrix.com or 888-248-1219.

Paperback
ISBN 13: 978-1-62733-975-9
ISBN 10: 1-62733-975-2

Ebook
ISBN 13: 978-1-5167-0464-4
ISBN 10: 1-5167-0464-9

Hardback
ISBN 13: 978-1-5167-0532-0
ISBN 10: 1-5167-0532-7

Dear Future Exam Success Story

First of all, **THANK YOU** for purchasing Mometrix study materials!

Second, congratulations! You are one of the few determined test-takers who are committed to doing whatever it takes to excel on your exam. **You have come to the right place.** We developed these study materials with one goal in mind: to deliver you the information you need in a format that's concise and easy to use.

In addition to optimizing your guide for the content of the test, we've outlined our recommended steps for breaking down the preparation process into small, attainable goals so you can make sure you stay on track.

We've also analyzed the entire test-taking process, identifying the most common pitfalls and showing how you can overcome them and be ready for any curveball the test throws you.

Standardized testing is one of the biggest obstacles on your road to success, which only increases the importance of doing well in the high-pressure, high-stakes environment of test day. Your results on this test could have a significant impact on your future, and this guide provides the information and practical advice to help you achieve your full potential on test day.

Your success is our success

We would love to hear from you! If you would like to share the story of your exam success or if you have any questions or comments in regard to our products, please contact us at **800-673-8175** or **support@mometrix.com**.

Thanks again for your business and we wish you continued success!

Sincerely,
The Mometrix Test Preparation Team

Table of Contents

Introduction

Thank you for purchasing this resource! You have made the choice to prepare yourself for a test that could have a huge impact on your future, and this guide is designed to help you be fully ready for test day. Obviously, it's important to have a solid understanding of the test material, but you also need to be prepared for the unique environment and stressors of the test, so that you can perform to the best of your abilities.

For this purpose, the first section that appears in this guide is the **Secret Keys**. We've devoted countless hours to meticulously researching what works and what doesn't, and we've boiled down our findings to the five most impactful steps you can take to improve your performance on the test. We start at the beginning with study planning and move through the preparation process, all the way to the testing strategies that will help you get the most out of what you know when you're finally sitting in front of the test.

We recommend that you start preparing for your test as far in advance as possible. However, if you've bought this guide as a last-minute study resource and only have a few days before your test, we recommend that you skip over the first two Secret Keys since they address a long-term study plan.

If you struggle with **test anxiety**, we strongly encourage you to check out our recommendations for how you can overcome it. Test anxiety is a formidable foe, but it can be beaten, and we want to make sure you have the tools you need to defeat it.

Secret Key #1 – Plan Big, Study Small

There's a lot riding on your performance. If you want to ace this test, you're going to need to keep your skills sharp and the material fresh in your mind. You need a plan that lets you review everything you need to know while still fitting in your schedule. We'll break this strategy down into three categories.

Information Organization

Start with the information you already have: the official test outline. From this, you can make a complete list of all the concepts you need to cover before the test. Organize these concepts into groups that can be studied together, and create a list of any related vocabulary you need to learn so you can brush up on any difficult terms. You'll want to keep this vocabulary list handy once you actually start studying since you may need to add to it along the way.

Time Management

Once you have your set of study concepts, decide how to spread them out over the time you have left before the test. Break your study plan into small, clear goals so you have a manageable task for each day and know exactly what you're doing. Then just focus on one small step at a time. When you manage your time this way, you don't need to spend hours at a time studying. Studying a small block of content for a short period each day helps you retain information better and avoid stressing over how much you have left to do. You can relax knowing that you have a plan to cover everything in time. In order for this strategy to be effective though, you have to start studying early and stick to your schedule. Avoid the exhaustion and futility that comes from last-minute cramming!

Study Environment

The environment you study in has a big impact on your learning. Studying in a coffee shop, while probably more enjoyable, is not likely to be as fruitful as studying in a quiet room. It's important to keep distractions to a minimum. You're only planning to study for a short block of time, so make the most of it. Don't pause to check your phone or get up to find a snack. It's also important to **avoid multitasking**. Research has consistently shown that multitasking will make your studying dramatically less effective. Your study area should also be comfortable and well-lit so you don't have the distraction of straining your eyes or sitting on an uncomfortable chair.

The time of day you study is also important. You want to be rested and alert. Don't wait until just before bedtime. Study when you'll be most likely to comprehend and remember. Even better, if you know what time of day your test will be, set that time aside for study. That way your brain will be used to working on that subject at that specific time and you'll have a better chance of recalling information.

Finally, it can be helpful to team up with others who are studying for the same test. Your actual studying should be done in as isolated an environment as possible, but the work of organizing the information and setting up the study plan can be divided up. In between study sessions, you can discuss with your teammates the concepts that you're all studying and quiz each other on the details. Just be sure that your teammates are as serious about the test as you are. If you find that your study time is being replaced with social time, you might need to find a new team.

Secret Key #2 – Make Your Studying Count

You're devoting a lot of time and effort to preparing for this test, so you want to be absolutely certain it will pay off. This means doing more than just reading the content and hoping you can remember it on test day. It's important to make every minute of study count. There are two main areas you can focus on to make your studying count.

Retention

It doesn't matter how much time you study if you can't remember the material. You need to make sure you are retaining the concepts. To check your retention of the information you're learning, try recalling it at later times with minimal prompting. Try carrying around flashcards and glance at one or two from time to time or ask a friend who's also studying for the test to quiz you.

To enhance your retention, look for ways to put the information into practice so that you can apply it rather than simply recalling it. If you're using the information in practical ways, it will be much easier to remember. Similarly, it helps to solidify a concept in your mind if you're not only reading it to yourself but also explaining it to someone else. Ask a friend to let you teach them about a concept you're a little shaky on (or speak aloud to an imaginary audience if necessary). As you try to summarize, define, give examples, and answer your friend's questions, you'll understand the concepts better and they will stay with you longer. Finally, step back for a big picture view and ask yourself how each piece of information fits with the whole subject. When you link the different concepts together and see them working together as a whole, it's easier to remember the individual components.

Finally, practice showing your work on any multi-step problems, even if you're just studying. Writing out each step you take to solve a problem will help solidify the process in your mind, and you'll be more likely to remember it during the test.

Modality

Modality simply refers to the means or method by which you study. Choosing a study modality that fits your own individual learning style is crucial. No two people learn best in exactly the same way, so it's important to know your strengths and use them to your advantage.

For example, if you learn best by visualization, focus on visualizing a concept in your mind and draw an image or a diagram. Try color-coding your notes, illustrating them, or creating symbols that will trigger your mind to recall a learned concept. If you learn best by hearing or discussing information, find a study partner who learns the same way or read aloud to yourself. Think about how to put the information in your own words. Imagine that you are giving a lecture on the topic and record yourself so you can listen to it later.

For any learning style, flashcards can be helpful. Organize the information so you can take advantage of spare moments to review. Underline key words or phrases. Use different colors for different categories. Mnemonic devices (such as creating a short list in which every item starts with the same letter) can also help with retention. Find what works best for you and use it to store the information in your mind most effectively and easily.

Secret Key #3 – Practice the Right Way

Your success on test day depends not only on how many hours you put into preparing, but also on whether you prepared the right way. It's good to check along the way to see if your studying is paying off. One of the most effective ways to do this is by taking practice tests to evaluate your progress. Practice tests are useful because they show exactly where you need to improve. Every time you take a practice test, pay special attention to these three groups of questions:

- The questions you got wrong
- The questions you had to guess on, even if you guessed right
- The questions you found difficult or slow to work through

This will show you exactly what your weak areas are, and where you need to devote more study time. Ask yourself why each of these questions gave you trouble. Was it because you didn't understand the material? Was it because you didn't remember the vocabulary? Do you need more repetitions on this type of question to build speed and confidence? Dig into those questions and figure out how you can strengthen your weak areas as you go back to review the material.

Additionally, many practice tests have a section explaining the answer choices. It can be tempting to read the explanation and think that you now have a good understanding of the concept. However, an explanation likely only covers part of the question's broader context. Even if the explanation makes perfect sense, **go back and investigate** every concept related to the question until you're positive you have a thorough understanding.

As you go along, keep in mind that the practice test is just that: practice. Memorizing these questions and answers will not be very helpful on the actual test because it is unlikely to have any of the same exact questions. If you only know the right answers to the sample questions, you won't be prepared for the real thing. **Study the concepts** until you understand them fully, and then you'll be able to answer any question that shows up on the test.

It's important to wait on the practice tests until you're ready. If you take a test on your first day of study, you may be overwhelmed by the amount of material covered and how much you need to learn. Work up to it gradually.

On test day, you'll need to be prepared for answering questions, managing your time, and using the test-taking strategies you've learned. It's a lot to balance, like a mental marathon that will have a big impact on your future. Like training for a marathon, you'll need to start slowly and work your way up. When test day arrives, you'll be ready.

Start with the strategies you've read in the first two Secret Keys—plan your course and study in the way that works best for you. If you have time, consider using multiple study resources to get different approaches to the same concepts. It can be helpful to see difficult concepts from more than one angle. Then find a good source for practice tests. Many times, the test website will suggest potential study resources or provide sample tests.

Practice Test Strategy

If you're able to find at least three practice tests, we recommend this strategy:

UNTIMED AND OPEN-BOOK PRACTICE

Take the first test with no time constraints and with your notes and study guide handy. Take your time and focus on applying the strategies you've learned.

TIMED AND OPEN-BOOK PRACTICE

Take the second practice test open-book as well, but set a timer and practice pacing yourself to finish in time.

TIMED AND CLOSED-BOOK PRACTICE

Take any other practice tests as if it were test day. Set a timer and put away your study materials. Sit at a table or desk in a quiet room, imagine yourself at the testing center, and answer questions as quickly and accurately as possible.

Keep repeating timed and closed-book tests on a regular basis until you run out of practice tests or it's time for the actual test. Your mind will be ready for the schedule and stress of test day, and you'll be able to focus on recalling the material you've learned.

Secret Key #4 – Pace Yourself

Once you're fully prepared for the material on the test, your biggest challenge on test day will be managing your time. Just knowing that the clock is ticking can make you panic even if you have plenty of time left. Work on pacing yourself so you can build confidence against the time constraints of the exam. Pacing is a difficult skill to master, especially in a high-pressure environment, so **practice is vital**.

Set time expectations for your pace based on how much time is available. For example, if a section has 60 questions and the time limit is 30 minutes, you know you have to average 30 seconds or less per question in order to answer them all. Although 30 seconds is the hard limit, set 25 seconds per question as your goal, so you reserve extra time to spend on harder questions. When you budget extra time for the harder questions, you no longer have any reason to stress when those questions take longer to answer.

Don't let this time expectation distract you from working through the test at a calm, steady pace, but keep it in mind so you don't spend too much time on any one question. Recognize that taking extra time on one question you don't understand may keep you from answering two that you do understand later in the test. If your time limit for a question is up and you're still not sure of the answer, mark it and move on, and come back to it later if the time and the test format allow. If the testing format doesn't allow you to return to earlier questions, just make an educated guess; then put it out of your mind and move on.

On the easier questions, be careful not to rush. It may seem wise to hurry through them so you have more time for the challenging ones, but it's not worth missing one if you know the concept and just didn't take the time to read the question fully. Work efficiently but make sure you understand the question and have looked at all of the answer choices, since more than one may seem right at first.

Even if you're paying attention to the time, you may find yourself a little behind at some point. You should speed up to get back on track, but do so wisely. Don't panic; just take a few seconds less on each question until you're caught up. Don't guess without thinking, but do look through the answer choices and eliminate any you know are wrong. If you can get down to two choices, it is often worthwhile to guess from those. Once you've chosen an answer, move on and don't dwell on any that you skipped or had to hurry through. If a question was taking too long, chances are it was one of the harder ones, so you weren't as likely to get it right anyway.

On the other hand, if you find yourself getting ahead of schedule, it may be beneficial to slow down a little. The more quickly you work, the more likely you are to make a careless mistake that will affect your score. You've budgeted time for each question, so don't be afraid to spend that time. Practice an efficient but careful pace to get the most out of the time you have.

Secret Key #5 – Have a Plan for Guessing

When you're taking the test, you may find yourself stuck on a question. Some of the answer choices seem better than others, but you don't see the one answer choice that is obviously correct. What do you do?

The scenario described above is very common, yet most test takers have not effectively prepared for it. Developing and practicing a plan for guessing may be one of the single most effective uses of your time as you get ready for the exam.

In developing your plan for guessing, there are three questions to address:

- When should you start the guessing process?
- How should you narrow down the choices?
- Which answer should you choose?

When to Start the Guessing Process

Unless your plan for guessing is to select C every time (which, despite its merits, is not what we recommend), you need to leave yourself enough time to apply your answer elimination strategies. Since you have a limited amount of time for each question, that means that if you're going to give yourself the best shot at guessing correctly, you have to decide quickly whether or not you will guess.

Of course, the best-case scenario is that you don't have to guess at all, so first, see if you can answer the question based on your knowledge of the subject and basic reasoning skills. Focus on the key words in the question and try to jog your memory of related topics. Give yourself a chance to bring the knowledge to mind, but once you realize that you don't have (or you can't access) the knowledge you need to answer the question, it's time to start the guessing process.

It's almost always better to start the guessing process too early than too late. It only takes a few seconds to remember something and answer the question from knowledge. Carefully eliminating wrong answer choices takes longer. Plus, going through the process of eliminating answer choices can actually help jog your memory.

Summary: Start the guessing process as soon as you decide that you can't answer the question based on your knowledge.

How to Narrow Down the Choices

The next chapter in this book (**Test-Taking Strategies**) includes a wide range of strategies for how to approach questions and how to look for answer choices to eliminate. You will definitely want to read those carefully, practice them, and figure out which ones work best for you. Here though, we're going to address a mindset rather than a particular strategy.

Your odds of guessing an answer correctly depend on how many options you are choosing from.

Number of options left	5	4	3	2	1
Odds of guessing correctly	20%	25%	33%	50%	100%

You can see from this chart just how valuable it is to be able to eliminate incorrect answers and make an educated guess, but there are two things that many test takers do that cause them to miss out on the benefits of guessing:

- Accidentally eliminating the correct answer
- Selecting an answer based on an impression

We'll look at the first one here, and the second one in the next section.

To avoid accidentally eliminating the correct answer, we recommend a thought exercise called **the $5 challenge**. In this challenge, you only eliminate an answer choice from contention if you are willing to bet $5 on it being wrong. Why $5? Five dollars is a small but not insignificant amount of money. It's an amount you could afford to lose but wouldn't want to throw away. And while losing $5 once might not hurt too much, doing it twenty times will set you back $100. In the same way, each small decision you make—eliminating a choice here, guessing on a question there—won't by itself impact your score very much, but when you put them all together, they can make a big difference. By holding each answer choice elimination decision to a higher standard, you can reduce the risk of accidentally eliminating the correct answer.

The $5 challenge can also be applied in a positive sense: If you are willing to bet $5 that an answer choice *is* correct, go ahead and mark it as correct.

Summary: Only eliminate an answer choice if you are willing to bet $5 that it is wrong.

Which Answer to Choose

You're taking the test. You've run into a hard question and decided you'll have to guess. You've eliminated all the answer choices you're willing to bet $5 on. Now you have to pick an answer. Why do we even need to talk about this? Why can't you just pick whichever one you feel like when the time comes?

The answer to these questions is that if you don't come into the test with a plan, you'll rely on your impression to select an answer choice, and if you do that, you risk falling into a trap. The test writers know that everyone who takes their test will be guessing on some of the questions, so they intentionally write wrong answer choices to seem plausible. You still have to pick an answer though, and if the wrong answer choices are designed to look right, how can you ever be sure that you're not falling for their trap? The best solution we've found to this dilemma is to take the decision out of your hands entirely. Here is the process we recommend:

Once you've eliminated any choices that you are confident (willing to bet $5) are wrong, select the first remaining choice as your answer.

Whether you choose to select the first remaining choice, the second, or the last, the important thing is that you use some preselected standard. Using this approach guarantees that you will not be enticed into selecting an answer choice that looks right, because you are not basing your decision on how the answer choices look.

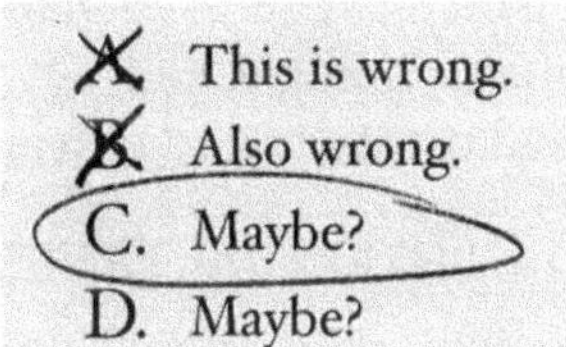

This is not meant to make you question your knowledge. Instead, it is to help you recognize the difference between your knowledge and your impressions. There's a huge difference between thinking an answer is right because of what you know, and thinking an answer is right because it looks or sounds like it should be right.

Summary: To ensure that your selection is appropriately random, make a predetermined selection from among all answer choices you have not eliminated.

Test-Taking Strategies

This section contains a list of test-taking strategies that you may find helpful as you work through the test. By taking what you know and applying logical thought, you can maximize your chances of answering any question correctly!

It is very important to realize that every question is different and every person is different: no single strategy will work on every question, and no single strategy will work for every person. That's why we've included all of them here, so you can try them out and determine which ones work best for different types of questions and which ones work best for you.

Question Strategies

✓ Read Carefully

Read the question and the answer choices carefully. Don't miss the question because you misread the terms. You have plenty of time to read each question thoroughly and make sure you understand what is being asked. Yet a happy medium must be attained, so don't waste too much time. You must read carefully and efficiently.

✓ Contextual Clues

Look for contextual clues. If the question includes a word you are not familiar with, look at the immediate context for some indication of what the word might mean. Contextual clues can often give you all the information you need to decipher the meaning of an unfamiliar word. Even if you can't determine the meaning, you may be able to narrow down the possibilities enough to make a solid guess at the answer to the question.

✓ Prefixes

If you're having trouble with a word in the question or answer choices, try dissecting it. Take advantage of every clue that the word might include. Prefixes can be a huge help. Usually, they allow you to determine a basic meaning. *Pre-* means before, *post-* means after, *pro-* is positive, *de-* is negative. From prefixes, you can get an idea of the general meaning of the word and try to put it into context.

✓ Hedge Words

Watch out for critical hedge words, such as *likely, may, can, often, almost, mostly, usually, generally, rarely,* and *sometimes.* Question writers insert these hedge phrases to cover every possibility. Often an answer choice will be wrong simply because it leaves no room for exception. Be on guard for answer choices that have definitive words such as *exactly* and *always.*

✓ Switchback Words

Stay alert for *switchbacks.* These are the words and phrases frequently used to alert you to shifts in thought. The most common switchback words are *but, although,* and *however.* Others include *nevertheless, on the other hand, even though, while, in spite of, despite,* and *regardless of.* Switchback words are important to catch because they can change the direction of the question or an answer choice.

✓ Face Value

When in doubt, use common sense. Accept the situation in the problem at face value. Don't read too much into it. These problems will not require you to make wild assumptions. If you have to go beyond creativity and warp time or space in order to have an answer choice fit the question, then you should move on and consider the other answer choices. These are normal problems rooted in reality. The applicable relationship or explanation may not be readily apparent, but it is there for you to figure out. Use your common sense to interpret anything that isn't clear.

Answer Choice Strategies

✓ Answer Selection

The most thorough way to pick an answer choice is to identify and eliminate wrong answers until only one is left, then confirm it is the correct answer. Sometimes an answer choice may immediately seem right, but be careful. The test writers will usually put more than one reasonable answer choice on each question, so take a second to read all of them and make sure that the other choices are not equally obvious. As long as you have time left, it is better to read every answer choice than to pick the first one that looks right without checking the others.

✓ Answer Choice Families

An answer choice family consists of two (in rare cases, three) answer choices that are very similar in construction and cannot all be true at the same time. If you see two answer choices that are direct opposites or parallels, one of them is usually the correct answer. For instance, if one answer choice says that quantity x increases and another either says that quantity x decreases (opposite) or says that quantity y increases (parallel), then those answer choices would fall into the same family. An answer choice that doesn't match the construction of the answer choice family is more likely to be incorrect. Most questions will not have answer choice families, but when they do appear, you should be prepared to recognize them.

✓ Eliminate Answers

Eliminate answer choices as soon as you realize they are wrong, but make sure you consider all possibilities. If you are eliminating answer choices and realize that the last one you are left with is also wrong, don't panic. Start over and consider each choice again. There may be something you missed the first time that you will realize on the second pass.

✓ Avoid Fact Traps

Don't be distracted by an answer choice that is factually true but doesn't answer the question. You are looking for the choice that answers the question. Stay focused on what the question is asking for so you don't accidentally pick an answer that is true but incorrect. Always go back to the question and make sure the answer choice you've selected actually answers the question and is not merely a true statement.

✓ Extreme Statements

In general, you should avoid answers that put forth extreme actions as standard practice or proclaim controversial ideas as established fact. An answer choice that states the "process should be used in certain situations, if…" is much more likely to be correct than one that states the "process should be discontinued completely." The first is a calm rational statement and doesn't even make a definitive, uncompromising stance, using a hedge word *if* to provide wiggle room, whereas the second choice is far more extreme.

⊘ Benchmark

As you read through the answer choices and you come across one that seems to answer the question well, mentally select that answer choice. This is not your final answer, but it's the one that will help you evaluate the other answer choices. The one that you selected is your benchmark or standard for judging each of the other answer choices. Every other answer choice must be compared to your benchmark. That choice is correct until proven otherwise by another answer choice beating it. If you find a better answer, then that one becomes your new benchmark. Once you've decided that no other choice answers the question as well as your benchmark, you have your final answer.

⊘ Predict the Answer

Before you even start looking at the answer choices, it is often best to try to predict the answer. When you come up with the answer on your own, it is easier to avoid distractions and traps because you will know exactly what to look for. The right answer choice is unlikely to be word-for-word what you came up with, but it should be a close match. Even if you are confident that you have the right answer, you should still take the time to read each option before moving on.

General Strategies

⊘ Tough Questions

If you are stumped on a problem or it appears too hard or too difficult, don't waste time. Move on! Remember though, if you can quickly check for obviously incorrect answer choices, your chances of guessing correctly are greatly improved. Before you completely give up, at least try to knock out a couple of possible answers. Eliminate what you can and then guess at the remaining answer choices before moving on.

⊘ Check Your Work

Since you will probably not know every term listed and the answer to every question, it is important that you get credit for the ones that you do know. Don't miss any questions through careless mistakes. If at all possible, try to take a second to look back over your answer selection and make sure you've selected the correct answer choice and haven't made a costly careless mistake (such as marking an answer choice that you didn't mean to mark). This quick double check should more than pay for itself in caught mistakes for the time it costs.

⊘ Pace Yourself

It's easy to be overwhelmed when you're looking at a page full of questions; your mind is confused and full of random thoughts, and the clock is ticking down faster than you would like. Calm down and maintain the pace that you have set for yourself. Especially as you get down to the last few minutes of the test, don't let the small numbers on the clock make you panic. As long as you are on track by monitoring your pace, you are guaranteed to have time for each question.

⊘ Don't Rush

It is very easy to make errors when you are in a hurry. Maintaining a fast pace in answering questions is pointless if it makes you miss questions that you would have gotten right otherwise. Test writers like to include distracting information and wrong answers that seem right. Taking a little extra time to avoid careless mistakes can make all the difference in your test score. Find a pace that allows you to be confident in the answers that you select.

✓ KEEP MOVING

Panicking will not help you pass the test, so do your best to stay calm and keep moving. Taking deep breaths and going through the answer elimination steps you practiced can help to break through a stress barrier and keep your pace.

Final Notes

The combination of a solid foundation of content knowledge and the confidence that comes from practicing your plan for applying that knowledge is the key to maximizing your performance on test day. As your foundation of content knowledge is built up and strengthened, you'll find that the strategies included in this chapter become more and more effective in helping you quickly sift through the distractions and traps of the test to isolate the correct answer.

Now that you're preparing to move forward into the test content chapters of this book, be sure to keep your goal in mind. As you read, think about how you will be able to apply this information on the test. If you've already seen sample questions for the test and you have an idea of the question format and style, try to come up with questions of your own that you can answer based on what you're reading. This will give you valuable practice applying your knowledge in the same ways you can expect to on test day.

Good luck and good studying!

Introduction

If you have to take a mechanical aptitude test for school or employment, you may be wondering exactly what these kinds of tests involve, and what their purpose is. Most tests measure how much a person knows. In a classroom, a teacher will give the class a test to make certain that her students have learned the subject matter. Schools give tests to make sure a person has acquired a certain amount of knowledge before awarding them a diploma. States require a person to pass a written test to get a driver's license to ensure that drivers know the rules of the road. We've all taken dozens if not hundreds of these kinds of tests. Measuring a person's knowledge about something is so important in so many situations that we encounter all through school and life.

An aptitude test on the other hand, does not measure knowledge you've already picked up; it measures *aptitude*, which is the natural ability to do well at something. There are billions of people on this planet, and each one is different. One person may have difficulty learning the basics of a subject or skill after weeks of diligent study or practice, while another will quickly excel at the same thing without breaking a sweat. The difference between the two is that the second person has an aptitude for the subject, while the first one does not. Schools and employers have found that people without a natural mechanical aptitude are going to struggle and be dissatisfied in certain courses or jobs, so they want to make sure that applicants have a natural ability in this area. They do this by giving mechanical aptitude tests.

Having a natural aptitude for something does not necessarily mean that a person will be able to easily demonstrate it on a test though. Test taking is a skill like any other, and it can be improved upon. You'll want to be thoroughly prepared for your test so you can make sure that you demonstrate your aptitude to the best of your ability, and this guide will help you do that. You'll find a wide variety of tips, tricks, and strategies that can help you maximize your score. The first half of the guide goes over several different types of questions you might see on your mechanical aptitude exam. There are plenty of definitions and illustrations to help you quickly grasp any concepts or principles of mechanics you're having trouble with. You'll also find a few practice questions at the end of each section to help you practice the strategies you've just read about. In the second half of the guide, you'll find a longer practice test to help you prepare for the real one.

No two mechanical aptitude tests are alike, so not all of the question types we cover here will appear on the test that you have to take. If you already know what types of questions to expect on your test, focus on just those questions. If not, practicing with all of these questions will give you the best chance to succeed on test day. Either way, we recommend taking the time to digest the material, carefully reading through each section and working the short sets of practice questions, before taking the larger practice test. This will help you maximize your chances of getting a great score on your mechanical aptitude test.

Physics Primer

If you're interested in going in depth into why things act the way they do in the physical world, having an adequate basis in physics is a necessity. This section can provide you with that basis.

Kinematics

To begin, we will look at the basics of physics. At its heart, physics is just a set of explanations for the ways in which matter and energy behave. There are three key concepts used to describe how matter moves:

1. Displacement
2. Velocity
3. Acceleration

Displacement

Concept: Where and how far an object has gone

Calculation: Final position – initial position

When something changes its location from one place to another, it is said to have undergone displacement. If a golf ball is hit across a sloped green into the hole, the displacement only takes into account the final and initial locations, not the path of the ball.

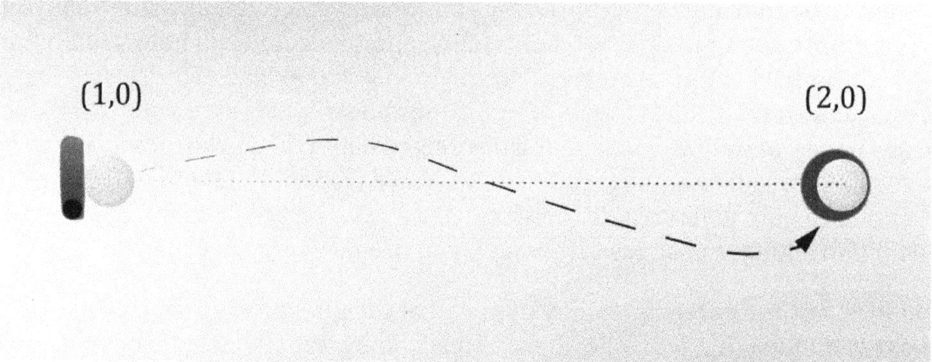

Displacement along a straight line is a very simple example of a vector quantity; it has both a magnitude and a direction. Direction is as important as magnitude in many measurements. If we can determine the original and final position of the object, then we can determine the total displacement with this simple equation:

$$\text{Displacement} = \text{final position} - \text{original position}$$

The hole (final position) is at the Cartesian coordinate location (2,0) and the ball is hit from the location (1,0). The displacement is:

$$\text{Displacement} = (2,0) - (1,0)$$

$$\text{Displacement} = (1,0)$$

The displacement has a magnitude of 1 and a direction of the positive x-direction.

Review Video: Displacement in Physics
Visit mometrix.com/academy and enter code: 236197

VELOCITY

Concept: The rate of moving from one position to another

Calculation: Change in position / change in time

Velocity answers the question, "How quickly is an object moving?" For example, if a car and a plane travel between two cities that are a hundred miles apart, but the car takes two hours and the plane takes one hour, the car has the same displacement as the plane but a smaller velocity.

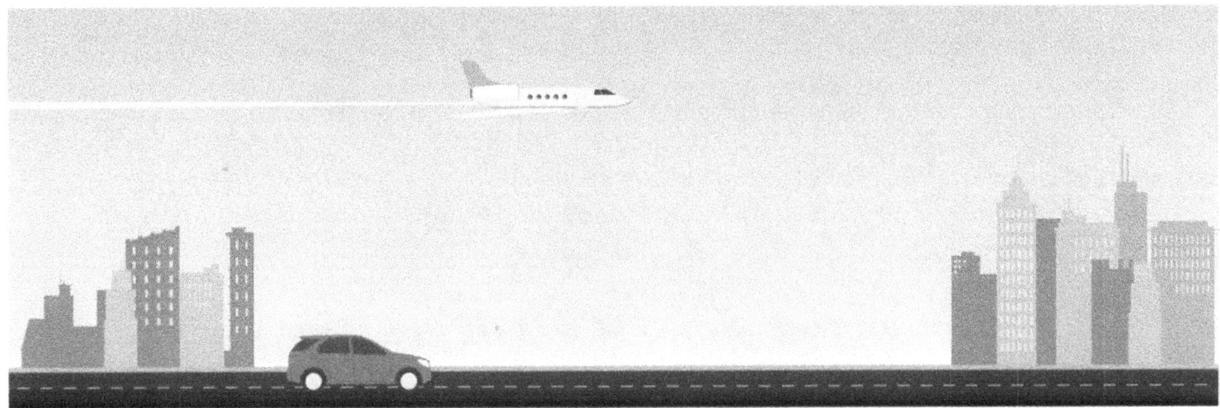

In order to solve some of the problems on the exam, you may need to assess the velocity of an object. If we want to calculate the average velocity of an object, we must know two things. First, we must know its displacement. Second, we must know the time it took to cover this distance. The formula for average velocity is quite simple:

$$\textbf{average velocity} = \frac{\textbf{displacement}}{\textbf{change in time}}$$

Or

$$\textbf{average velocity} = \frac{\textbf{final position} - \textbf{original position}}{\textbf{final time} - \textbf{original time}}$$

To complete the example, the velocity of the plane is calculated to be:

$$\text{plane average velocity} = \frac{100 \text{ miles}}{1 \text{ hour}} = 100 \text{ miles per hour}$$

The velocity of the car is less:

$$\text{car average velocity} = \frac{100 \text{ miles}}{2 \text{ hours}} = 50 \text{ miles per hour}$$

Often, people confuse the words *speed* and *velocity*. There is a significant difference. The average velocity is based on the amount of displacement, a vector. Alternately, the average speed is based on the distance covered or the path length. The equation for speed is:

$$\textbf{average speed} = \frac{\textbf{total distance traveled}}{\textbf{change in time}}$$

Notice that we used total distance and *not* change in position, because speed is path-dependent.

If the plane traveling between cities had needed to fly around a storm on its way, making the distance traveled 50 miles greater than the distance the car traveled, the plane would still have the same total displacement as the car.

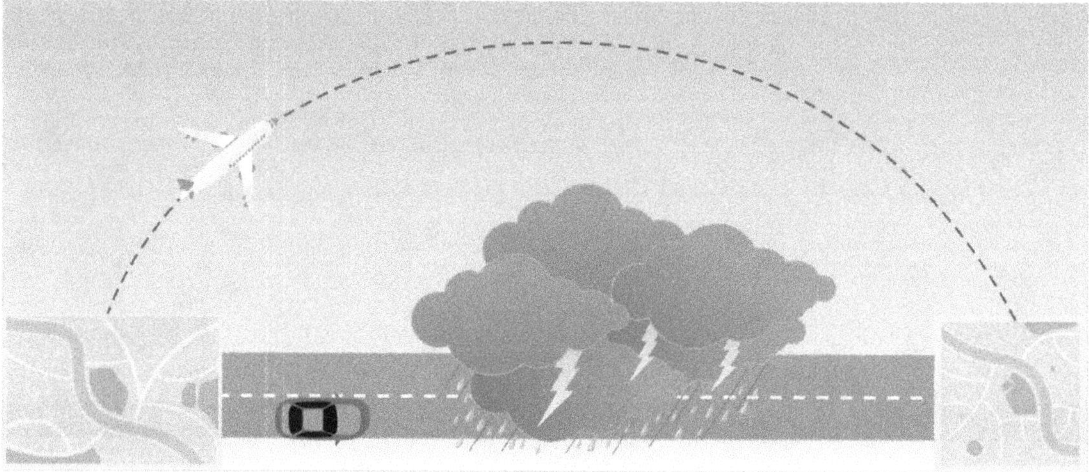

For this reason, the average speed can be calculated:

$$\text{plane average speed} = \frac{150 \text{ miles}}{1 \text{ hour}} = 150 \text{ miles per hour}$$

$$\text{car average speed} = \frac{100 \text{ miles}}{2 \text{ hours}} = 50 \text{ miles per hour}$$

Acceleration

Concept: How quickly something changes from one velocity to another

Calculation: Change in velocity / change in time

Acceleration is the rate of change of the velocity of an object. If a car accelerates from zero velocity to 60 miles per hour (88 feet per second) in two seconds, the car has an impressive acceleration.

But if a car performs the same change in velocity in eight seconds, the acceleration is much lower and not as impressive.

To calculate average acceleration, we may use the equation:

$$\textbf{average acceleration} = \frac{\textbf{change in velocity}}{\textbf{change in time}}$$

The acceleration of the cars is found to be:

$$\text{Car \#1 average acceleration} = \frac{\text{88 feet per second}}{\text{2 seconds}} = 44\ \frac{\text{feet}}{\text{second}^2}$$

$$\text{Car \#2 average acceleration} = \frac{\text{88 feet per second}}{\text{8 seconds}} = 11\ \frac{\text{feet}}{\text{second}^2}$$

Acceleration will be expressed in units of distance divided by time squared; for instance, meters per second squared or feet per second squared.

Review Video: Displacement, Velocity, and Acceleration
Visit mometrix.com/academy and enter code: 671849

Projectile Motion

A specific application of the study of motion is projectile motion. Simple projectile motion occurs when an object is in the air and experiencing only the force of gravity. We will disregard drag for this topic. Some common examples of projectile motion are thrown balls, flying bullets, and falling rocks. The characteristics of projectile motion are:

1. The horizontal component of velocity doesn't change
2. The vertical acceleration due to gravity affects the vertical component of velocity

Because gravity only acts downwards, objects in projectile motion only experience acceleration in the y-direction (vertical). The horizontal component of the object's velocity does not change in flight. This means that if a rock is thrown out off a cliff, the horizontal velocity (think of the shadow if the sun is directly overhead) will not change until the ball hits the ground.

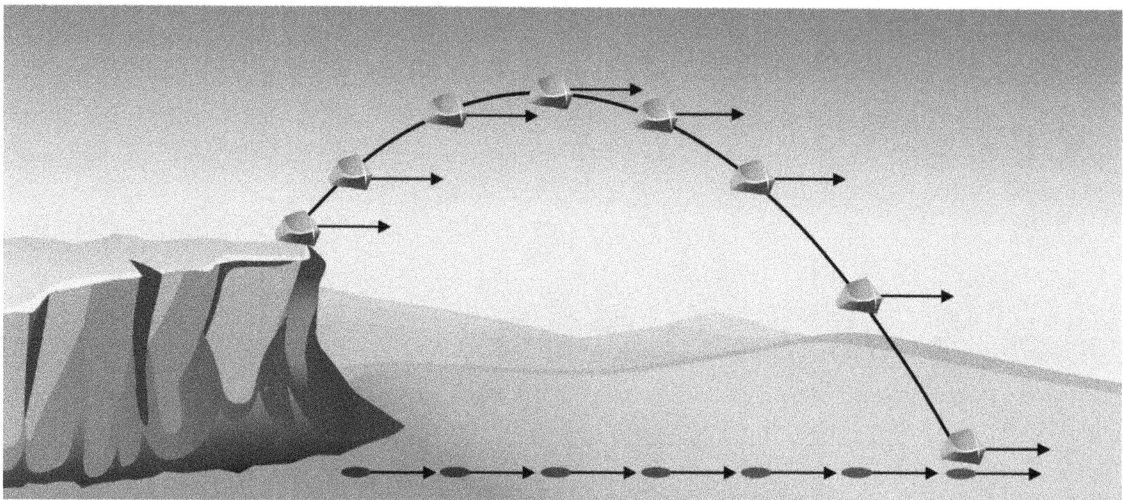

The velocity in the vertical direction is affected by gravity. Gravity imposes an acceleration of $g = 9.8\frac{\text{m}}{\text{s}^2}$ or $32\frac{\text{ft}}{\text{s}^2}$ downward on projectiles. The vertical component of velocity at any point is equal to:

$$\textbf{vertical velocity} = \textbf{original vertical velocity} - \textbf{g} \times \textbf{time}$$

When these characteristics are combined, there are three points of particular interest in a projectile's flight. At the beginning of a flight, the object has a horizontal component and a vertical component giving it a large speed. At the top of a projectile's flight, the vertical velocity equals zero, making the top the slowest part of travel. When the object passes the same height as the launch, the vertical velocity is opposite of the initial vertical velocity, making the speed equal to the initial speed.

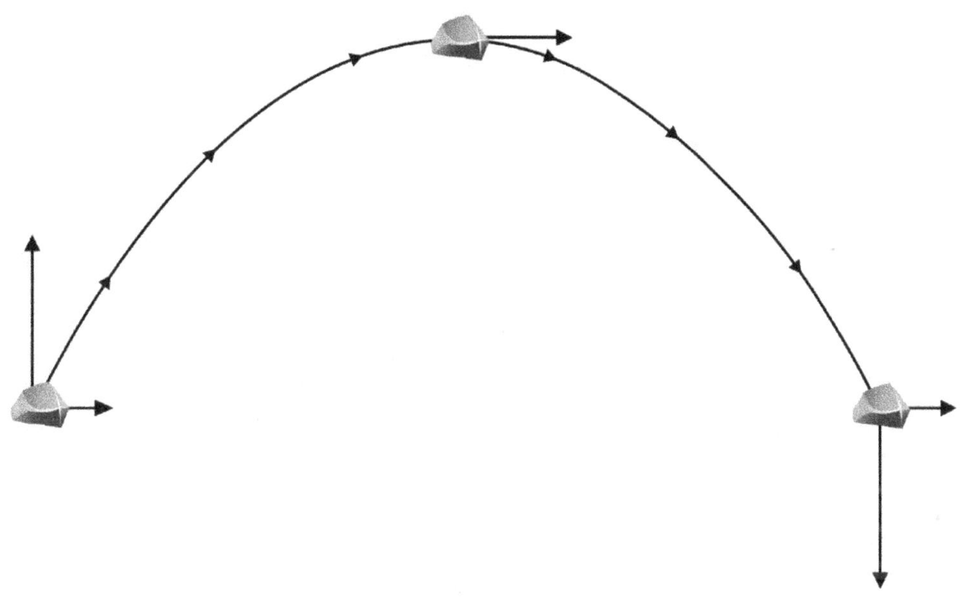

If the object continues falling below the initial height from which it was launched (e.g., it was launched from the edge of a cliff), it will have an even greater velocity than it did initially from that point until it hits the ground.

Review Video: Projectile Motion
Visit mometrix.com/academy and enter code: 719700

Rotational Kinematics

Concept: Increasing the radius increases the linear speed

Calculation: Linear speed = radius × rotational speed

Another interesting application of the study of motion is rotation. In practice, simple rotation is when an object rotates around a point at a constant speed. Most questions covering rotational kinematics will provide the distance from a rotating object to the center of rotation (radius) and ask about the linear speed of the object. A point will have a greater linear speed when it is farther from the center of rotation.

If a potter is spinning his wheel at a constant speed of one revolution per second, the clay six inches away from the center will be going faster than the clay three inches from the center. The clay directly in the center of the wheel will not have any linear velocity.

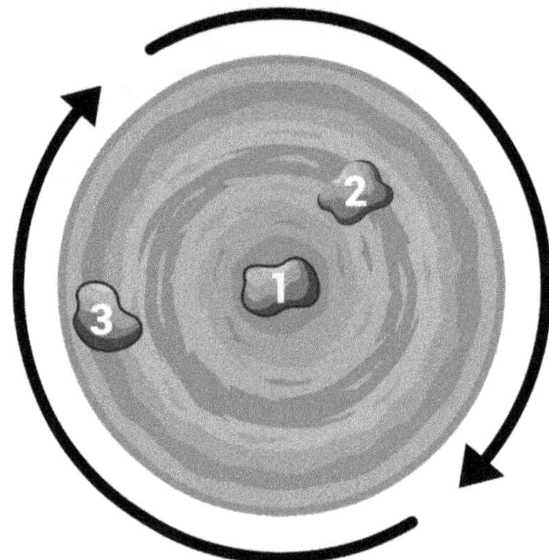

To find the linear speed of rotating objects using radians, we use the equation:

$$\textbf{linear speed} = (\textbf{rotational speed [in radians]}) \times (\textbf{radius})$$

Using degrees, the equation is:

$$\textbf{linear speed} = (\textbf{rotational speed [in degrees]}) \times \frac{\boldsymbol{\pi}\textbf{ radians}}{\textbf{180 degrees}} \times (\textbf{radius})$$

To find the speed of the pieces of clay, we use the known values (rotational speed of 1 revolution per second, radii of 0 inches, 3 inches, and 6 inches) and the knowledge that one revolution = 2π.

$$\text{clay \#1 speed} = \left(2\pi\frac{\text{rad}}{\text{s}}\right) \times (0 \text{ inches}) = 0\frac{\text{inches}}{\text{second}}$$

$$\text{clay \#2 speed} = \left(2\pi\frac{\text{rad}}{\text{s}}\right) \times (3 \text{ inches}) = 18.8\frac{\text{inches}}{\text{second}}$$

$$\text{clay \#3 speed} = \left(2\pi\frac{\text{rad}}{\text{s}}\right) \times (6 \text{ inches}) = 37.7\frac{\text{inches}}{\text{second}}$$

Review Video: Linear Speed
Visit mometrix.com/academy and enter code: 327101

CAMS

In the study of motion, a final application often tested is the cam. A cam and follower system allows mechanical systems to have timed, specified, and repeating motion. Although cams come in varied forms, tests focus on rotary cams. In engines, a cam shaft coordinates the valves for intake and exhaust. Cams are often used to convert rotational motion into repeating linear motion.

Cams rotate around one point. The follower sits on the edge of the cam and moves along with the edge. To understand simple cams, count the number of bumps on the cam. Each bump will cause the follower to move outwards.

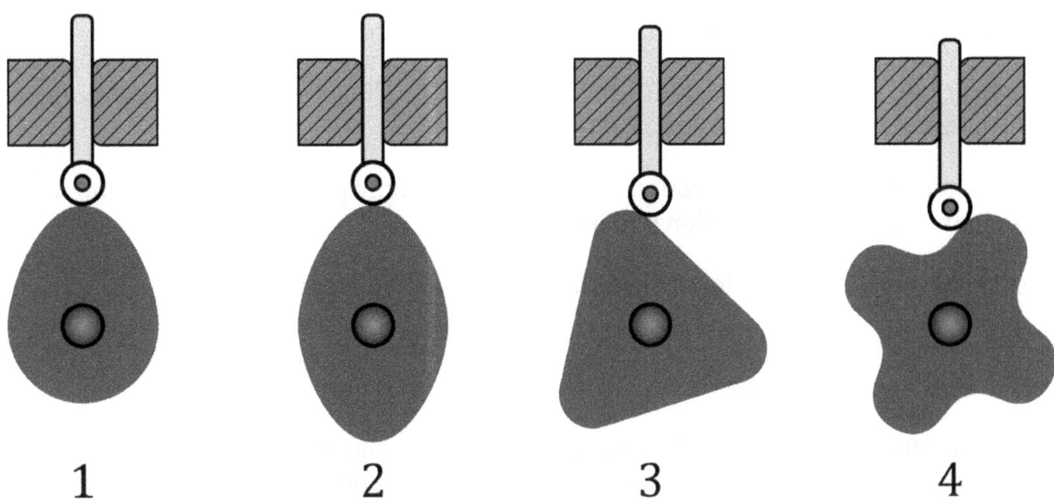

Another way to consider cams is to unravel the cam profile into a straight object. The follower will then follow the top of the profile.

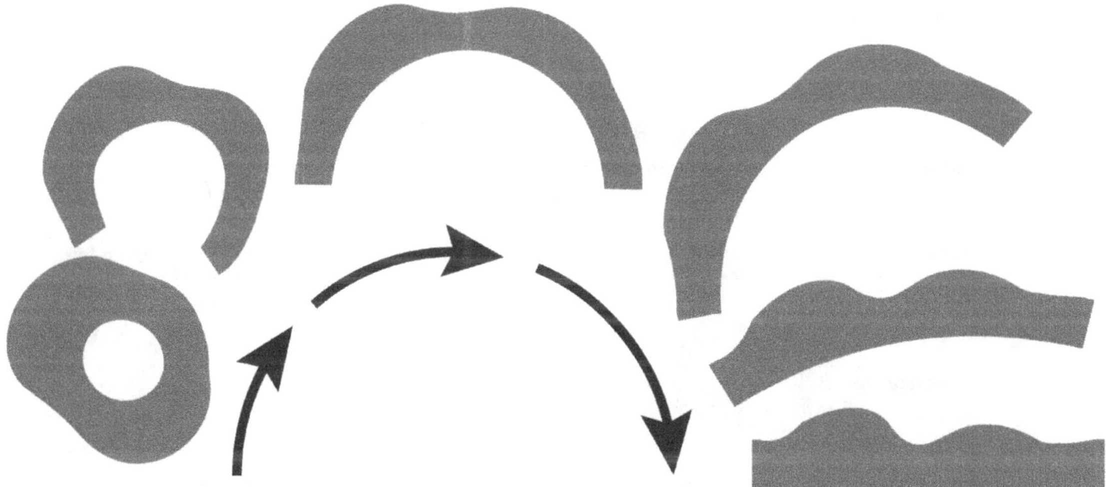

Kinetics

Newton's Three Laws of Mechanics

The questions on the exam may require you to demonstrate familiarity with the concepts expressed in Newton's three laws of motion which relate to the concept of force.

Newton's first law – A body at rest tends to remain at rest, while a body in motion tends to remain in motion, unless acted upon by an external force.

Newton's second law – The acceleration of an object is directly proportional to the force being exerted on it and inversely proportional to its mass.

Newton's third law – For every force, there is an equal and opposite force.

First Law

Concept: Unless something interferes, an object won't start or stop moving

Although intuition supports the idea that objects do not start moving until a force acts on them, the idea of an object continuing forever without any forces can seem odd. Before Newton formulated his laws of mechanics, general thought held that some force had to act on an object continuously in order for it to move at a constant velocity. This seems to make sense; when an object is briefly pushed, it will eventually come to a stop. Newton, however, determined that unless some other force acted on the object (most notably friction or air resistance), it would continue in the direction it was pushed at the same velocity forever.

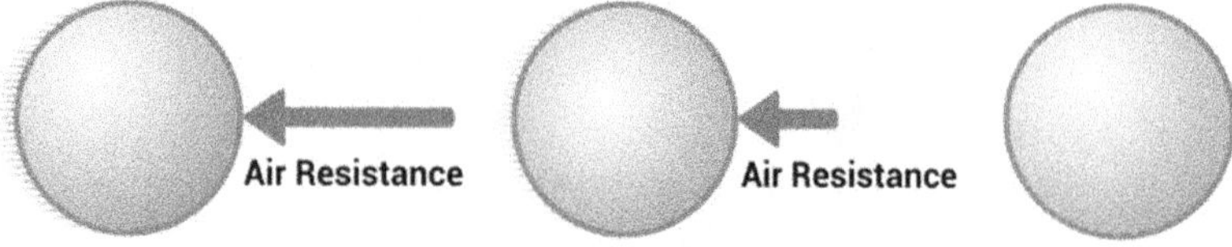

As time moves forward, the air resistance stops one ball, but the ball without air resistance has no stopping force.

Review Video: Newton's First Law of Motion
Visit mometrix.com/academy and enter code: 590367

Second Law

Concept: Acceleration increases linearly with force.

Although Newton's second law can be conceptually understood as a series of relationships describing how an increase in one factor will decrease another factor, the law can be understood best in equation format:

$$\textbf{Force} = \textbf{mass} \times \textbf{acceleration}$$

Or

$$\text{Acceleration} = \frac{\text{force}}{\text{mass}}$$

Or

$$\text{Mass} = \frac{\text{force}}{\text{acceleration}}$$

Each of the forms of this equation allows for a different look at the same relationships. To examine the relationships, change one factor and observe the result. If a steel ball with a diameter of 6.3 cm has a mass of 1 kg and an acceleration of 1 m/s^2, then the net force on the ball will be 1 Newton.

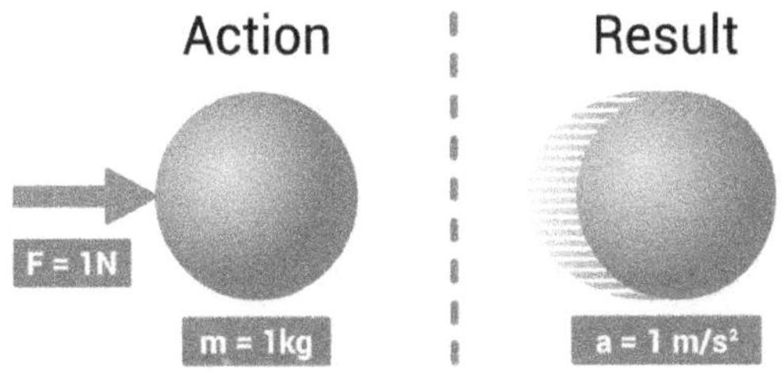

Review Video: Newton's Second Law of Motion
Visit mometrix.com/academy and enter code: 737975

Third Law

Concept: Nothing can push or pull without being pushed or pulled in return.

When any object exerts a force on another object, the other object exerts the opposite force back on the original object. To observe this, consider two spring-based fruit scales, both tipped on their sides as shown with the weighing surfaces facing each other. If fruit scale #1 is pressing fruit scale #2 into the wall, it exerts a force on fruit scale #2, measurable by the reading on scale #2. However, because fruit scale #1 is exerting a force on scale #2, scale #2 is exerting a force on scale #1 with an opposite direction, but the same magnitude.

Review Video: Newton's Third Law of Motion
Visit mometrix.com/academy and enter code: 838401

FORCE

Concept: A push or pull on an object

Calculation: Force = mass × acceleration

A force is a vector that causes acceleration of a body. Force has both magnitude and direction. Furthermore, multiple forces acting on one object combine in vector addition. This can be demonstrated by considering an object placed at the origin of the coordinate plane. If it is pushed along the positive direction of the *x*-axis, it will move in this direction. If the force acting on it is in the positive direction of the *y*-axis, it will move in that direction.

However, if both forces are applied at the same time, then the object will move at an angle to both the *x*- and *y*-axes, an angle determined by the relative amount of force exerted in each direction. In this way, we may see that the resulting force is a vector sum; a net force that has both magnitude and direction.

Resultant vectors from applied forces:

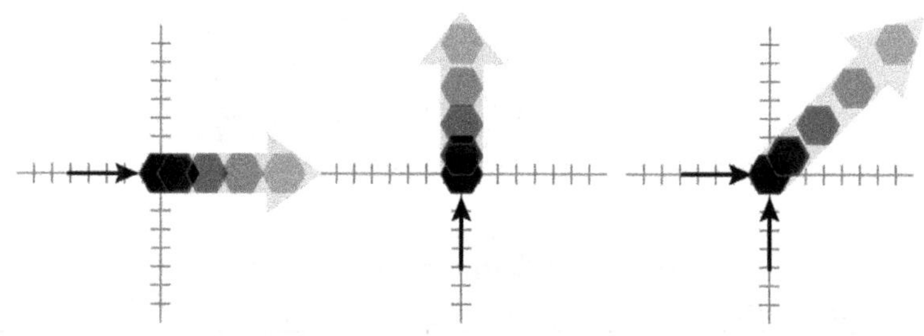

Review Video: Forces: Push-Pull
Visit mometrix.com/academy and enter code: 104731

MASS

Concept: The amount of matter

Mass can be defined as the quantity of matter in an object. If we apply the same force to two objects of different mass, we will find that the resulting acceleration is different. In other words, the acceleration of an object is directly proportional to the force being exerted on it and inversely proportional to its mass.

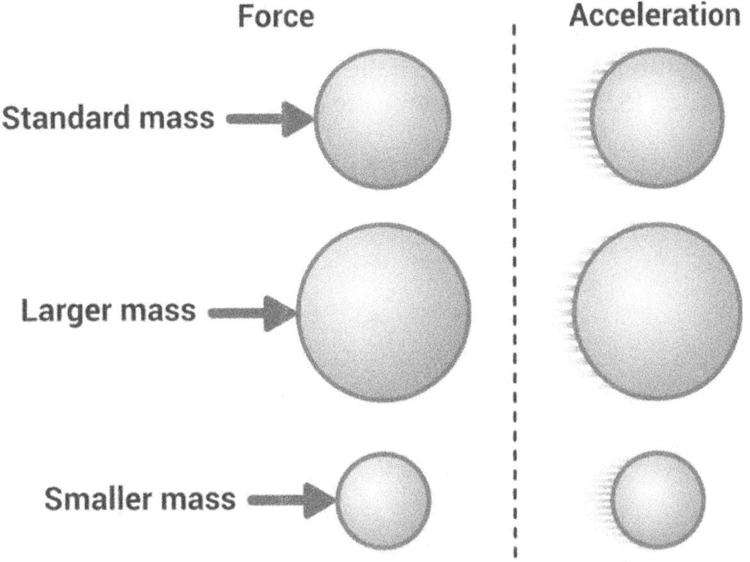

GRAVITY

Gravity is a force that exists between all objects with matter. Gravity is a pulling force between objects, meaning that the forces on the objects point toward the opposite object. When Newton's third law is applied to gravity, the force pairs from gravity are shown to be equal in magnitude and opposite in direction.

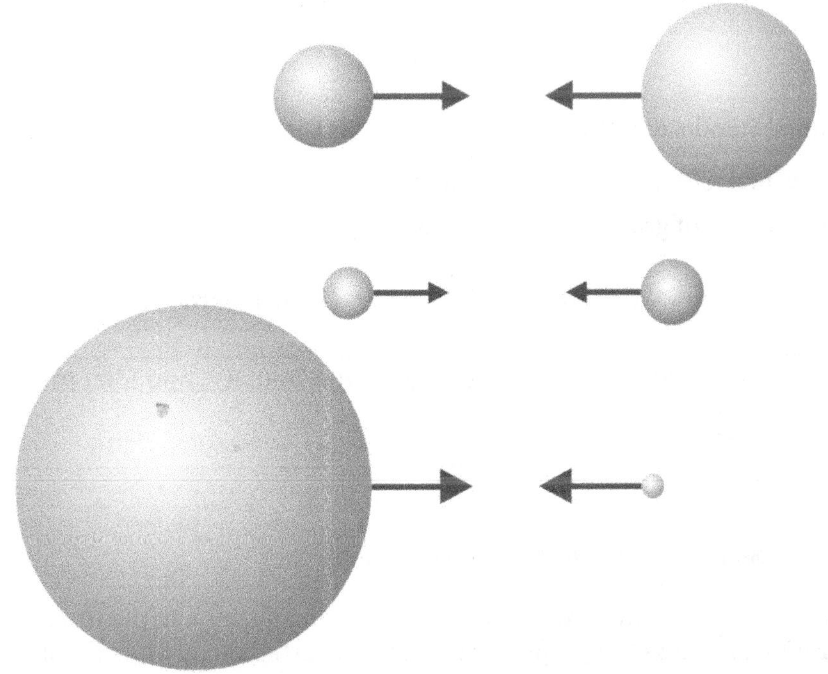

Review Video: Newton's Law of Gravitation
Visit mometrix.com/academy and enter code: 709086

WEIGHT

Weight is sometimes confused with mass. While mass is the amount of matter, weight is the force exerted by the earth on an object with matter by gravity. The earth pulls every object of mass toward its center while every object of mass pulls the earth toward its center. The object's pull on the earth is equal in magnitude to the pull which the earth exerts, but, because the mass of the earth is very large in comparison (5.97×10^{24} kg), only the object appears to be affected by the force.

The gravity of the earth causes a constant acceleration due to gravity (g) at a specific altitude. For most earthbound applications, the acceleration due to gravity is 32.2 ft/s^2 or 9.8 m/s^2 in a downward direction. The equation for the force of gravity (weight) on an object is the equation from Newton's Second Law with the constant acceleration due to gravity (g).

$$\textbf{Weight} = \textbf{mass} \times \textbf{acceleration due to gravity}$$

$$\mathbf{W = m \times g}$$

The SI (International Standard of Units) unit for weight is the Newton $\left(\frac{\text{kg}\times\text{m}}{\text{s}^2}\right)$. The English Engineering unit system uses the pound, or lb, as the unit for weight and force $\left(\frac{\text{slug}\times\text{ft}}{\text{s}^2}\right)$. Thus, a 2 kg object under the influence of gravity would have a weight of:

$$W = 2\text{ kg} \times 9.8\frac{\text{m}}{\text{s}^2} = 19.6\text{ N downward}$$

Review Video: Mass, Weight, Volume, Density, and Specific Gravity
Visit mometrix.com/academy and enter code: 920570

NORMAL FORCE

Concept: The force perpendicular to a contact surface

The word *normal* is used in mathematics to mean perpendicular, and so the force known as normal force should be remembered as the perpendicular force exerted on an object that is resting on some other surface. For instance, if a box is resting on a horizontal surface, we may say that the normal force is directed upwards through the box (the opposite, downward force is the weight of the box).

If the box is resting on a wedge, the normal force from the wedge is not vertical but is perpendicular to the wedge edge.

Tension

Concept: A pulling force like that from a cord or rope.

Another force that may come into play on the exam is called tension. Anytime a cord is attached to a body and pulled so that it is taut, we may say that the cord is under tension. The cord in tension applies a pulling tension force on the connected objects. This force is pointed away from the body and along the cord at the point of attachment. In simple considerations of tension, the cord is assumed to be both without mass and incapable of stretching. In other words, its only role is as the connector between two bodies. The cord is also assumed to pull on both ends with the same magnitude of tension force.

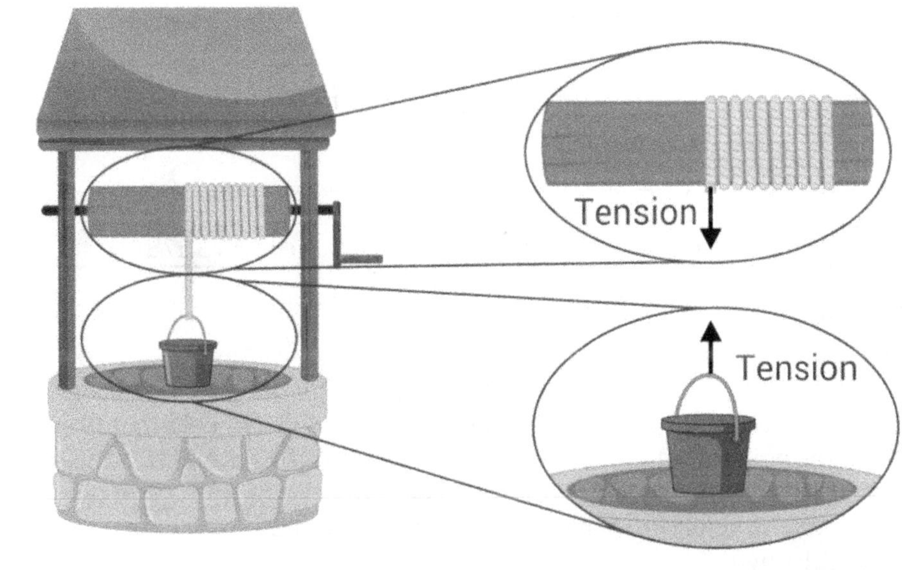

Friction

Concept: Friction is a resistance to motion between contacting surfaces

In order to illustrate the concept of friction, let us imagine a book resting on a table. As it sits, the force of its weight is equal to and opposite of the normal force. If, however, we were to exert a force on the book, attempting to push it to one side, a frictional force would arise, equal and opposite to our force. This kind of frictional force is known as static frictional force.

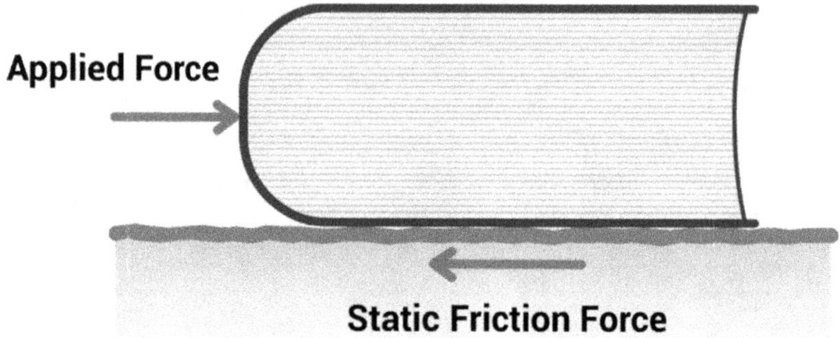

As we increase our force on the book, however, we will eventually cause it to accelerate in the direction of our force. At this point, the frictional force opposing us will be known as kinetic friction. For many combinations of surfaces, the magnitude of the kinetic frictional force is lower than that of the static frictional force, and consequently, the amount of force needed to maintain the movement of the book will be less than that needed to initiate the movement.

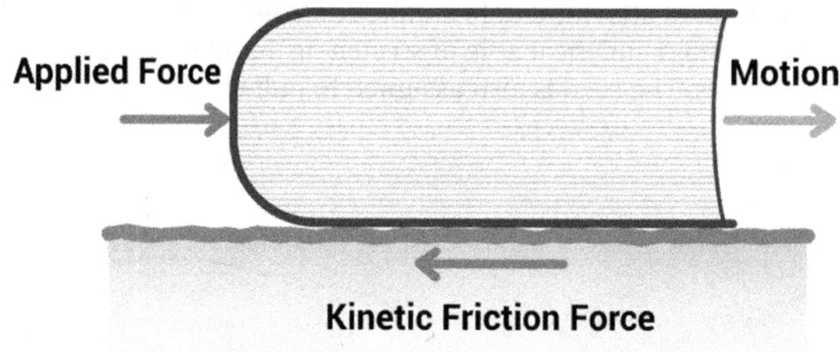

Review Video: Friction
Visit mometrix.com/academy and enter code: 716782

Rolling Friction

Occasionally, a question will ask you to consider the amount of friction generated by an object that is rolling. If a wheel is rolling at a constant speed, then the point at which it touches the ground will not slide, and there will be no friction between the ground and the wheel inhibiting movement. In fact, the friction at the point of contact between the wheel and the ground is static friction necessary to propel with wheels. When a vehicle accelerates, the static friction between the wheels and the ground allows the vehicle to achieve acceleration. Without this friction, the vehicle would spin its wheels and go nowhere.

Although the static friction does not impede movement for the wheels, a combination of frictional forces can resist rolling motion. One such frictional force is bearing friction. Bearing friction is the kinetic friction between the wheel and an object it rotates around, such as a stationary axle.

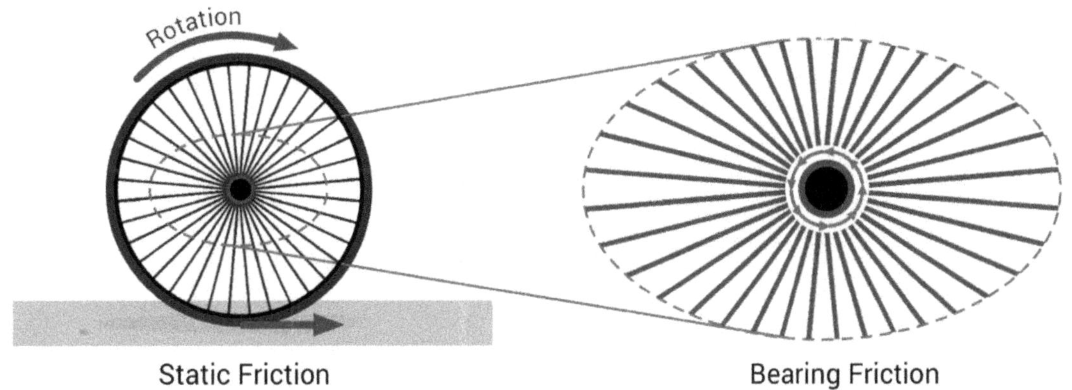

Drag Force

Friction can also be generated when an object is moving through air or liquid. A drag force occurs when a body moves through some fluid (either liquid or gas) and experiences a force that opposes the motion of the body. The drag force is greater if the air or fluid is thicker or is moving in the direction opposite to the object. Obviously, the higher the drag force, the greater amount of positive force required to keep the object moving forward.

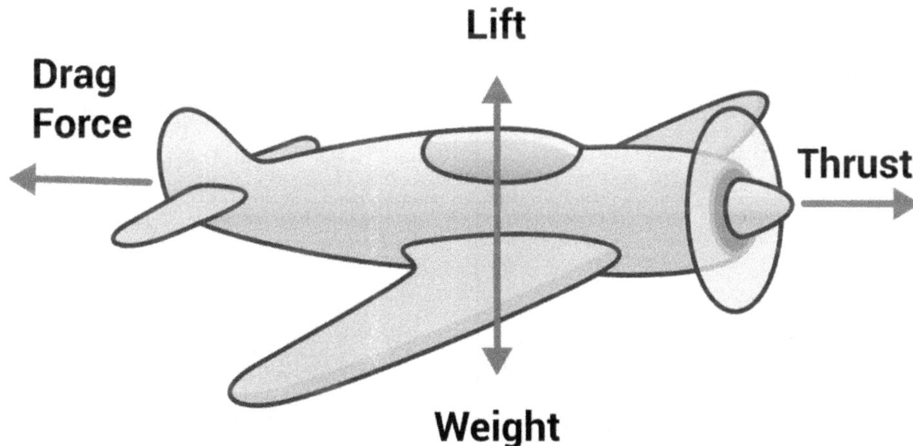

Balanced Forces

An object is in equilibrium when the sum of all forces acting on the object is zero. When the forces on an object sum to zero, the object does not accelerate. Equilibrium can be obtained when forces in the y-direction sum to zero, forces in the x-direction sum to zero, or forces in both directions sum to zero.

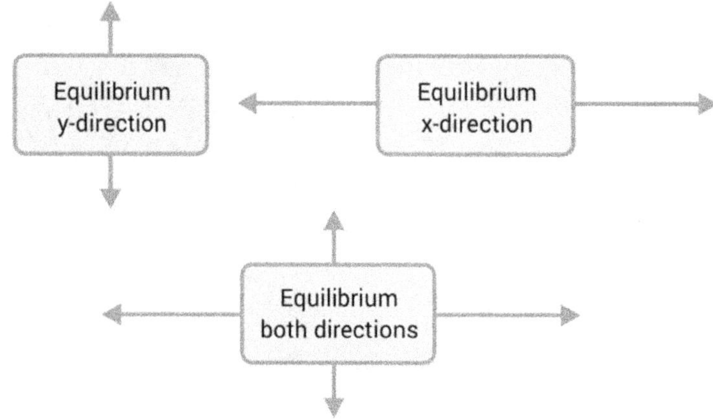

In most cases, a problem will provide one or more forces acting on an object and ask for a force to balance the system. The force will be the opposite of the current force or sum of current forces.

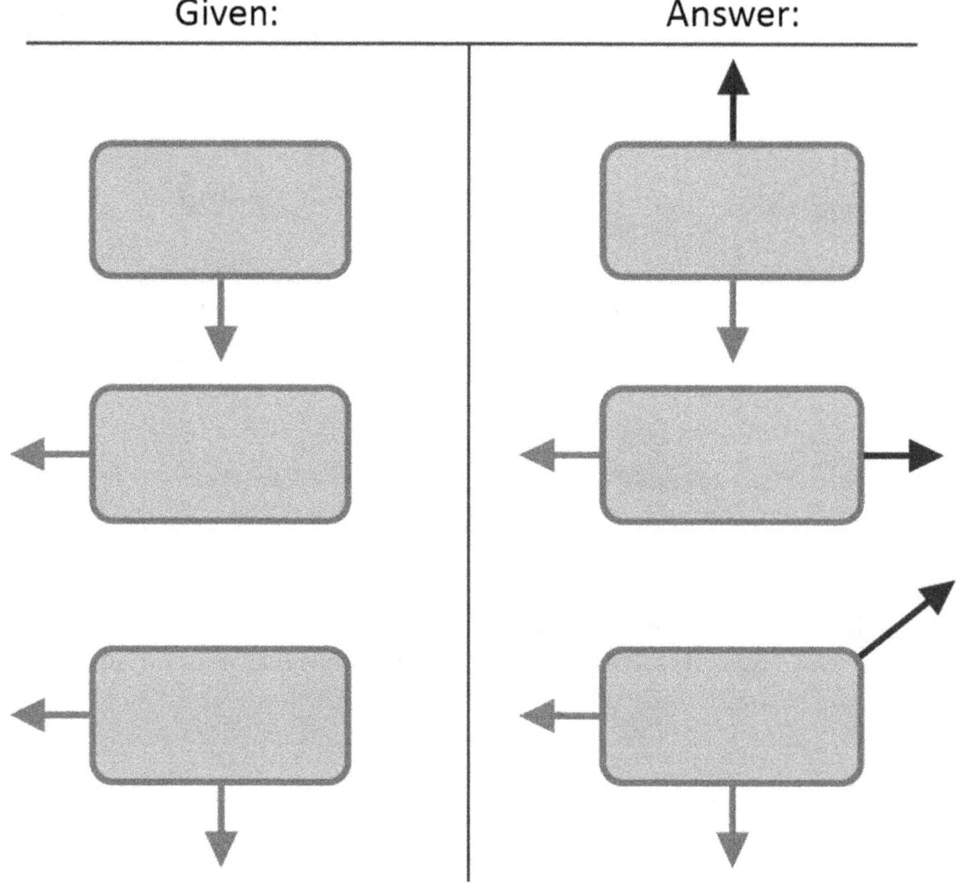

Rotational Kinetics

Many equations and concepts in linear kinematics and kinetics transfer to rotation. For example, angular position is an angle. Angular velocity, like linear velocity, is the change in the position (angle) divided by the time. Angular acceleration is the change in angular velocity divided by time. Although most tests will not require you to perform angular calculations, they will expect you to understand the angular version of force: torque.

Concept: Torque is a twisting force on an object

Calculation: Torque = radius × force

Torque, like force, is a vector and has magnitude and direction. As with force, the sum of torques on an object will affect the angular acceleration of that object. The key to solving problems with torque is understanding the lever arm. A better description of the torque equation is:

Torque = force × the distance perpedicular to the force from the center of rotation

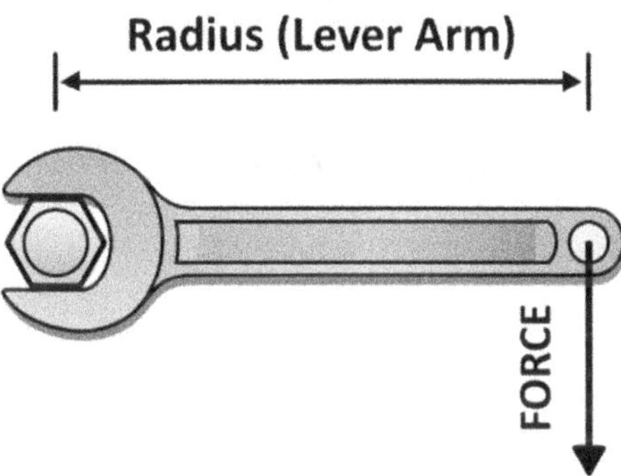

Because torque is directly proportional to the radius, or lever arm, a greater lever arm will result in a greater torque with the same amount of force. The wrench on the right has twice the radius and, as a result, twice the torque.

Alternatively, a greater force also increases torque. The wrench on the right has twice the force and twice the torque.

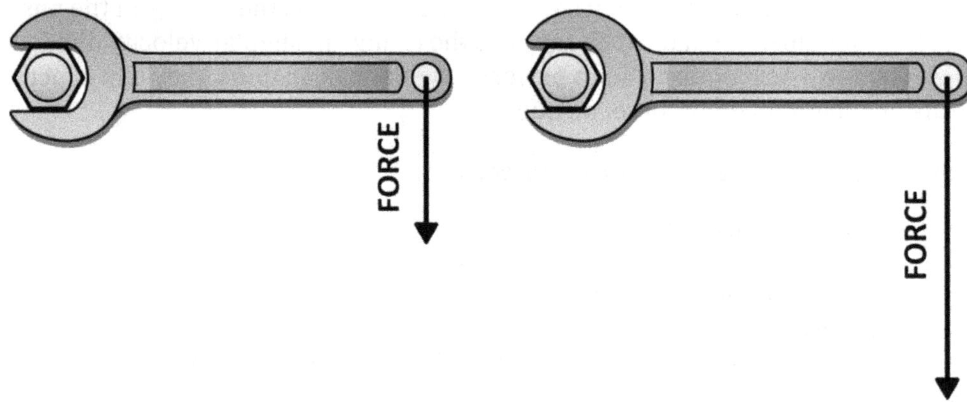

Work/Energy

Work

Concept: Work is the transfer of energy from one object to another

Calculation: Work = force × displacement

The equation for work in one dimension is fairly simple: $W = F \times d$ In the equation, the force and the displacement are the magnitude of the force exerted and the total change in position of the object on which the force is exerted, respectively. If force and displacement have the same direction, then the work is positive. If they are in opposite directions, however, the work is negative.

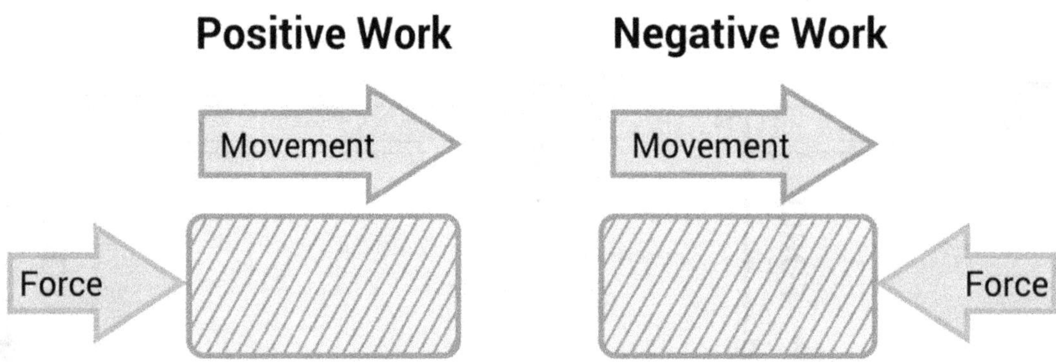

For two-dimensional work, the equation is a bit more complex:

$$\textbf{Work} = \textbf{Force} \times \textbf{displacement} \times \cos(\boldsymbol{\theta} \textbf{ between displacement and force})$$

$$\mathbf{W = F \times d \times \cos(\boldsymbol{\theta})}$$

The angle in the equation is the angle between the direction of the force and the direction of the displacement. Thus, the work done when a box is pulled at a 20 degree angle with a force of 100 lb for 20 ft will be less than the work done when a differently weighted box is pulled horizontally with a force of 100 lb for 20 ft.

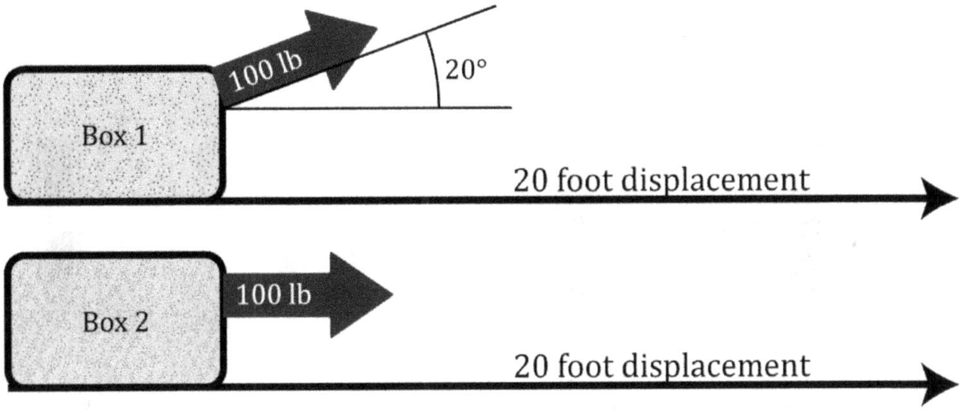

$$W_1 = 100\text{lb} \times 20\text{ft} \times \cos(20°) = 1880 \text{ ft} \cdot \text{lb}$$

$$W_2 = 100\text{lb} \times 20\text{ft} \times \cos(0°) = 2000 \text{ ft} \cdot \text{lb}$$

The unit ft · lb is the unit for both work and energy.

Review Video: Work
Visit mometrix.com/academy and enter code: 681834

Energy

Concept: The ability of a body to do work on another object

Energy is a word that has developed several different meanings in the English language, but in physics, it refers to the measure of a body's ability to do work. In physics, energy may not have a million meanings, but it does have many forms. Each of these forms, such as chemical, electric, and nuclear, is the capability of an object to perform work. However, for the purpose of most tests, mechanical energy and mechanical work are the only forms of energy worth understanding in depth. Mechanical energy is the sum of an object's kinetic and potential energies. Although they will be introduced in greater detail, these are the forms of mechanical energy:

Kinetic Energy – energy an object has by virtue of its motion

Gravitational Potential Energy – energy by virtue of an object's height

Elastic Potential Energy – energy stored in compression or tension

Neglecting frictional forces, mechanical energy is conserved.

As an example, imagine a ball moving perpendicular to the surface of the earth, in other words straight up and down, with its weight being the only force acting on it. As the ball rises, the weight will be doing work on the ball, decreasing its speed and its kinetic energy and slowing it down until it momentarily stops. During this ascent, the potential energy of the ball will be rising. Once the ball begins to fall back down, it will lose potential energy as it gains kinetic energy. Mechanical energy is conserved throughout; the potential energy of the ball at its highest point is equal to the kinetic energy of the ball at its lowest point prior to impact.

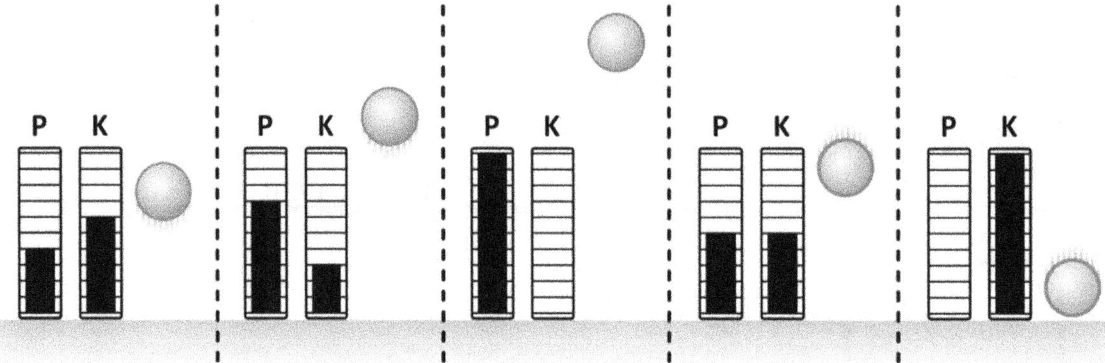

In systems where friction and air resistance are not negligible, we observe a different sort of result. For example, imagine a block sliding across the floor until it comes to a stop due to friction. Unlike a compressed spring or a ball flung into the air, there is no way for this block to regain its energy with a return trip. Therefore, we cannot say that the lost kinetic energy is being stored as potential energy. Instead, it has been dissipated and cannot be recovered. The total mechanical energy of the block-floor system has been not conserved in this case but rather reduced. The total energy of the system has not decreased, since the kinetic energy has been converted into thermal energy, but that energy is no longer useful for work.

Energy, though it may change form, will be neither created nor destroyed during physical processes. However, if we construct a system and some external force performs work on it, the result may be slightly different. If the work is positive, then the overall store of energy is increased; if it is negative, however, we can say that the overall energy of the system has decreased.

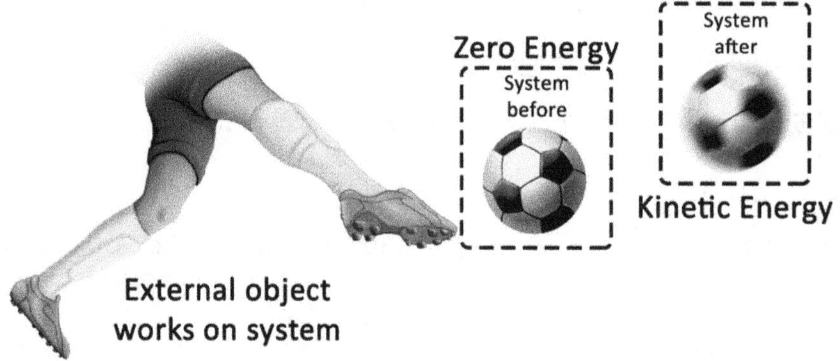

Kinetic Energy

The kinetic energy of an object is the amount of energy it possesses by reason of being in motion. Kinetic energy cannot be negative. Changes in kinetic energy will occur when a force does work on an object, such that the motion of the object is altered. This change in kinetic energy is equal to the amount of work that is done. This relationship is commonly referred to as the work-energy theorem.

One interesting application of the work-energy theorem is that of objects in a free fall. To begin with, let us assert that the force acting on such an object is its weight, which is equal to its mass times g (the force of gravity). The work done by this force will be positive, as the force is exerted in the direction in which the object is traveling. Kinetic energy will, therefore, increase, according to the work-kinetic energy theorem.

If the object is dropped from a great enough height, it eventually reaches its terminal velocity, where the drag force is equal to the weight, so the object is no longer accelerating and its kinetic energy remains constant.

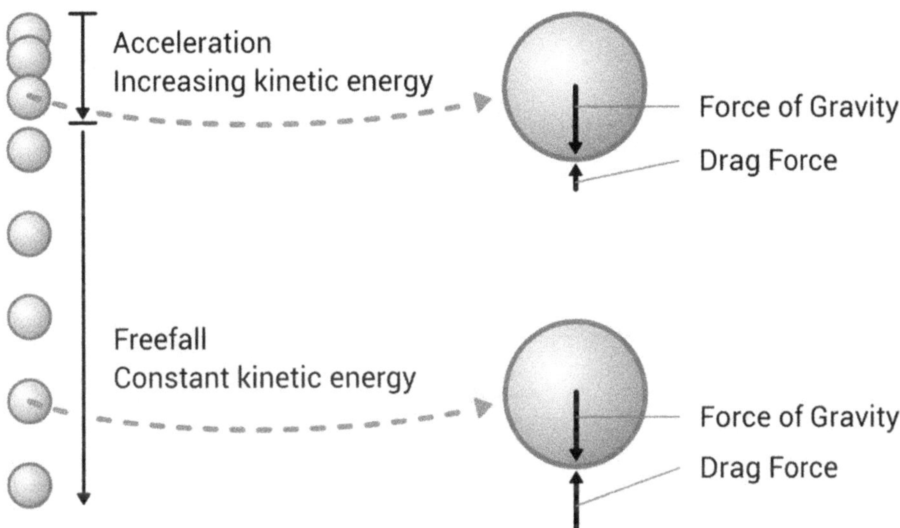

Gravitational Potential Energy

Gravitational potential energy is simply the potential for a certain amount of work to be done by one object on another using gravity. For objects on earth, the gravitational potential energy is equal to the amount of work which the earth can act on the object. The work which gravity performs on objects moving entirely or partially in the vertical direction is equal to the force exerted by the earth (weight) times the distance traveled in the direction of the force (height above the ground or reference point): Work from gravity = weight × height above the ground. Thus, the gravitational potential energy is the same as the potential work.

Gravitational Potential Energy = weight × height

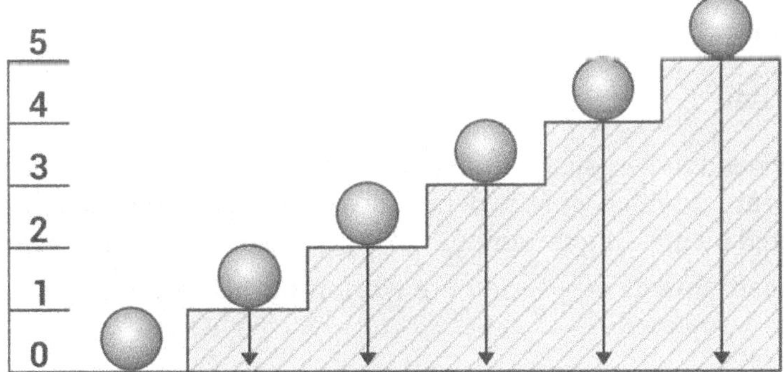

Elastic Potential Energy

Elastic potential energy is the potential for a certain amount of work to be done by one object on another using elastic compression or tension. The most common example is the spring. A spring will resist any compression or tension away from its equilibrium position (natural position). A small buggy is pressed into a large spring. The spring contains a large amount of elastic potential energy. If the buggy and spring are released, the spring will exert a force on the buggy, pushing it for a distance. This work will put kinetic energy into the buggy. The energy can be imagined as a liquid poured from one container into another. The spring pours its elastic energy into the buggy, which receives the energy as kinetic energy.

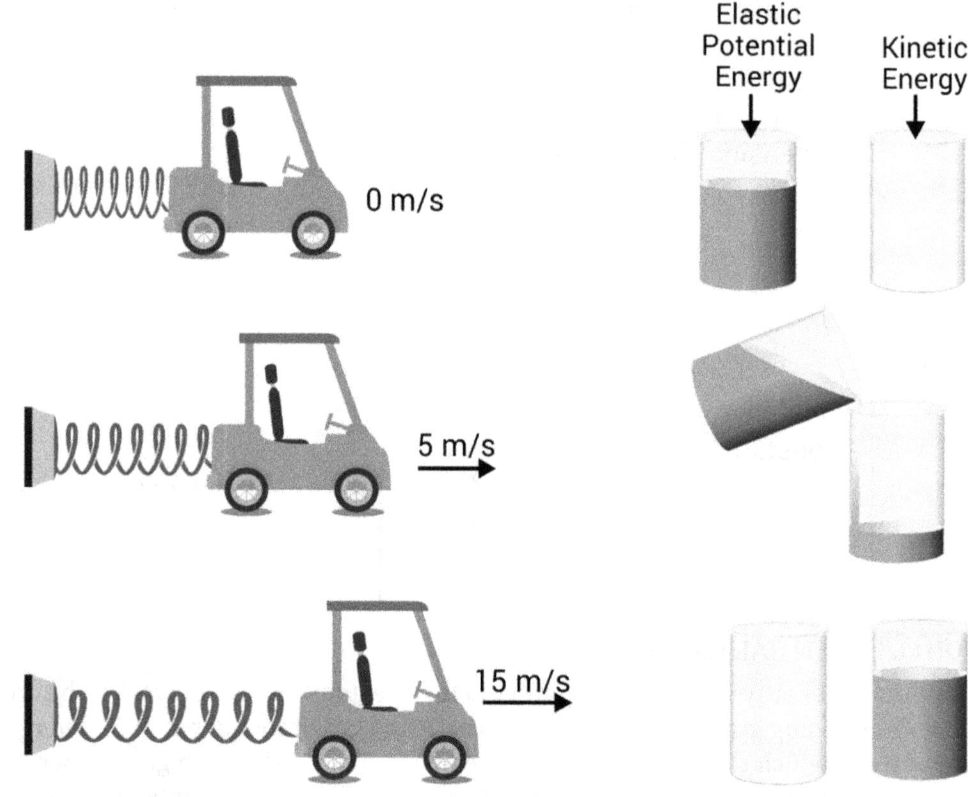

Review Video: Potential and Kinetic Energy
Visit mometrix.com/academy and enter code: 491502

Power

Concept: The rate of work

Calculation: Work/time

On occasion, you may need to demonstrate an understanding of power as it is defined in applied physics. Power is the rate at which work is done. Power, like work and energy, is a scalar quantity. Power can be calculated by dividing the amount of work performed by the amount of time in which the work was performed: **Power** $= \frac{\textbf{work}}{\textbf{time}}$. If more work is performed in a shorter amount of time, more power has been exerted. Power can be expressed in a variety of units. The preferred metric expression is one of watts or joules per seconds. Engine power is often expressed in horsepower.

Machines

SIMPLE MACHINES

Concept: Tools which transform forces to make tasks easier.

As their job is to transform forces, simple machines have an input force and an output force or forces. Simple machines transform forces in two ways: direction and magnitude. A machine can change the direction of a force, with respect to the input force, like a single stationary pulley which only changes the direction of the output force. A machine can also change the magnitude of the force like a lever.

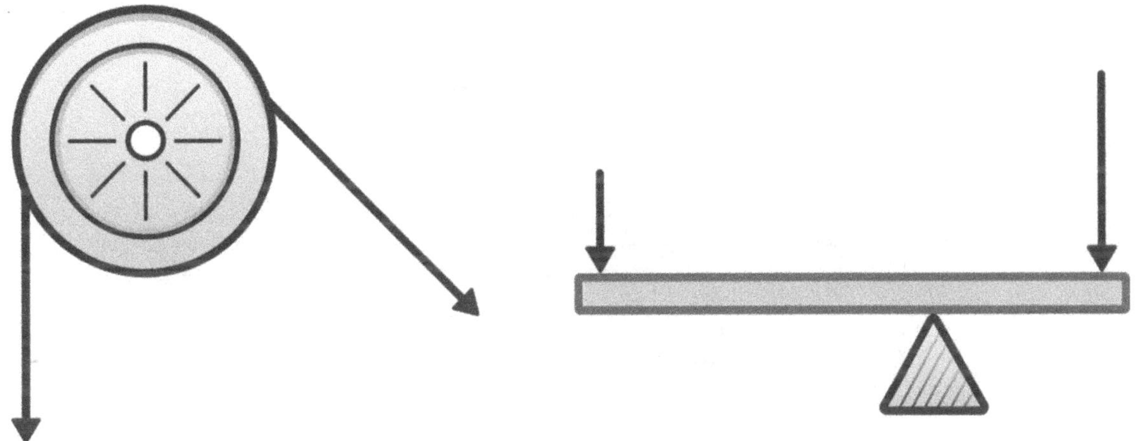

Review Video: Simple Machines
Visit mometrix.com/academy and enter code: 950789

Simple machines include the inclined plane, the wedge, the screw, the pulley, the lever, and the wheel.

Mechanical Advantage

Concept: The amount of change a simple machine provides to the magnitude of a force

Calculation: Output force/input force

Mechanical advantage is the measure of the output force divided by the input force. Thus, mechanical advantage measures the change performed by a machine. Machines cannot create energy, only transform it. Thus, in frictionless, ideal machines, the input work equals the output work.

$$\textbf{Work}_{\textbf{input}} = \textbf{Work}_{\textbf{output}}$$

$$\textbf{force}_{\textbf{input}} \times \textbf{distance}_{\textbf{input}} = \textbf{force}_{\textbf{output}} \times \textbf{distance}_{\textbf{output}}$$

This means that a simple machine can increase the force of the output by decreasing the distance which the output travels or it can increase the distance of the output by decreasing the force at the output.

By moving parts of the equation for work, we can arrive at the equation for mechanical advantage.

$$\textbf{Mechanical Advantage} = \frac{\textbf{force}_{\textbf{output}}}{\textbf{force}_{\textbf{input}}} = \frac{\textbf{distance}_{\textbf{input}}}{\textbf{distance}_{\textbf{output}}}$$

If the mechanical advantage is greater than one, the output force is greater than the input force and the input distance is greater than the output distance. Conversely, if the mechanical advantage is less than one, the input force is greater than the output force and the output distance is greater than the input distance. In equation form this is:

If Mechanical Advantage > 1:

$$\mathbf{force_{input} < force_{output} \text{ and } distance_{output} < distance_{input}}$$

If Mechanical Advantage < 1:

$$\mathbf{force_{input} > force_{output} \text{ and } distance_{output} > distance_{input}}$$

INCLINED PLANE

The inclined plane is perhaps the most common of the simple machines. It is simply a flat surface that elevates as you move from one end to the other; a ramp is an easy example of an inclined plane. Consider how much easier it is for an elderly person to walk up a long ramp than to climb a shorter but steeper flight of stairs; this is because the force required is diminished as the distance increases. Indeed, the longer the ramp, the easier it is to ascend.

On the exam, this simple fact will most often be applied to moving heavy objects. For instance, if you have to move a heavy box onto the back of a truck, it is much easier to push it up a ramp than to lift it directly onto the truck bed. The longer the ramp, the greater the mechanical advantage, and the easier it will be to move the box. The mechanical advantage of an inclined plane is equal to the slant length divided by the rise of the plane.

$$\textbf{Mechanical Advantage} = \frac{\textbf{slant length}}{\textbf{rise}}$$

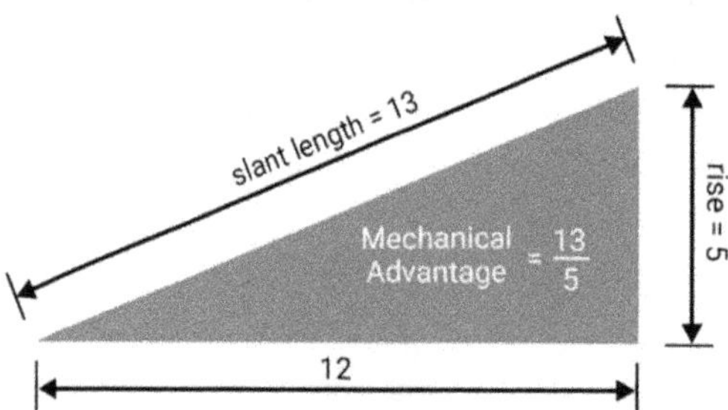

As you solve this kind of problem, however, remember that the same amount of work is being performed whether the box is lifted directly or pushed up a twenty-foot ramp; a simple machine only changes the force and the distance.

WEDGE

A wedge is a variation on the inclined plane, in which the wedge moves between objects or parts and forces them apart. The unique characteristic of a wedge is that, unlike an inclined plane, it is designed to move. Perhaps the most familiar use of the wedge is in splitting wood. A wedge is driven into the wood by hitting the flat back end. The thin end of a wedge is easier to drive into the wood since it has less surface area and, therefore, transmits more force per area. As the wedge is driven in, the increased width helps to split the wood.

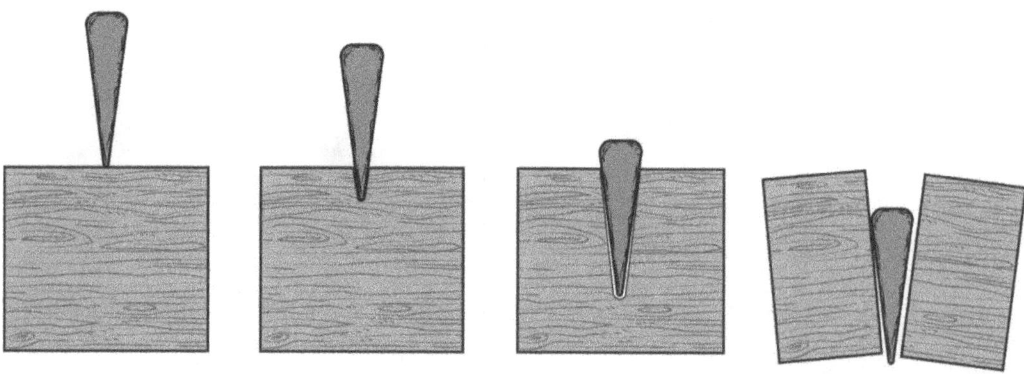

The exam may require you to select the wedge that has the highest mechanical advantage. This should be easy: the longer and thinner the wedge, the greater the mechanical advantage. The equation for mechanical advantage is:

$$\textbf{Mechanical Advantage} = \frac{\textbf{Length}}{\textbf{Width}}$$

SCREW

A screw is simply an inclined plane that has been wound around a cylinder so that it forms a sort of spiral.

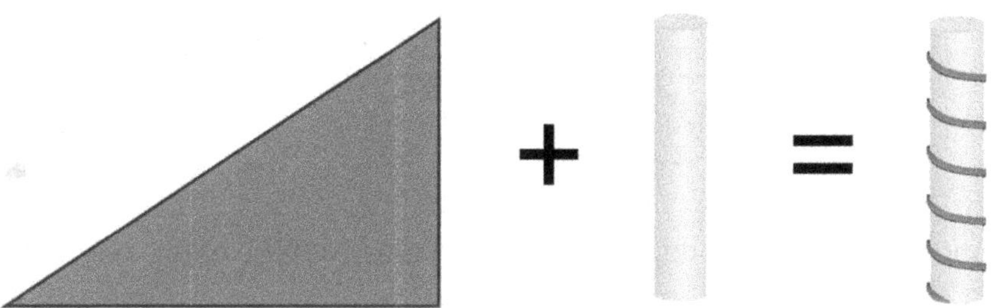

When it is placed into some medium, as for instance wood, the screw will move either forward or backward when it is rotated. The principle of the screw is used in a number of different objects, from jar lids to flashlights. On the exam, you are unlikely to see many questions regarding screws, though you may be presented with a given screw rotation and asked in which direction the screw will move. However, for consistency's sake, the equation for the mechanical advantage is a modification of the inclined plane's equation. Again, the formula for an inclined plane is:

$$\textbf{Mechanical Advantage} = \frac{\textbf{slant length}}{\textbf{rise}}$$

Because the rise of the inclined plane is the length along a screw, length between rotations = rise. Also, the slant length will equal the circumference of one rotation = $2\pi r$.

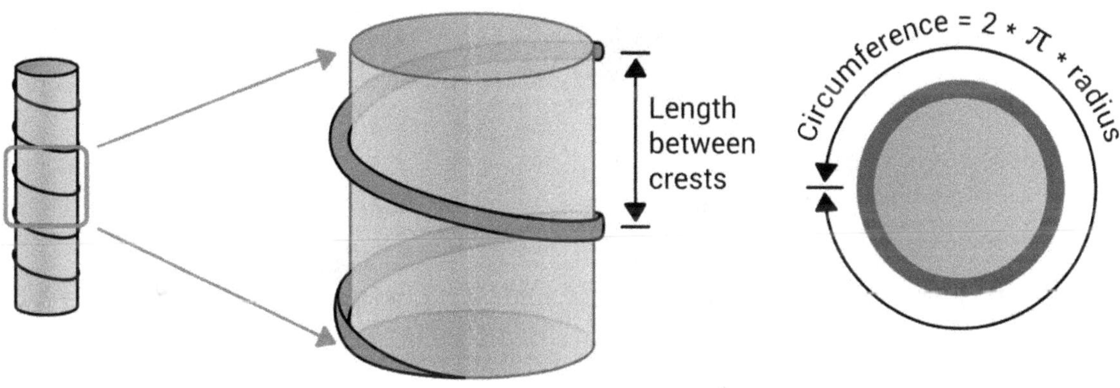

$$\textbf{Mechanical Advantage} = \frac{\textbf{2} \times \pi \times \textbf{radius}}{\textbf{length between crests}}$$

LEVER

The lever is the most common kind of simple machine. See-saws, shovels, and baseball bats are all examples of levers. There are three classes of levers which are differentiated by the relative orientations of the fulcrum, resistance, and effort. The fulcrum is the point at which the lever rotates, the effort is the point on the lever where force is applied, and the resistance is the part of the lever that acts in response to the effort.

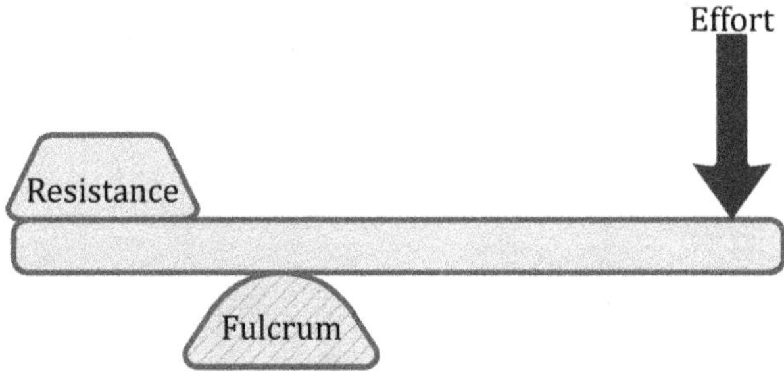

The mechanical advantage of a lever depends on the distances of the effort and resistance from the fulcrum.

$$\textbf{Mechanical Advantage} = \frac{\textbf{effort distance}}{\textbf{resistance distance}}$$

Each class of lever has a different arrangement of effort, fulcrum, and resistance:

First-Class Lever

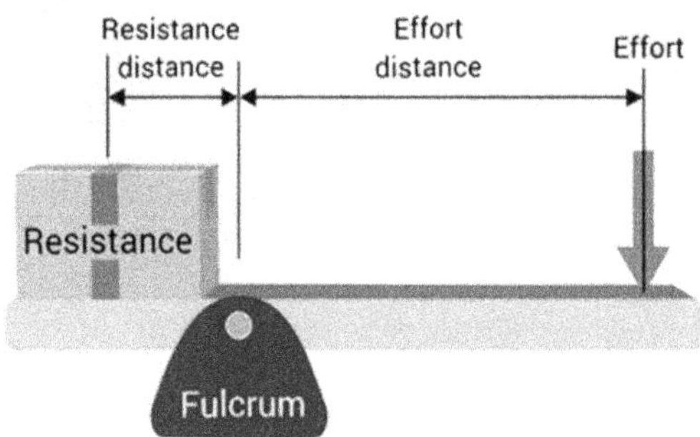

First-Class Lever

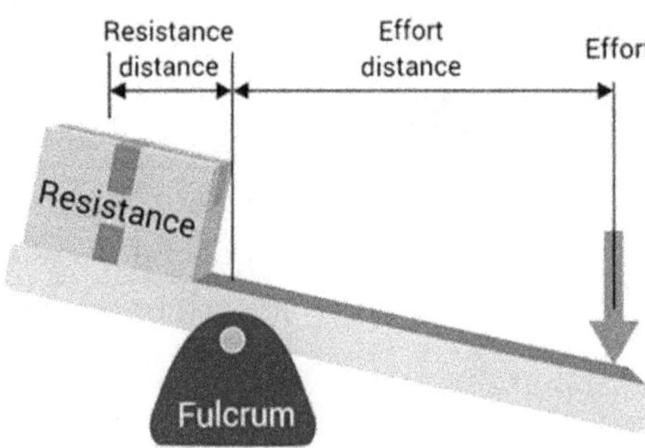

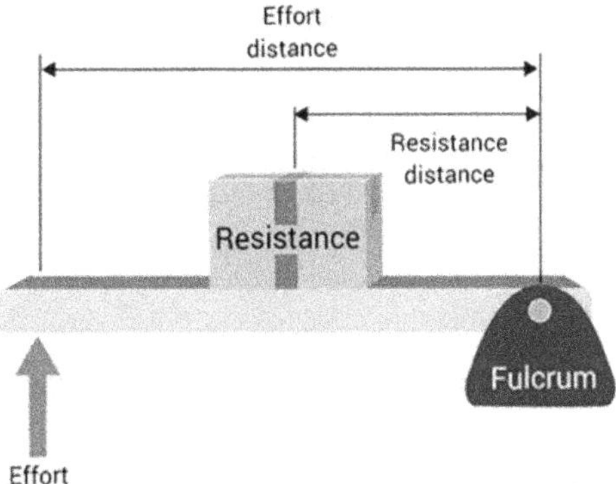
Second-Class Lever
Effort distance
Resistance distance
Resistance
Fulcrum
Effort

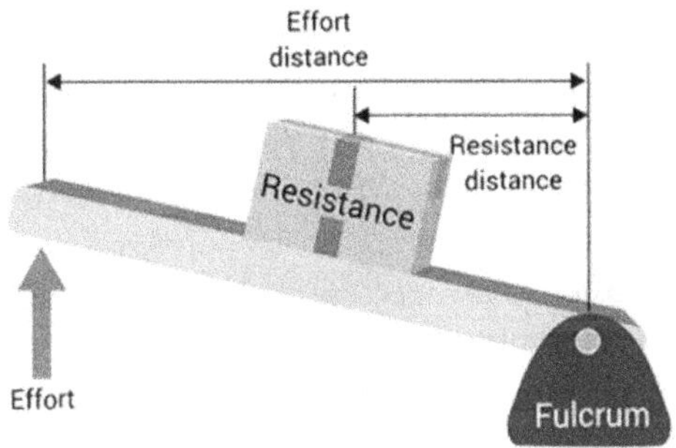
Second-Class Lever
Effort distance
Resistance distance
Resistance
Effort
Fulcrum

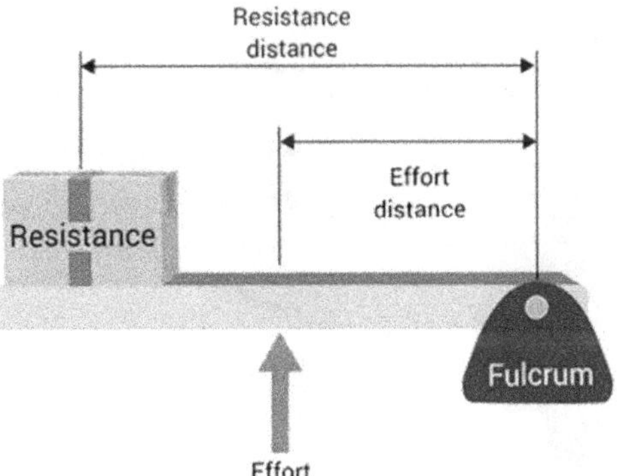
Third-Class Lever
Resistance distance
Effort distance
Resistance
Fulcrum
Effort

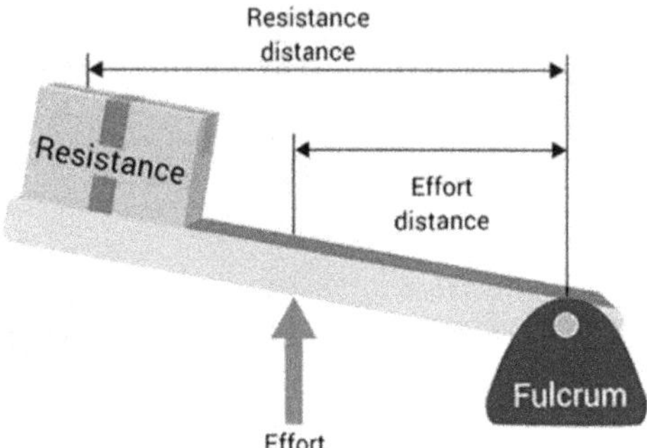

In a first-class lever, the fulcrum is between the effort and the resistance. A seesaw is a good example of a first-class lever when effort is applied to force one end up, the other end goes down, and vice versa. The shorter the distance between the fulcrum and the resistance, the easier it will be to move the resistance. As an example, consider whether it is easier to lift another person on a see-saw when they are sitting close to the middle or all the way at the end. A little practice will show you that it is much more difficult to lift a person the farther away he or she is on the see-saw.

In a second-class lever, the resistance is in between the fulcrum and the effort. While a first-class lever is able to increase force and distance through mechanical advantage, a second-class lever is only able to increase force. A common example of a second-class lever is the wheelbarrow; the force exerted by your hand at one end of the wheelbarrow is magnified at the load. Basically, with a second-class lever, you are trading distance for force; by moving your end of the wheelbarrow a bit farther, you produce greater force at the load.

Third-class levers are used to produce greater distance. In a third-class lever, the force is applied in between the fulcrum and the resistance. A baseball bat is a classic example of a third-class lever; the bottom of the bat, below where you grip it, is considered the fulcrum. The end of the bat, where the ball is struck, is the resistance. By exerting effort at the base of the bat, close to the fulcrum, you are able to make the end of the bat fly quickly through the air. The closer your hands are to the base of the bat, the faster you will be able to make the other end of the bat travel.

Review Video: Levers
Visit mometrix.com/academy and enter code: 103910

PULLEY

The pulley is a simple machine in which a rope is carried by the rotation of a wheel. Another name for a pulley is a block. Pulleys are typically used to allow the force to be directed from a convenient location. For instance, imagine you are given the task of lifting a heavy and tall bookcase. Rather than tying a rope to the bookcase and trying to lift it, it would make sense to tie a pulley system to a rafter above the bookcase and run the rope through it, so that you could pull down on the rope and lift the bookcase. Pulling down allows you to incorporate your weight (normal force) into the act of lifting, thereby making it easier.

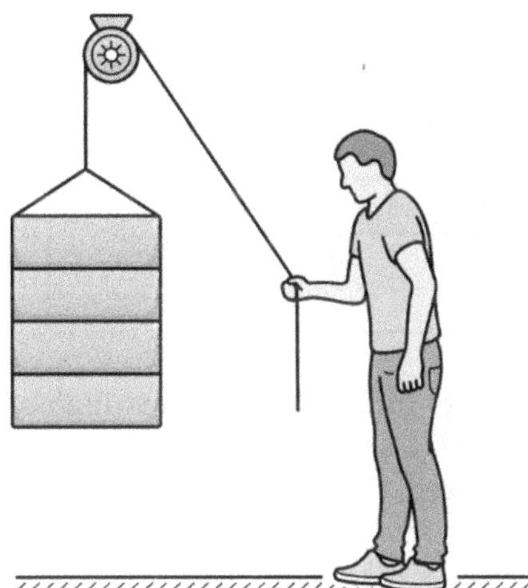

If there is just one pulley above the bookcase, you have created a first-class lever that will not diminish the amount of force that needs to be applied to lift the bookcase. There is another way to use a pulley, however, that can make the job of lifting a heavy object considerably easier. First, tie the rope directly to the rafter. Then, attach a pulley to the top of the bookcase and run the rope through it. If you can then stand so that you are above the bookcase, you will have a much easier time lifting this heavy object. Why? Because the weight of the bookcase is now being distributed: half of it is acting on the rafter, and half of it is acting on you. In other words, this arrangement allows you to lift an object with half the force. This simple pulley system, therefore, has a mechanical advantage of 2. Note that in this arrangement, the unfixed pulley is acting like a second-class lever. The price you pay for your mechanical advantage is that whatever distance you raise your end of the rope, the bookcase will only be lifted half as much.

Of course, it might be difficult for you to find a place high enough to enact this system. If this is the case, you can always tie another pulley to the rafter and run the rope through it and back down to the floor. Since this second pulley is fixed, the mechanical advantage will remain the same.

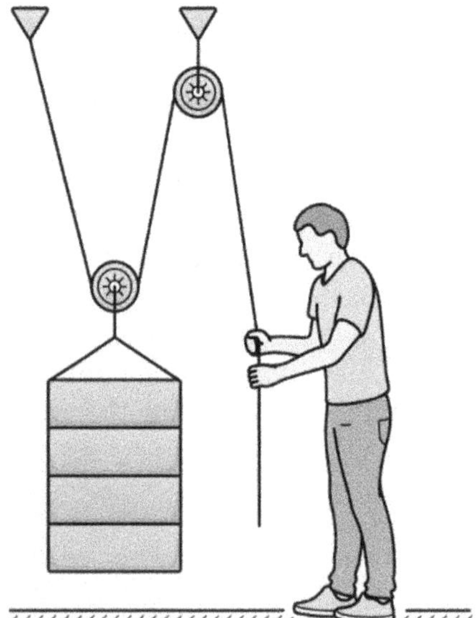

There are other, slightly more complex ways to obtain an even greater mechanical advantage with a system of pulleys. On the exam, you may be required to determine the pulley and tackle (rope) arrangement that creates the greatest mechanical advantage. The easiest way to determine the answer is to count the number of ropes that are going to and from the unfixed pulley; the more ropes coming and going, the greater the mechanical advantage.

Wheel and Axle

Another basic arrangement that makes use of simple machines is called the wheel and axle. When most people think of a wheel and axle, they immediately envision an automobile tire. The steering wheel of the car, however, operates on the same mechanical principle, namely that the force required to move the center of a circle is much greater than the force required to move the outer rim of a circle. When you turn the steering wheel, you are essentially using a second-class lever by increasing the output force by increasing the input distance. The force required to turn the wheel from the outer rim is much less than would be required to turn the wheel from its center. Just imagine how difficult it would be to drive a car if the steering wheel was the size of a saucer!

Conceptually, the mechanical advantage of a wheel is easy to understand. For instance, all other things being equal, the mechanical advantage created by a system will increase along with the radius. In other words, a steering wheel with a radius of 12 inches has a greater mechanical advantage than a steering wheel with a radius of ten inches; the same amount of force exerted on the rim of each wheel will produce greater force at the axis of the larger wheel.

Review Video: Simple Machines - Wheel and Axle
Visit mometrix.com/academy and enter code: 574045

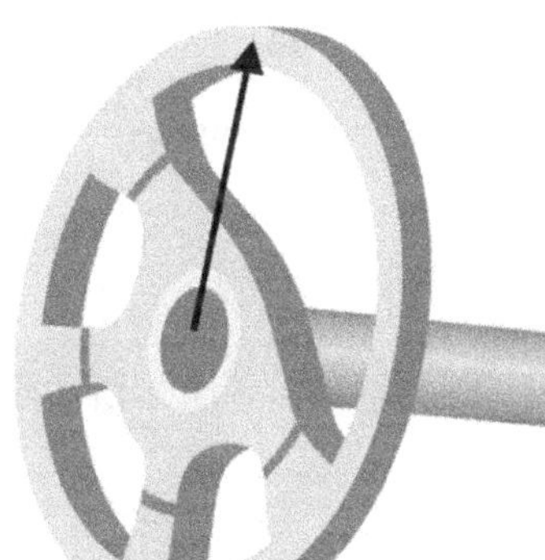

The equation for the mechanical advantage of a wheel and axle is:

$$\textbf{Mechanical Advantage} = \frac{\textbf{radius}_{\textbf{wheel}}}{\textbf{radius}_{\textbf{axle}}}$$

Thus, the mechanical advantage of the steering wheel with a larger radius will be:

$$\textbf{Mechanical Advantage} = \frac{\textbf{12 inches}}{\textbf{2 inches}} = \textbf{6}$$

Gears

The exam may ask you questions involving some slightly more complex mechanisms. It is very common, for instance, for there to be a couple of questions concerning gears. Gears are a system of interlocking wheels that can create immense mechanical advantages. The amount of mechanical advantage, however, will depend on the gear ratio; that is, on the relation in size between the gears.

When a small gear is driving a big gear, the speed of the big gear is relatively slow; when a big gear is driving a small gear, the speed of the small gear is relatively fast.

The equation for the mechanical advantage is:

$$\textbf{Mechanical Advantage} = \frac{\text{Torque}_{\text{output}}}{\text{Torque}_{\text{input}}} = \frac{r_{\text{output}}}{r_{\text{input}}} = \frac{\#\text{ of teeth}_{\text{output}}}{\#\text{ of teeth}_{\text{input}}}$$

Note that mechanical advantage is greater than 1 when the output gear is larger. In these cases, the output velocity (ω) will be lower. The equation for the relative speed of a gear system is:

$$\frac{\omega_{\text{input}}}{\omega_{\text{output}}} = \frac{r_{\text{output}}}{r_{\text{input}}}$$

$$\textit{Mechanical Advantage} = \frac{\textit{teeth}_{\textit{output}}}{\textit{teeth}_{\textit{input}}} = \frac{20}{10} = 2$$

$$\textit{Mechanical Advantage} = \frac{\textit{teeth}_{\textit{output}}}{\textit{teeth}_{\textit{input}}} = \frac{16}{8} = 2$$

USES OF GEARS

Gears are used to change the direction, location, and amount of output torque, as well as change the angular velocity of output.

Change output direction

Change torque amount

Change output velocity

GEAR RATIOS

A gear ratio is a measure of how much the speed and torque are changing in a gear system. It is the ratio of output speed to input speed. Because the number of teeth is directly proportional to the speed in meshing gears, a gear ratio can also be calculated using the number of teeth on the gears. When the driving gear has 30 teeth and the driven gear has 10 teeth, the gear ratio is 3:1.

$$\text{Gear Ratio} = \frac{\#\text{ of teeth}_{\text{driving}}}{\#\text{ of teeth}_{\text{driven}}} = \frac{30}{10} = \frac{3}{1} = 3:1$$

This means that the smaller, driven gear rotates 3 times for every 1 rotation of the driving gear.

The Hydraulic Jack

The hydraulic jack is a simple machine using two tanks and two pistons to change the amount of an output force.

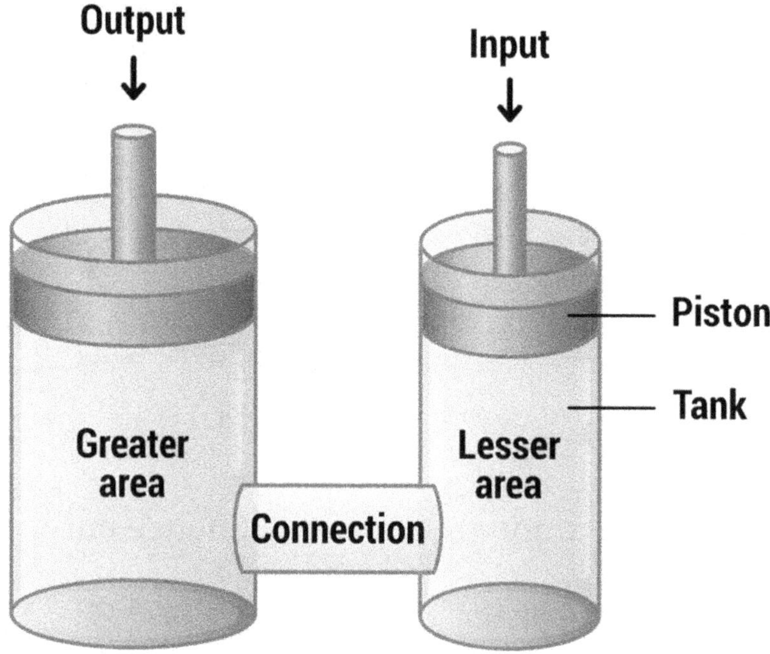

Since fluids are effectively incompressible, when you apply pressure to one part of a contained fluid, that pressure will have to be relieved in equal measure elsewhere in the container. Suppose the input piston has half the surface area of the output piston (10 in^2 compared to 20 in^2), and it is being pushed downward with 50 pounds of force. The pressure being applied to the fluid is 50 lb ÷ $10\ \text{in}^2 = 5\frac{\text{lb}}{\text{in}^2}$ or 5 psi. When that 5 psi of pressure is applied to the output piston, it pushes that piston upward with a force of $5\frac{\text{lb}}{\text{in}^2} \times 20\ \text{in}^2 = 100\ \text{lb}$.

The hydraulic jack functions similarly to a first-class lever, but with the important factor being the area of the pistons rather than the length of the lever arms. Note that the mechanical advantage is based on the relative areas, not the relative radii, of the pistons. The radii must be squared to compute the relative areas.

$$\textbf{Mechanical Advantage} = \frac{\textbf{Force}_{\textbf{output}}}{\textbf{Force}_{\textbf{input}}} = \frac{\textbf{area}_{\textbf{output}}}{\textbf{area}_{\textbf{input}}} = \frac{\textbf{radius}_{\textbf{output}}^{\ 2}}{\textbf{radius}_{\textbf{input}}^{\ 2}}$$

Pulleys and Belts

Another system involves two pulleys connected by a drive belt (a looped band that goes around both pulleys). The operation of this system is similar to that of gears, with the exception that the pulleys will rotate in the same direction, while interlocking gears will rotate in opposite directions.

A smaller pulley will always spin faster than a larger pulley, though the larger pulley will generate more torque.

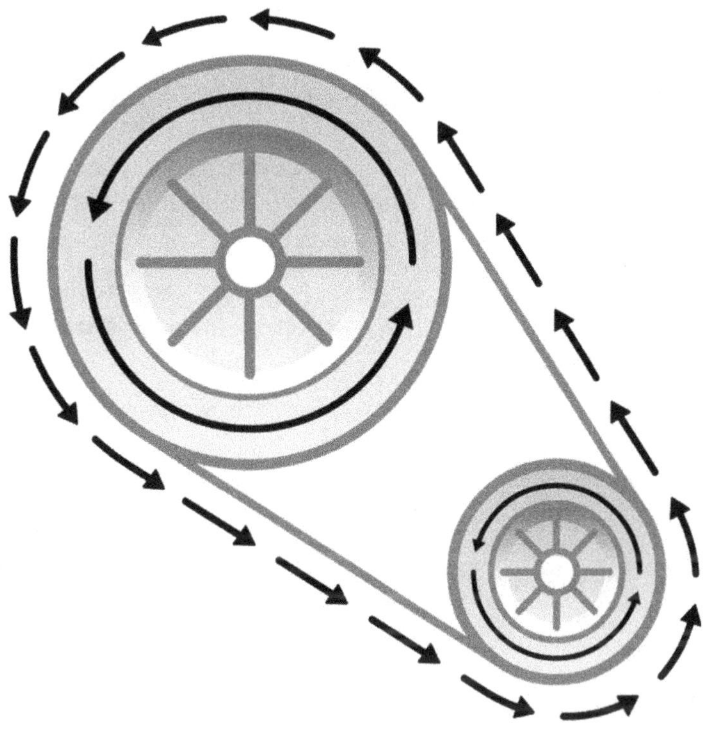

The speed ratio between the pulleys can be determined by comparing their radii; for instance, a 4-inch pulley and a 12-inch pulley will have a speed ratio of 3:1.

Momentum/Impulse

Linear Momentum

Concept: How much a body will resist stopping

Calculation: Momentum = mass × velocity

In physics, linear momentum can be found by multiplying the mass and velocity of an object. Momentum and velocity will always be in the same direction. Newton's second law describes momentum, stating that the rate of change of momentum is proportional to the force exerted and is in the direction of the force. If we assume a closed and isolated system (one in which no objects leave or enter, and upon which the sum of external forces is zero), then we can assume that the momentum of the system will neither increase nor decrease. That is, we will find that the momentum is a constant. The law of conservation of linear momentum applies universally in physics, even in situations of extremely high velocity or with subatomic particles.

Collisions

This concept of momentum takes on new importance when we consider collisions. A collision is an isolated event in which a strong force acts between each of two or more colliding bodies for a brief period of time. However, a collision is more intuitively defined as one or more objects hitting each other.

When two bodies collide, each object exerts a force on the opposite member. These equal and opposite forces change the linear momentum of the objects. However, when both bodies are considered, the net momentum in collisions is conserved.

There are two types of collisions: elastic and inelastic. The difference between the two lies in whether kinetic energy is conserved. If the total kinetic energy of the system is conserved, the collision is elastic. Visually, elastic collisions are collisions in which objects bounce perfectly. If some of the kinetic energy is transformed into heat or another form of energy, the collision is inelastic. Visually, inelastic collisions are collisions in which the objects stick to each other or bounce but do not return to their original height.

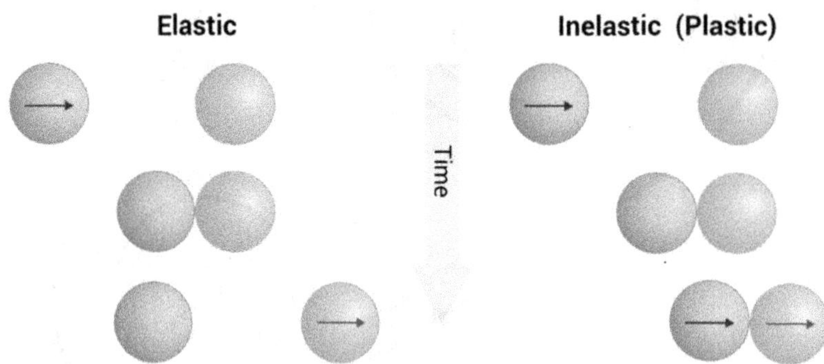

If the two bodies involved in an elastic collision have the same mass, then the body that was moving will stop completely, and the body that was at rest will begin moving at the same velocity as the projectile was moving before the collision.

Fluids

FLUIDS

Concept: Liquids and gasses

A few of the questions on the exam will probably require you to consider the behavior of fluids. It sounds obvious, perhaps, but fluids can best be defined as substances that flow. A fluid will conform, slowly or quickly, to any container in which it is placed. Both liquids and gasses are considered to be fluids. Fluids are essentially those substances in which the atoms are not arranged in any permanent, rigid way. In ice, for instance, atoms are all lined up in what is known as a crystalline lattice, while in water and steam, the only intermolecular arrangements are haphazard connections between neighboring molecules.

FLOW RATES

When liquids flow in and out of containers at certain rates, the change in volume is the volumetric flow in minus the volumetric flow out. Volumetric flow is essentially the amount of volume moved past some point divided by the time it took for the volume to pass.

$$\textbf{Volumetric flow rate} = \frac{\textbf{volume moved}}{\textbf{time for the movement}}$$

If the flow into a container is greater than the flow out, the container will fill with the fluid. However, if the flow out of a container is greater than the flow into a container, the container will drain of the fluid.

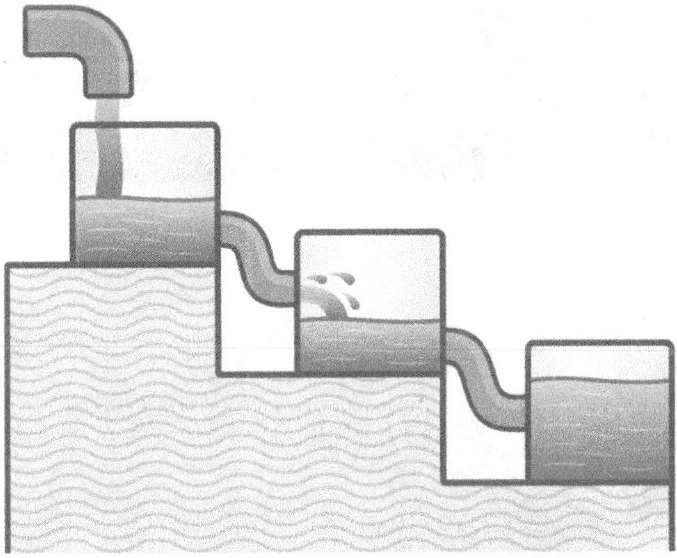

DENSITY

Concept: How much mass is in a specific volume of a substance

Calculation: $\textbf{Density} = \rho = \frac{\text{mass}}{\text{volume}}$

Density is essentially how much stuff there is in a volume or space. The density of a fluid is generally expressed with the symbol ρ (the Greek letter *rho*). Density is a scalar property, meaning that it has no direction component.

PRESSURE

Concept: The amount of force applied per area

Calculation: $\textbf{Pressure} = \frac{\text{force}}{\text{area}}$

Pressure, like fluid density, is a scalar and does not have a direction. The equation for pressure is concerned only with the magnitude of that force, not with the direction in which it is pointing. The SI unit of pressure is the Newton per square meter, or Pascal.

As every deep-sea diver knows, the pressure of water becomes greater the deeper you go below the surface; conversely, experienced mountain climbers know that air pressure decreases as they gain a higher altitude. These pressures are typically referred to as hydrostatic pressures because they involve fluids at rest.

Pascal's Principle

The exam may also require you to demonstrate some knowledge of how fluids move. Anytime you squeeze a tube of toothpaste, you are demonstrating the idea known as Pascal's principle. This principle states that a change in the pressure applied to an enclosed fluid is transmitted undiminished to every portion of the fluid as well as to the walls of the containing vessel.

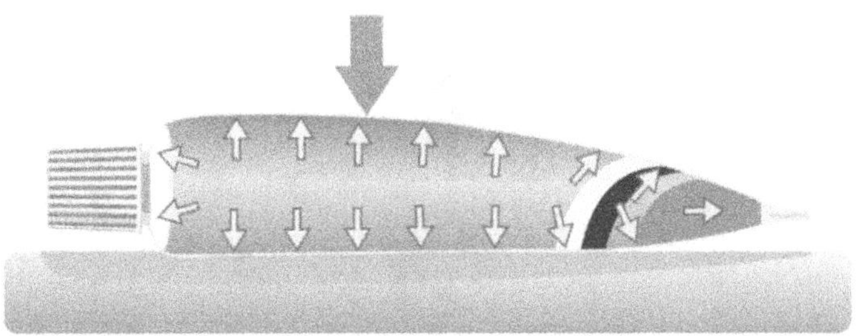

Buoyant Force

If an object is submerged in water, it will have a buoyant force exerted on it in the upward direction. Often, of course, this buoyant force is much too small to keep an object from sinking to the bottom. Buoyancy is summarized in Archimedes' principle; a body wholly or partially submerged in a fluid will be buoyed up by a force equal to the weight of the fluid that the body displaces.

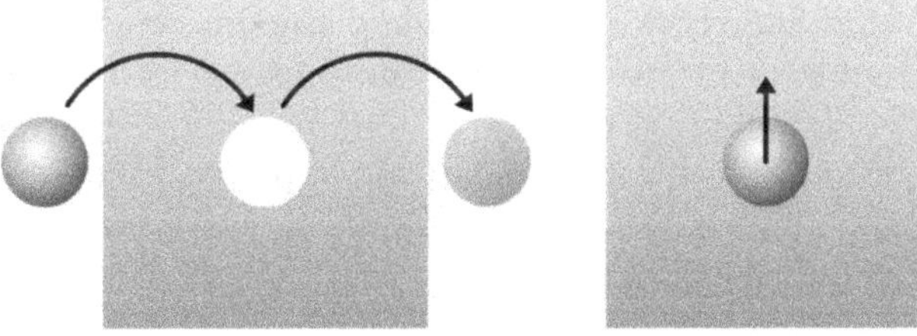

If the buoyant force is greater than the weight of an object, the object will go upward. If the weight of the object is greater than the buoyant force, the object will sink. When an object is floating on the surface, the buoyant force has the same magnitude as the weight.

Even though the weight of a floating object is precisely balanced by a buoyant force, these forces will not necessarily act at the same point. The weight will act from the center of mass of the object, while the buoyancy will act from the center of mass of the hole in the water made by the object (known as the center of buoyancy). If the floating object is tilted, then the center of buoyancy will shift and the object may be unstable. In order to remain in equilibrium, the center of buoyancy must always shift in such a way that the buoyant force and weight provide a restoring torque, one that will restore the body to its upright position. This concept is, of course, crucial to the construction of boats which must always be made to encourage restoring torque.

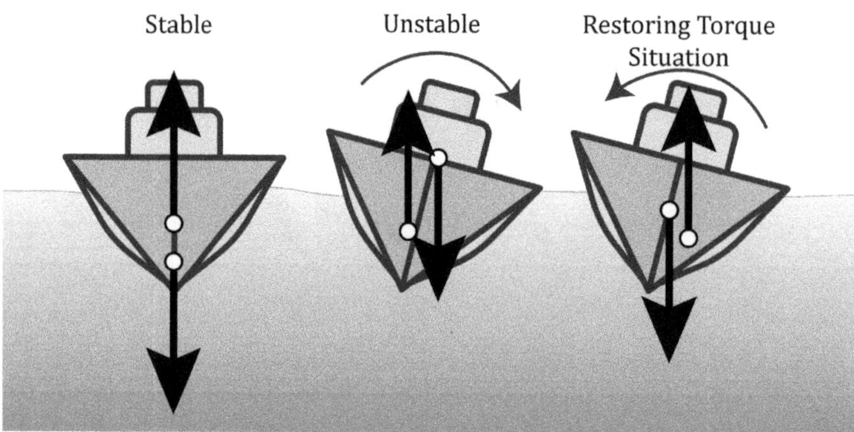

Ideal Fluids

Because the motion of actual fluids is extremely complex, the exam usually assumes ideal fluids when they set up their problems. Using ideal fluids in fluid dynamics problems is like discounting friction in other problems. Therefore, when we deal with ideal fluids, we are making four assumptions. It is important to keep these in mind when considering the behavior of fluids on the exam. First, we are assuming that the flow is steady; in other words, the velocity of every part of the fluid is the same. Second, we assume that fluids are incompressible and therefore have a consistent density. Third, we assume that fluids are nonviscous, meaning that they flow easily and without resistance. Fourth, we assume that the flow of ideal fluids is irrotational: that is, particles in the fluid will not rotate around a center of mass.

Bernoulli's Principle

When fluids move, they do not create or destroy energy; this modification of Newton's second law for fluid behavior is called Bernoulli's principle. It is essentially just a reformulation of the law of conservation of mechanical energy for fluid mechanics.

The most common application of Bernoulli's principle is that pressure and speed are inversely related, assuming constant altitude. Thus, if the elevation of the fluid remains constant and the speed of a fluid particle increases as it travels along a streamline, the pressure will decrease. If the fluid slows down, the pressure will increase.

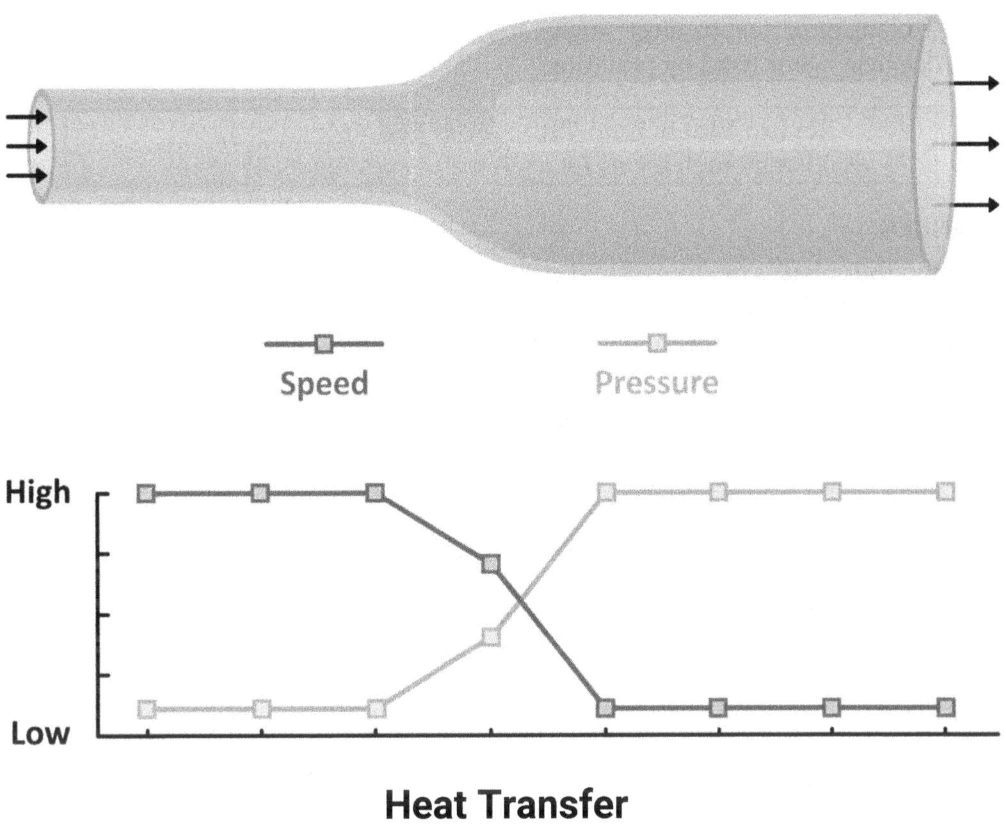

Heat Transfer

HEAT TRANSFER

Heat is a type of energy. Heat transfers from the hot object to the cold object through the three forms of heat transfer: conduction, convection, and radiation.

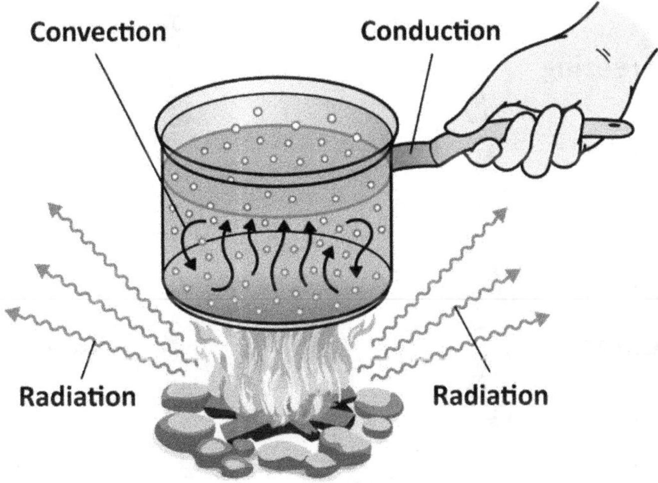

Conduction is the transfer of heat by physical contact. When you touch a hot pot, the pot transfers heat to your hand by conduction.

Convection is the transfer of heat by the movement of fluids. When you put your hand in steam, the steam transfers heat to your hand by convection.

Radiation is the transfer of heat by electromagnetic waves. When you put your hand near a campfire, the fire heats your hand by radiation.

Review Video: Heat Transfer at the Molecular Level
Visit mometrix.com/academy and enter code: 451646

Phase Changes

Materials exist in four phases or states: solid, liquid, gas, and plasma. However, as most tests will not cover plasma, we will focus on solids, liquids, and gases. The solid state is the densest in almost all cases (water is the most notable exception), followed by liquid, and then gas.

The catalyst for phase change (changing from one phase to another) is heat. When a solid is heated, it will change into a liquid. The same process of heating will change a liquid into a gas.

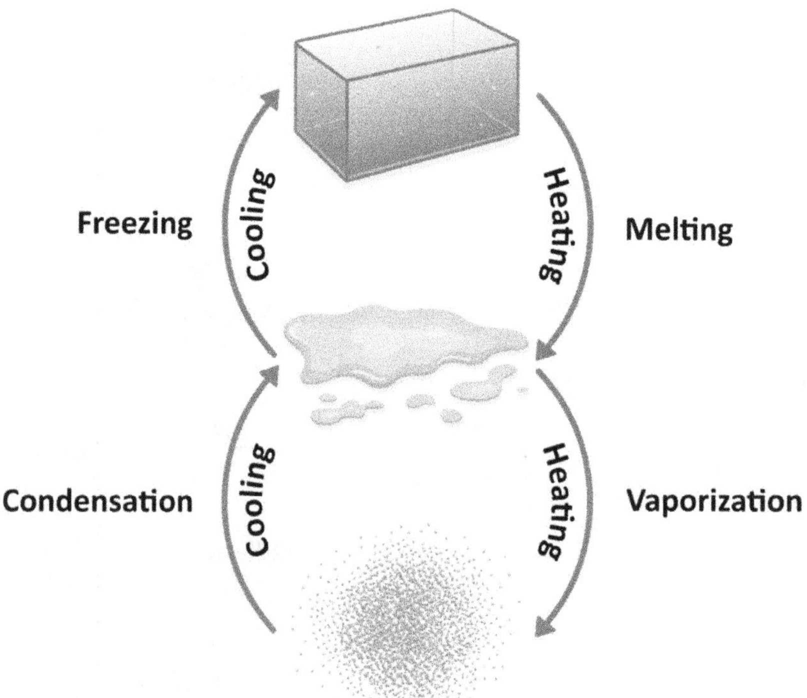

Review Video: States of Matter
Visit mometrix.com/academy and enter code: 742449

Optics

Optics

Lenses change the way light travels. Lenses are able to achieve this by the way in which light travels at different speeds in different mediums. The essentials to optics with lenses deal with concave and convex lenses. Concave lenses make objects appear smaller, while convex lenses make objects appear larger.

Convex Lens

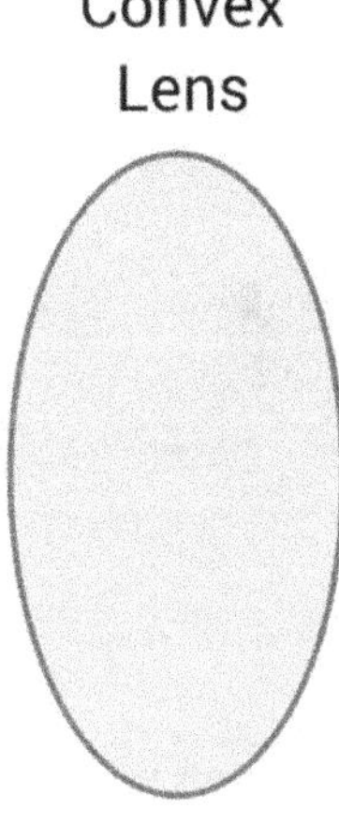

View through a convex lens

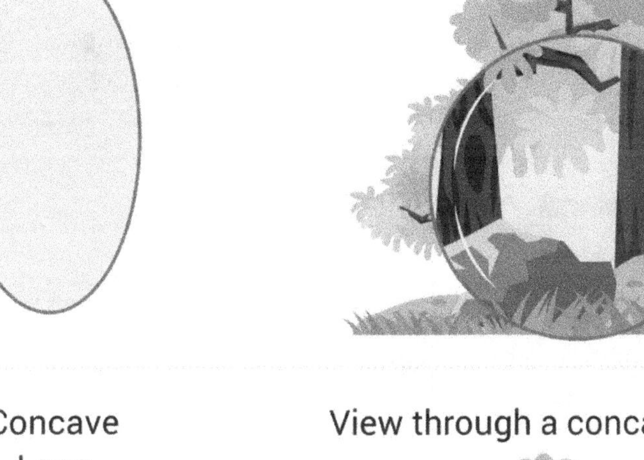

Concave Lens

View through a concave lens

Electricity

Electric Charge

Much like gravity, electricity is an everyday observable phenomenon which is very complex, but may be understood as a set of behaviors. As the gravitational force exists between objects with mass, the electric force exists between objects with electrical charge. In all atoms, the protons have a positive charge, the electrons have a negative charge, and the neutrons have no charge. An imbalance of electrons and protons in an object results in a net charge. Unlike gravity, which only pulls, electrical forces can push objects apart as well as pull them together.

Similar electric charges repel each other. Opposite charges attract each other.

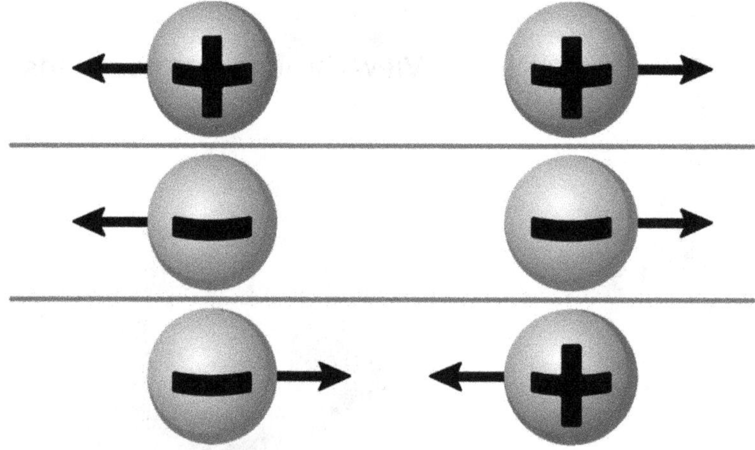

Review Video: Electric Charge
Visit mometrix.com/academy and enter code: 323587

CURRENT

Electrons (and electrical charge with it) move through conductive materials by switching quickly from one atom to another. This electrical flow can manipulate energy like mechanical systems.

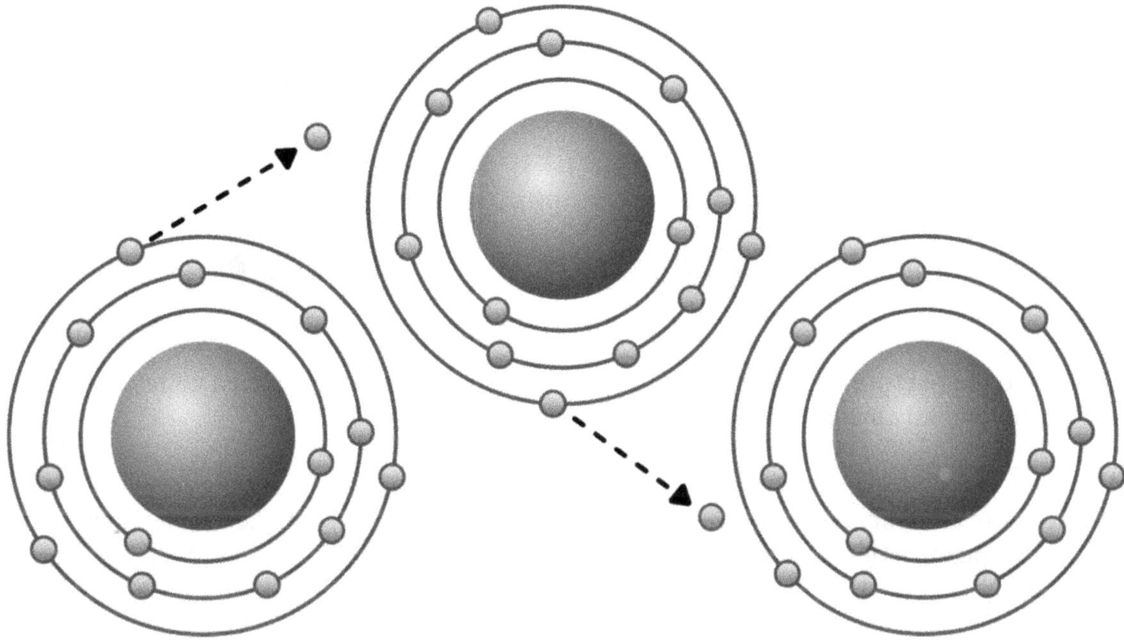

The term for the rate at which the charge flows through a conductive material is *current*. Because each electron carries a specific charge, current can be thought of as the number of electrons passing a point in a length of time. Current is measured in Amperes (A), each unit of which is approximately 6.24×10^{18} electrons per second.

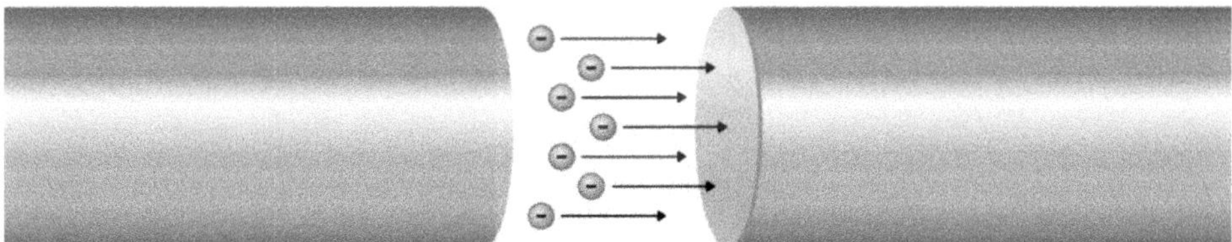

Electric current carries energy much like moving balls carry energy.

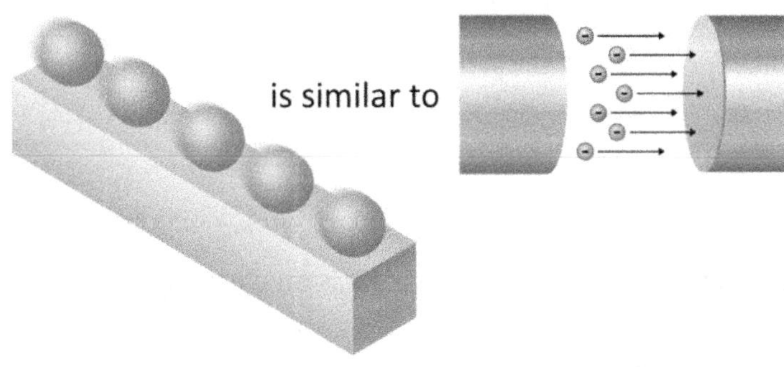

Voltage

Voltage is the potential for electric work. It can also be thought of as the *push* behind electrical work. Voltage is similar to gravitational potential energy.

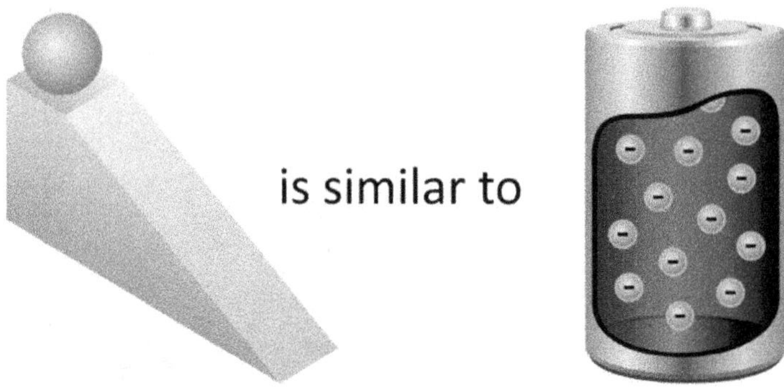

Anything used to generate a voltage, such as a battery or a generator, is called a voltage source. Voltage is conveniently measured in Volts (V).

Resistance

Resistance is the amount something hinders the flow of electrical current. Electrical resistance is much like friction, resisting flow and dissipating energy.

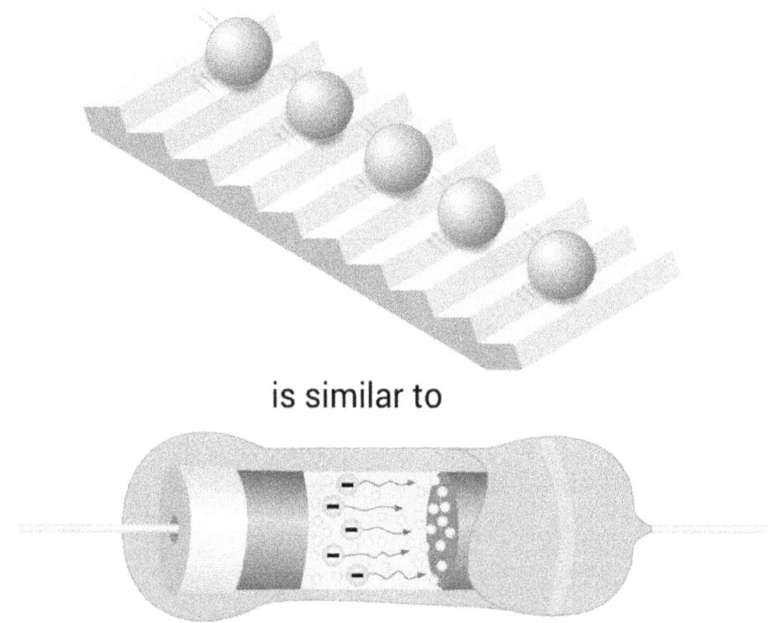

Different objects have different resistances. A resistor is an electrical component designed to have a specific resistance, measured in Ohms (Ω).

Review Video: Resistance of Electric Currents
Visit mometrix.com/academy and enter code: 668423

BASIC CIRCUITS

A circuit is a closed loop through which current can flow. A simple circuit contains a voltage source and a resistor. The current flows from the positive side of the voltage source through the resistor to the negative side of the voltage source.

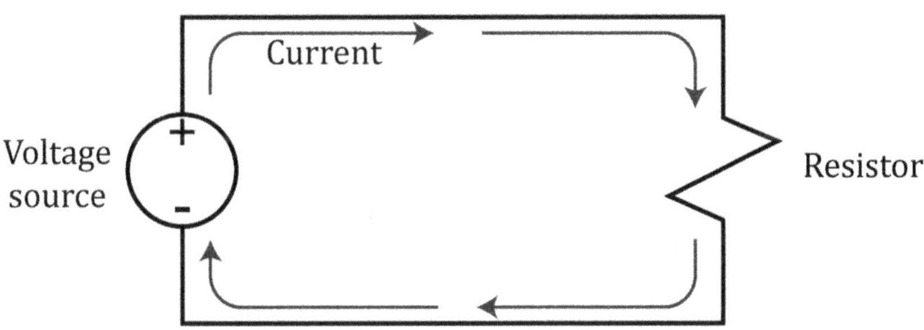

If we plot the voltage of a simple circuit, the similarities to gravitational potential energy appear.

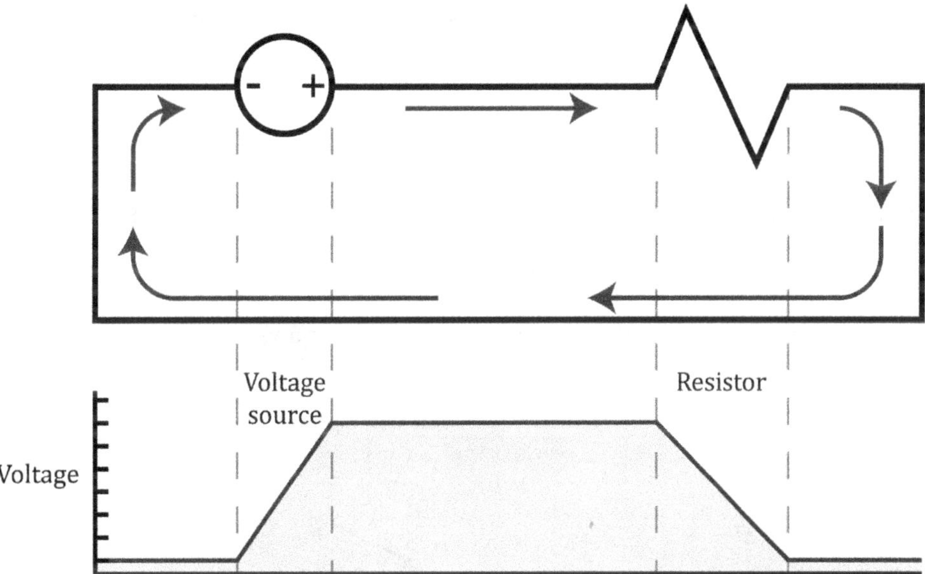

If we consider the circuit to be a track, the electrons would be balls, the voltage source would be a powered lift, and the resistor would be a sticky section of the track. The lift raises the balls, increasing their potential energy. This potential energy is expended as the balls roll down the sticky section of the track.

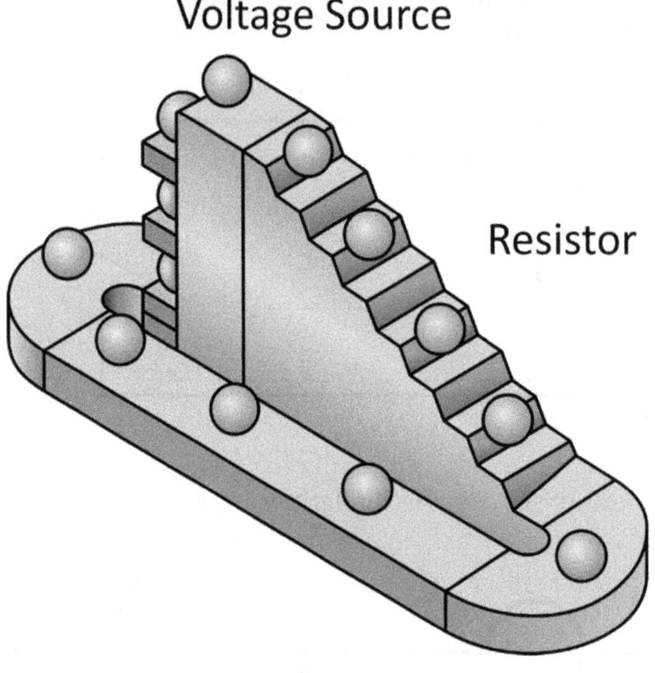

OHM'S LAW

A principle called Ohm's Law explains the relationship between the voltage, current, and resistance. The voltage drop over a resistance is equal to the amount of current times the resistance:

Voltage (V) = current (I) × resistance (R)

We can gain a better understanding of this equation by looking at a reference simple circuit and then changing one variable at a time to examine the results.

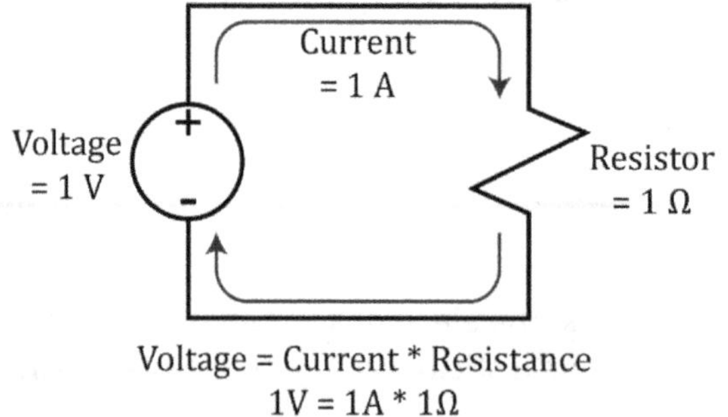

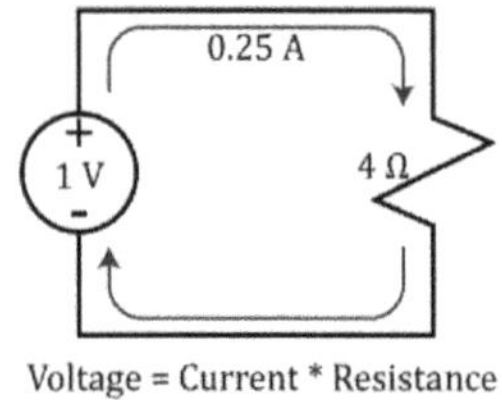

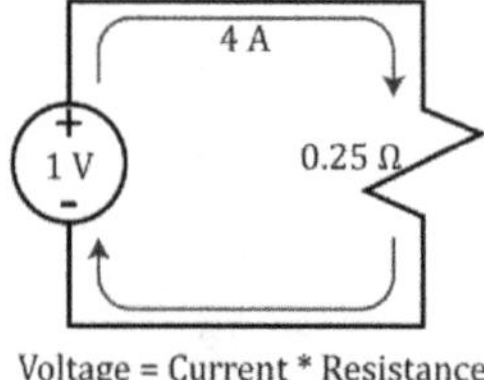

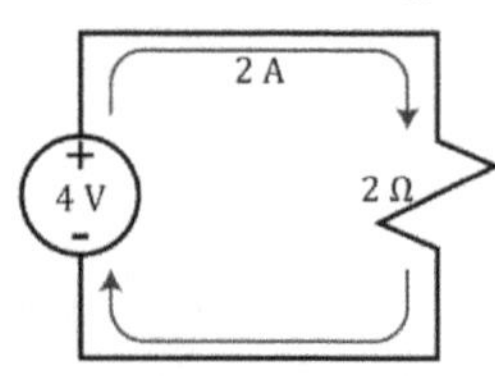

Series Circuits

A series circuit is a circuit with two or more resistors on the same path. The same current runs through both resistors. However, the total voltage drop splits between the resistors. The resistors in series can be added together to make an equivalent basic circuit.

$$R_{equiv} = R_1 + R_2$$

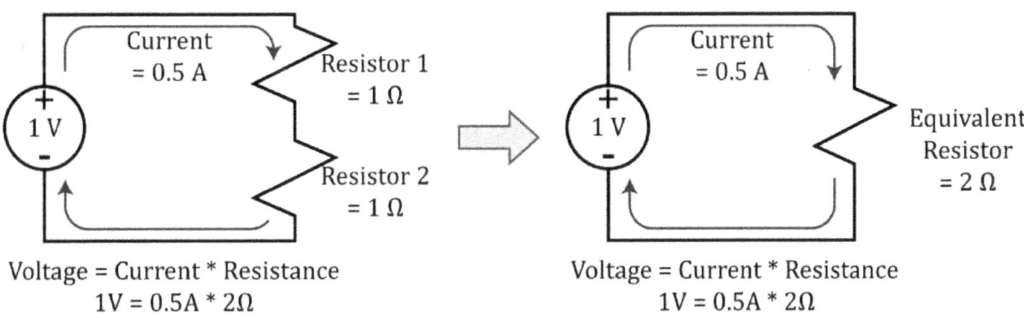

Parallel Circuits

A parallel circuit is a circuit with two or more resistors on different, parallel paths. Unlike the series circuit, the current splits between the different paths in a parallel circuit. Resistors in parallel can be reduced to an equivalent circuit, but not by simply adding the resistances. The inverse of the equivalent resistance of parallel resistors is equal to the sum of the inverses of the resistance of each leg of the parallel circuit. In equation form that means:

$$\frac{1}{R_{equiv}} = \frac{1}{R_1} + \frac{1}{R_2}$$

Or when solved for equivalent resistance:

$$R_{equiv} = \frac{1}{\frac{1}{R_1} + \frac{1}{R_2}}$$

Current
= 0.5 A
Resistor 1
= 1 Ω
Resistor 2
= 1 Ω
1 V
Current
= 0.5 A
1 V
Equivalent
Resistor
= 0.5 Ω

$$R_{equiv} = \frac{1}{\frac{1}{1\,\Omega} + \frac{1}{1\,\Omega}} = 0.5\ \Omega$$

Electrical Power

Electrical power, or the energy output over time, is equal to the current resulting from a voltage source times the voltage of that source:

$$\textbf{Power(P)} = \textbf{current (I)} \times \textbf{voltage (V)}$$

Thanks to Ohm's Law, we can write this relation in two other ways:

$$\mathbf{P = I^2R}$$

$$\mathbf{P = \frac{V^2}{R}}$$

For instance, if a circuit is composed of a 9 Volt battery and a 3 Ohm resistor, the power output of the battery will be:

$$\text{Power} = \frac{V^2}{R} = \frac{9^2}{3} = 27 \text{ Watts}$$

AC vs. DC

Up until this point, current has been assumed to flow in one direction. One directional flow is called Direct Current (DC). However, there is another type of electric current: Alternating Current (AC). Many circuits use AC power sources, in which the current flips back and forth rapidly between directions.

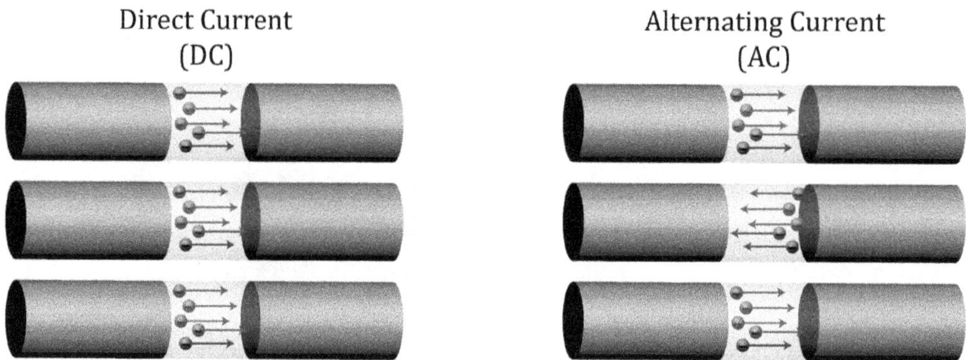

Capacitors

Capacitors are electrical components which store voltage. Capacitors are made from two conductive surfaces separated from each other by a space and/or insulation. Capacitors resist changes to voltage. Capacitors don't stop AC circuits (although they do affect the current flow), but they do stop DC circuits, acting as open circuits.

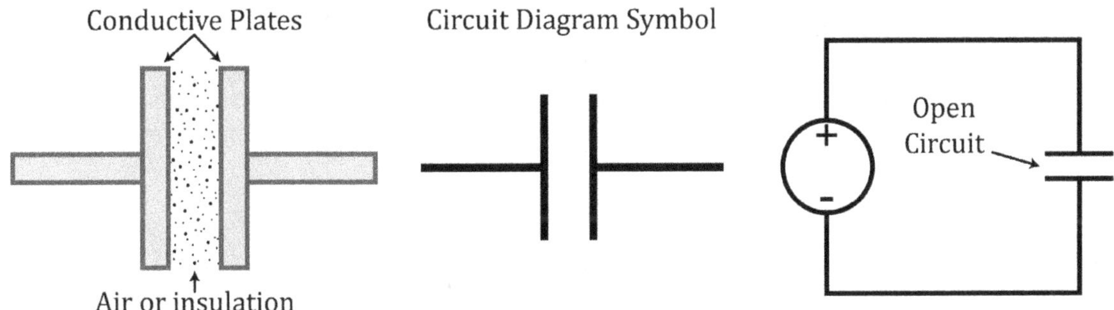

Inductors

Inductors are electrical components which effectively store current. Inductors use the relationship between electricity and magnetism to resist changes in current by running the current through coils of wire. Inductors don't stop DC circuits, but they do resist AC circuits as AC circuits utilize changing currents.

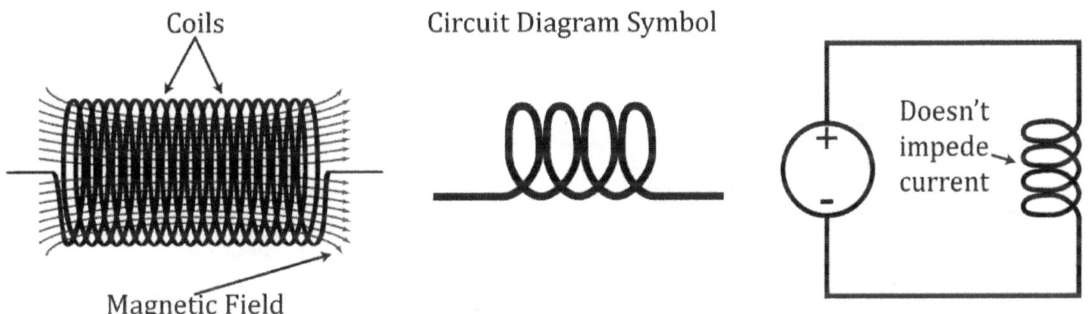

Diodes

Diodes are electrical components which limit the flow of electricity to one direction. If current flows through a diode in the intended direction, the diode will allow the flow. However, a diode will stop current if it runs the wrong way.

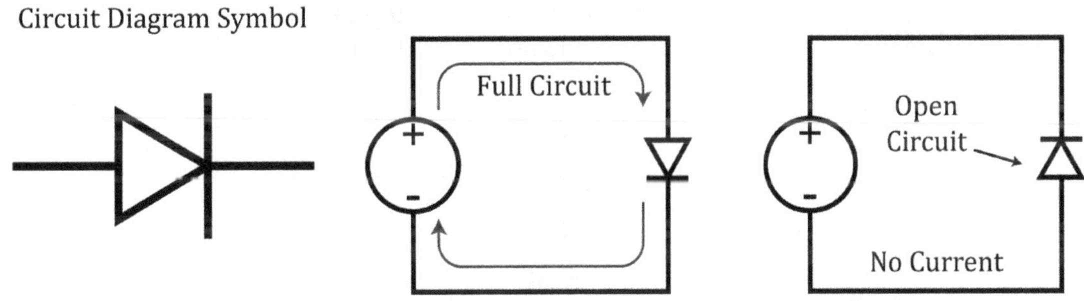

Magnetism

Magnetism

Magnetism is an attraction between opposite poles of magnetic materials and a repulsion between similar poles of magnetic materials. Magnetism can be natural or induced with the use of electric currents. Magnets almost always exist with two polar sides: north and south. A magnetic force exists between two poles on objects. Different poles attract each other. Like poles repel each other.

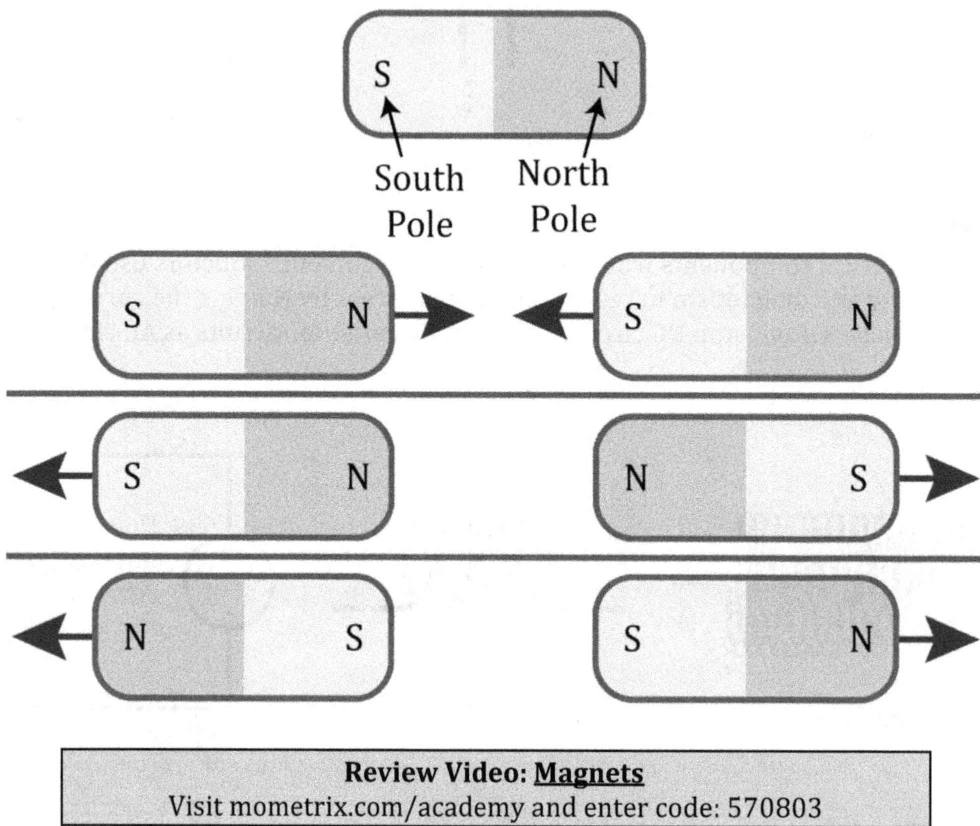

Review Video: Magnets
Visit mometrix.com/academy and enter code: 570803

Final Notes

This concludes the review of basic physics. Hopefully, a lot of this material was familiar to you, but if not, be sure to reread any sections you had difficulty with until you have a solid grasp of the important concepts. The following sections go into detail about specific types of questions that may appear on the exam, and strategies you can use to approach them.

Good luck and good studying!

Pulleys

What Are These Questions Testing?

These questions test your understanding of pulley physics, particularly the relationships among forces, distances, and directions when using a pulley.

What Is the Question Format?

The test will show a pulley system with a rope and one or more wheels and weights. The question will usually ask you to determine one or more of the following, based on the information given in the picture: a) what force is needed to lift a weight; b) whether the weights will move; c) how far the rope has to be pulled to move the pulley a certain distance.

Basics of Pulleys

In order to answer the test questions, there are several properties of pulleys you need to understand.

1. What is a pulley?

A pulley is a mechanical device that consists of one or more wheels and a flexible rope. Typically, pulleys are used to lift heavy weights more easily. Pulleys can be arranged so that less force is required to lift a given weight, or so that force can be applied in a different direction.

For example, the figure below illustrates a very simple pulley. To lift the 100-pound weight *upward*, the operator pulls *downward* on the rope with 100 pounds of force. Although he still has to use 100 pounds of force to move the weight, the pulley allows him to apply that force in a different direction from that in which the weight moves.

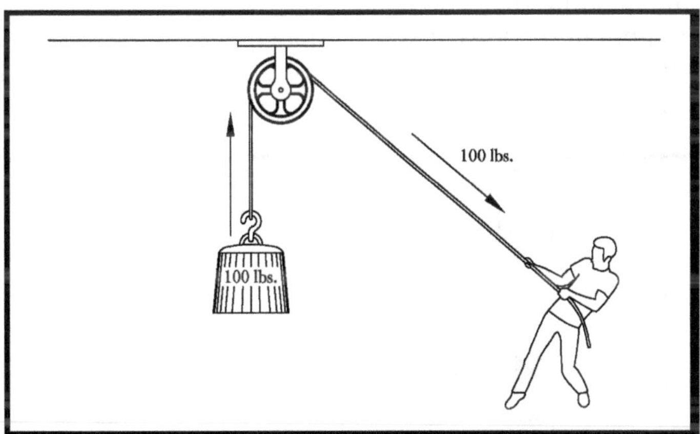

More sophisticated pulleys can actually allow the operator to use *less than* 100 pounds of force to lift the 100-pound weight. This concept is explained below.

2. How do pulleys allow you to lift a weight with less force?

To understand how pulleys operate, you need to first understand the concept of work. As used in physics, work is the product of force times distance. For example, if you lift a weight that weighs 100 pounds a distance of 5 feet, you have done 5 * 100 = 500 foot-pounds of work. The total amount of work needed to move a certain object a certain distance is always the same: if you want to move a 100-pound weight over a distance of 5 feet, you will always have to do 500 foot-pounds of work.

However, while pulleys can't change the *total* amount of work you have to do, they *can* make it easier by allowing you to apply a smaller force over a larger distance, as shown in the picture below. In this pulley system, two pulley wheels are used instead of one. The rope and wheels are arranged so that whenever you pull the rope downward a length of 10 feet, for example, the 100-pound weight still moves upward only 5 feet. However, because the total amount of work (force times distance) is the same, you only need to apply half the force (50 pounds) to move the weight, since you are applying that force over twice the distance. In this way, pulleys allow people to lift heavy weights they normally couldn't.

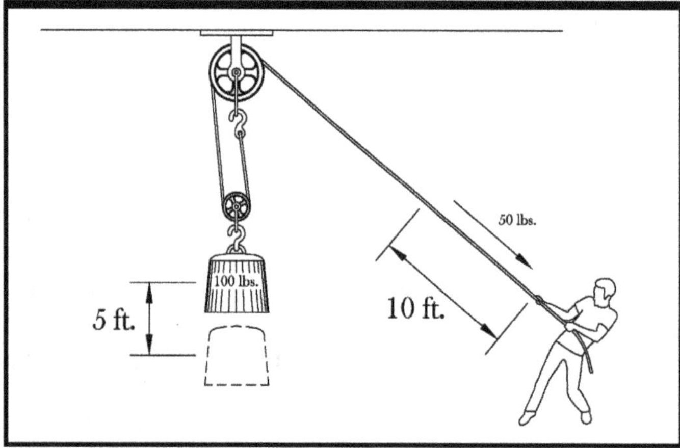

Note that in the above picture, there are two sections of rope supporting the weight, instead of just one. As a result, you would need to apply only half the force you normally would in order to lift the weight. In general, the amount of force you need to apply to lift a certain weight is equal to the weight divided by the number of sections of rope supporting it. In the drawing below, a 100-pound weight is supported by four sections of rope. Therefore, 25 pounds of force are required to move the weight.

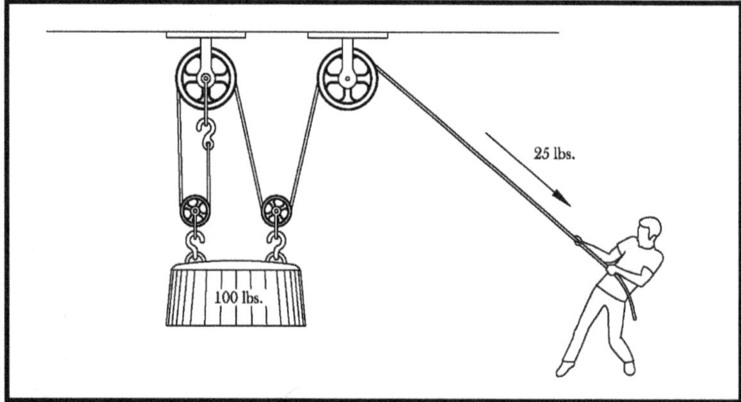

3. How to tell whether pulleys will move

Some questions may show a pulley system with multiple weights and ask you whether the weights will move. There are several possible configurations, and they are best explained through examples.

The figure below shows a very simple two-weight pulley system. The pulley has equal weights on each end of the rope. Because equal forces are exerted on each end of the rope, the weights will not move.

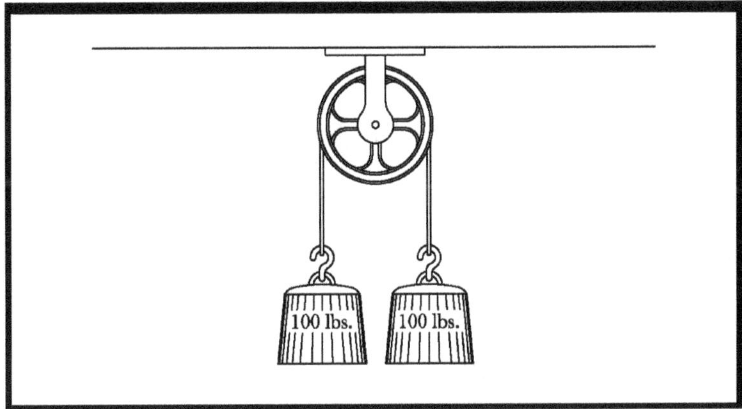

The figure below also shows a one-wheel pulley system; however, this pulley has uneven weights on each end of the rope. Because a greater force is being applied to the left side of the rope, the weight on the left side will move downward, and the weight on the right side will move upward. The weights will continue to move until they reach the position shown on the right side of the picture.

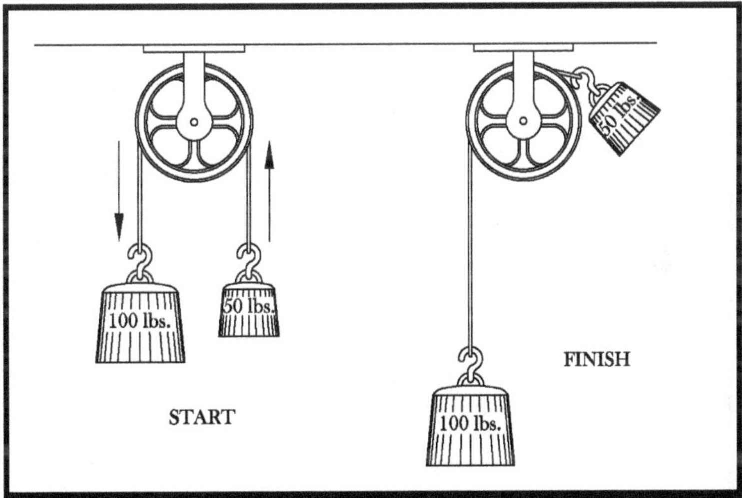

When analyzing more complex pulley systems, you must not only look at the weights, but also the number of rope sections supporting each weight. In the figure below, the 100-pound weight is supported by two sections of rope, and a 50-pound weight is attached to the other end of the rope.

At first glance, it may seem like the 100-pound weight would move the 50-pound weight. However, because the 100-pound weight is supported by two rope sections, only 50 pounds are required on the other end of the rope to balance the pulley, so the weights won't move at all.

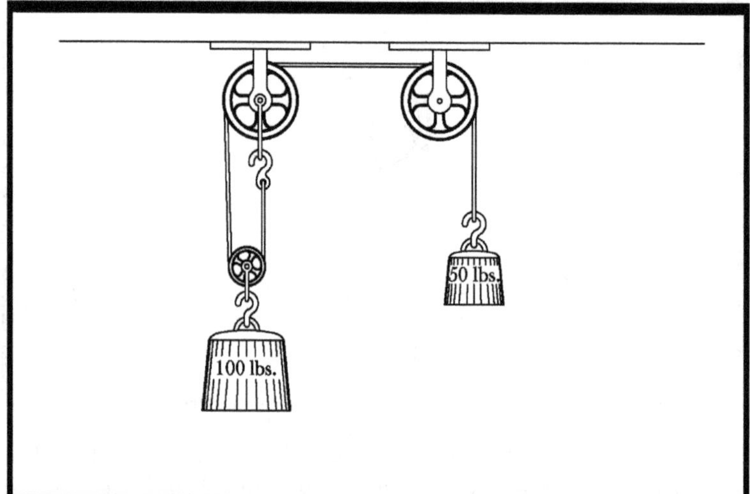

The pulley system in the left part of picture below shows two weighted wheels placed on a flexible rope. In this scenario, the weights will pull the rope downward, and the wheels will roll to the center of the rope and meet there, as shown on the right side of the picture.

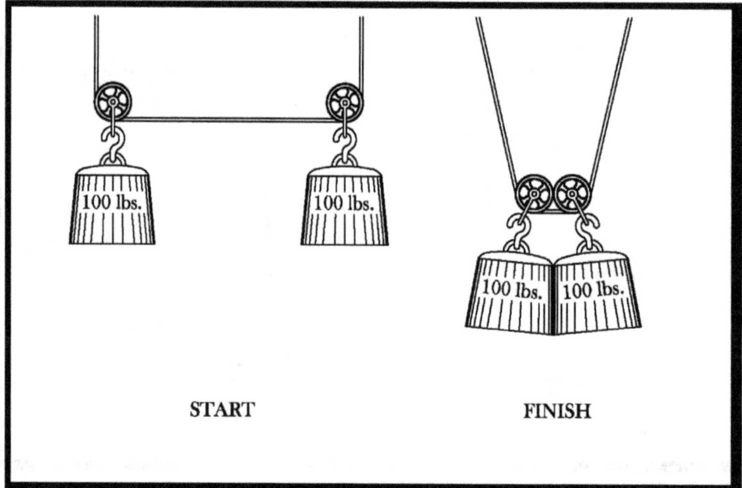

Important Points to Remember

- Pulleys cannot change the amount of work (force times distance) required to move a weight, but they can allow you to apply a *smaller force* over a *larger distance.*
- For simple pulleys in which each weight is supported by only one rope section, the amount of force you must apply to move the weight *equals the weight on the other end.*
- For pulleys in which one weight is supported by *multiple rope sections,* the amount of force you must apply to move the weight equals the *weight on the other end divided by the number of supporting sections.*

Practice Questions

1. Using the pulley below, how many pounds of force does the operator need to apply to the rope in order to move the weight?

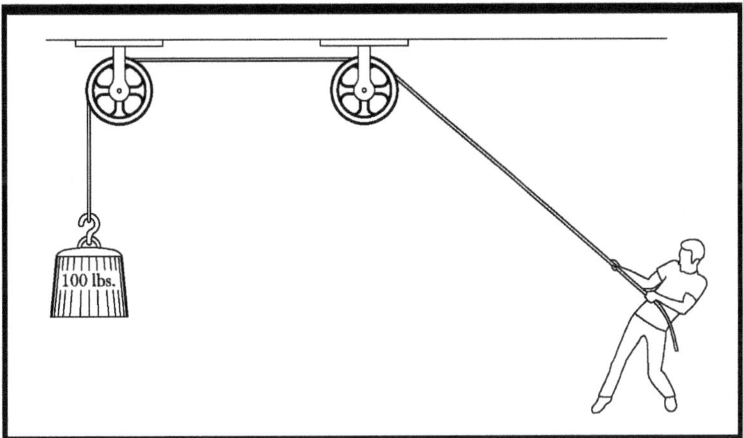

2. Using the pulley below, how many pounds of force does the man need to use to move the weight? How far does he need to pull the rope in order to move the weight upward by two feet?

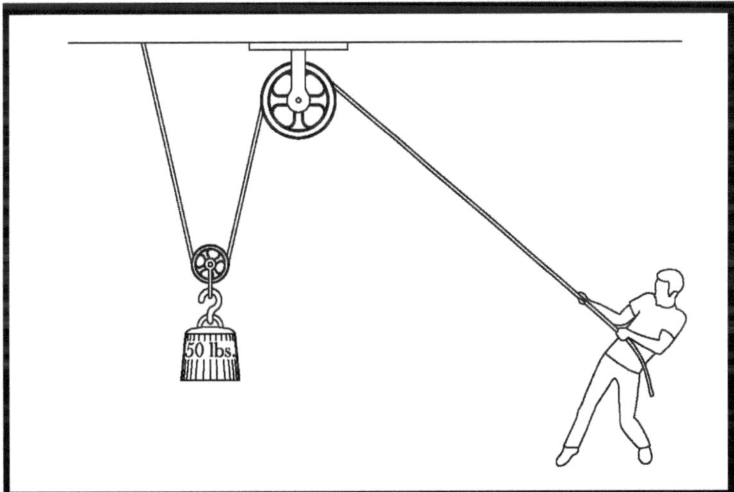

Practice Answers

1. The operator needs to pull the rope with 100 pounds of force to move the weight. Even though the rope is supported by two different wheels, there is only one rope section supporting the weight, so the weight is equal to the force required to move it.

2. The man will need to pull the rope for 4 feet using 25 pounds of force. In order to move a 50-pound weight for 2 feet, the man must do 50 * 2 = 100 foot-pounds of work. The 50-pound weight is supported by two sections of rope, so the man must use half the force that he would normally have to use. However, in order to do the same amount of work, he must apply that force over twice the distance that he would otherwise.

Gears

What Are These Questions Testing?

These questions test your understanding of how gears interact. In particular, the questions test how the size, rotational direction and speed, and relative positions of gears affect other gears in the gear system.

What Is the Question Format?

The test will show a gear system having two or more connected gears and give you information about the size or movement of at least one of the gears. Based on that information, you'll have to determine how another gear in the system moves.

Properties of Gears

Before you can answer these questions, there are several properties of gears you need to know:

1. What is a gear?

A gear is a mechanical device that can be rotated, and has a set of evenly-spaced teeth along its edge. These teeth interlock with teeth on another device, usually another gear, so that when one gear (called the driving gear) is rotated, it also causes the attached gear (called the following gear) to rotate.

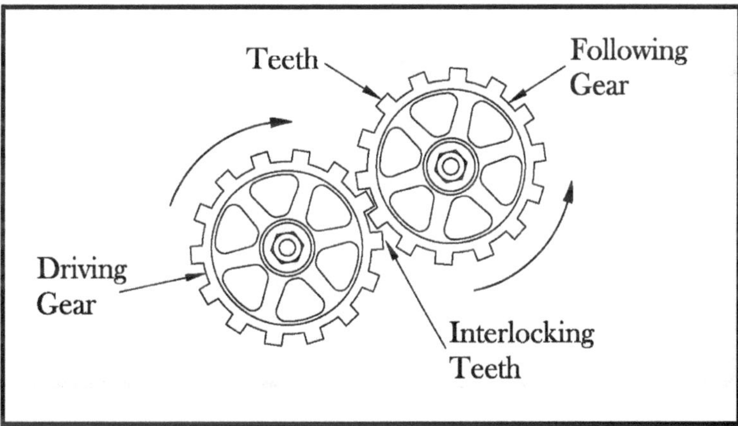

2. Direction of gears

When one gear rotates, the interlocking gears (also called mating gears) rotate in the opposite direction. For example, if Gear A in the picture above rotates in a clockwise direction, Gear B will rotate in a counterclockwise direction, and vice versa.

This principle remains true even if multiple following gears are attached to the driving gear. In the picture below, for example, gear A is driving following gears B and C. If A rotates in a clockwise direction, B and C rotate in a counterclockwise direction, and vice versa.

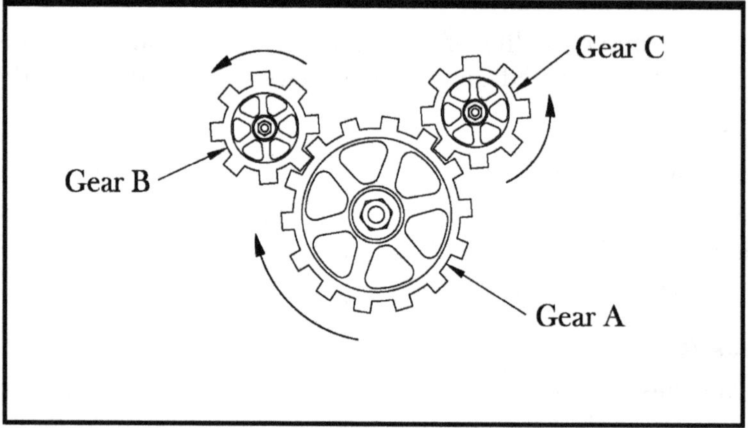

It is also possible to create a "gear chain" in which each of the gears rotates in the opposite direction of the gears next to it. For example, the picture below shows driving gear A connected to following gear B. Following gear B is connected to following gear C, and so on. If A rotates counterclockwise, then B rotates clockwise, C rotates counterclockwise, and so on.

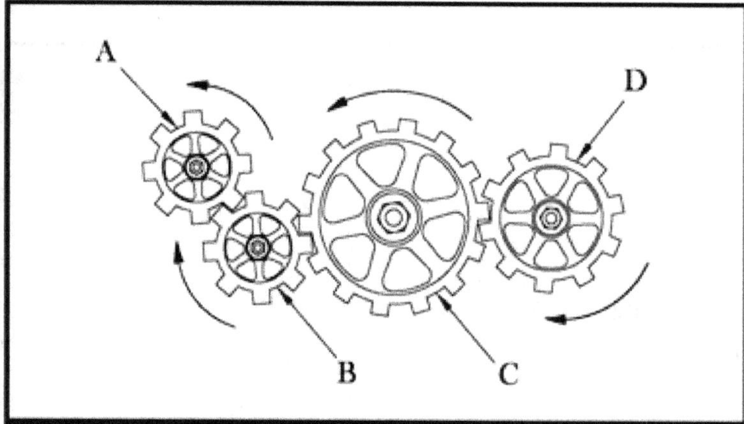

Note that if the number of gears in the chain is odd, the first and last gears in the chain will rotate in the same direction. If the number of gears is even, the first and last gears will rotate in the opposite direction.

3. Gear speed

Interlocking gears turn at different speeds depending on their sizes. The larger the gear within the gear system, the more slowly that gear will rotate relative to the other gears. The speeds of the gears vary proportionally based on their relative diameters.

For example, the picture below shows interlocking gears A, B, and C rotating at different speeds. A has a diameter of 10 cm, B has a diameter of 20 cm, and C has a diameter of 5 cm. If A rotates at 10 revolutions per minute (RPM), B will rotate at half that speed (5 RPM) because its diameter is twice as large as A's diameter. C will rotate at twice the speed of A (20 RPM) because its diameter is half as large as A's.

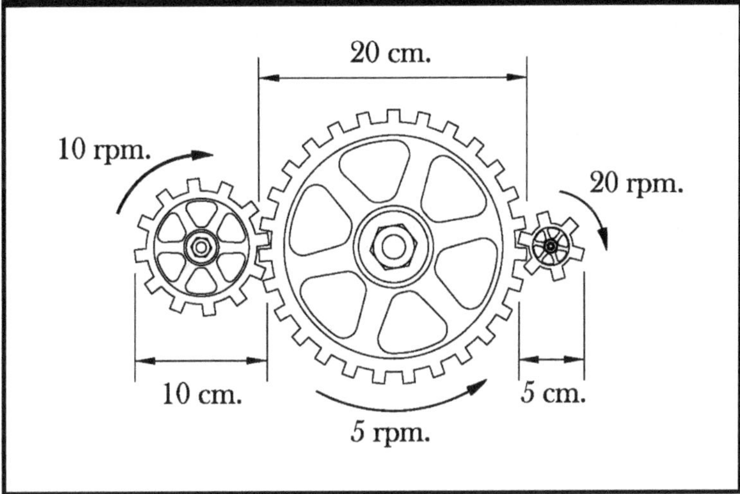

Note in the picture above that the number of teeth on each gear is directly related to its size. That is, gear B has twice as many teeth as gear A, and gear C has half as many teeth as gear A. Thus, you can determine the relative speeds of interlocking gears by counting the number of teeth they have. Gears with more teeth rotate more slowly than gears with fewer teeth.

In summary:

- If interlocking gears have different sizes, the *largest* gear with *the most teeth* will rotate *the most slowly;* and the *smallest* gear with the *fewest teeth* will rotate *the most quickly.*
- If interlocking gears have the same size and number of teeth, they will rotate at the same speed.

Important Points to Remember

GEAR DIRECTION: When gears are interlocked, the gears will always rotate in the *opposite* direction of the adjacent gears. If there are several gears in series, the gears will continuously alternate directions.

GEAR SPEED: In a gear system, the slowest gear will always be the largest, measured in terms of either diameter or number of teeth. The fastest gear will always be the smallest.

Practice Questions

1. Gears W, X, Y, and Z are interlocked as shown. If gear W is rotating clockwise, in what direction is gear Z rotating?

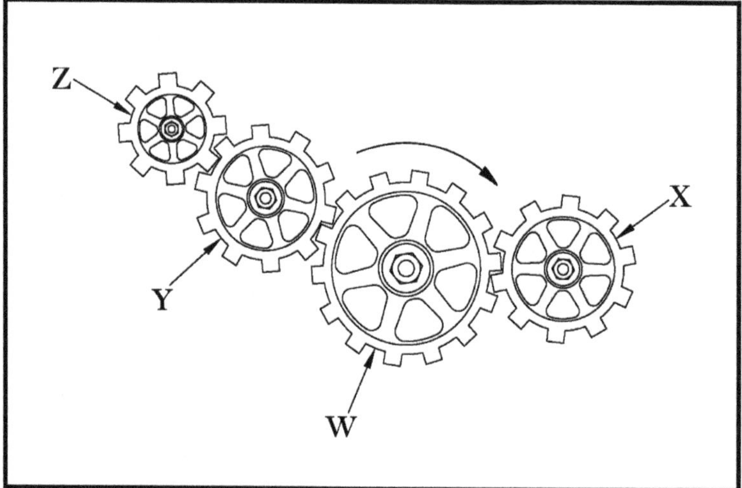

2. In the picture above, which of the gears W, X, Y, and Z is rotating most quickly? Least quickly?

Practice Answers

1. Gear Z is rotating in a clockwise direction. Because W is interlocked with Y, and W is rotating clockwise, Y must rotate in the opposite direction—counterclockwise. Y is interlocked with Z, so Y must turn in the opposite direction from Z—clockwise.

2. Gear W is the largest gear in the system, so it must also be the slowest gear. Gear Z is the smallest gear in the system, so it must also be the fastest gear.

Note that you can also answer this question by counting the number of teeth on each gear. Gear W has the most teeth, so it must be the slowest gear. Gear Z has the fewest teeth, so it must be the fastest gear.

Mechanical Concepts

What Are These Questions Testing?

These questions test your ability to use mechanical intuition and knowledge of physics to determine the outcome in a variety of situations.

What Is the Question Format?

Each question visually outlines a situation and asks you to make a determination about what is or will be taking place in the situation. Below is an example.

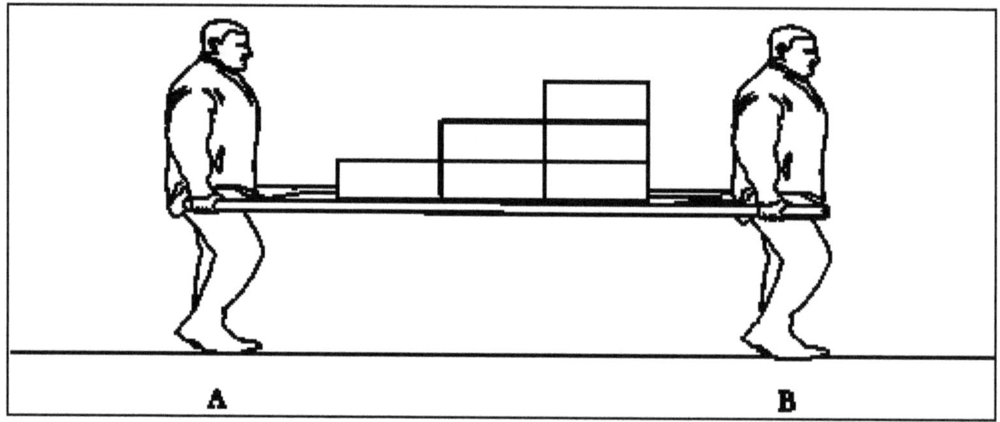

Here you are shown a picture of two men jointly carrying a stacked load of boxes balanced on a board between them. The question will ask you to decide which man is carrying more of the weight, or if they are carrying equal weight.

The question can be solved intuitively by saying most of the boxes are closer to the man on the right so he is carrying more weight. Alternatively, you can use knowledge of physics to estimate the torque about the center of the board. Suppose each box weighs 20 pounds and the boxes are 1 foot wide. The stack of two boxes is directly over the center, so they do not affect the torque. The single box on the left generates a counterclockwise torque of 20 pounds times 1 foot, or 20 foot-pounds. The three boxes on the right generate a clockwise torque of 60 pounds times 1 foot, or 60 foot-pounds. This is a net of 40 foot-pounds in the clockwise direction. This means that the man on the right must be generating 40 foot-pounds of torque more than the man on the left to balance out the torque.

How Can I Improve My Ability to Answer These Questions?

Since intuition is the most effective way to answer these questions quickly, it is difficult to cram for this section. The best way to develop your intuition about mechanical concepts is to see them in action and interact with them. Solving lots of practice problems the long way using physics can also be a good way to build intuition over time.

Practice Questions

1. Which car (A or B) will travel a greater distance on the given track? (If equal, mark C)

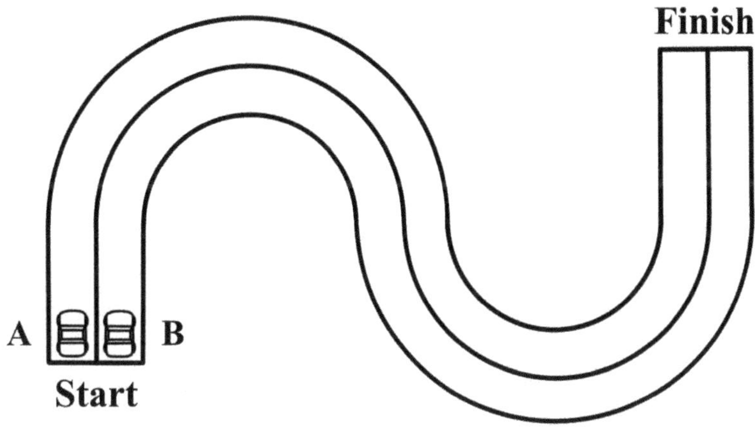

2. In which direction (A or B) will the ball move once the sticks of dynamite explode? (If neither, mark C)

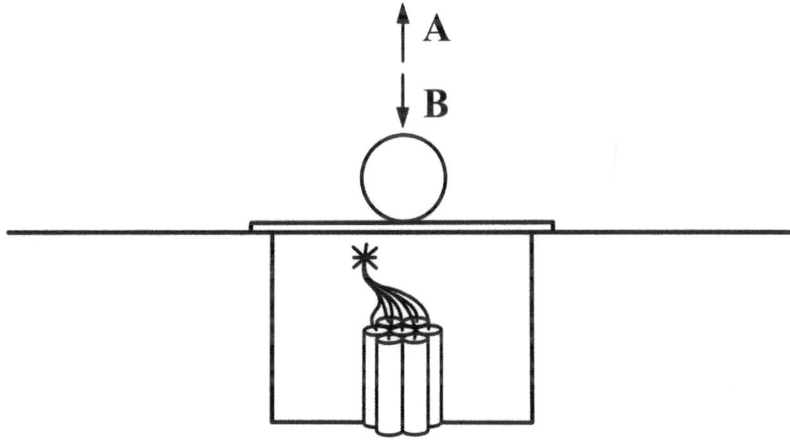

3. In which direction (A or B) will pulley 4 spin if pulley 1 is spinning counter-clockwise? (If none, mark C)

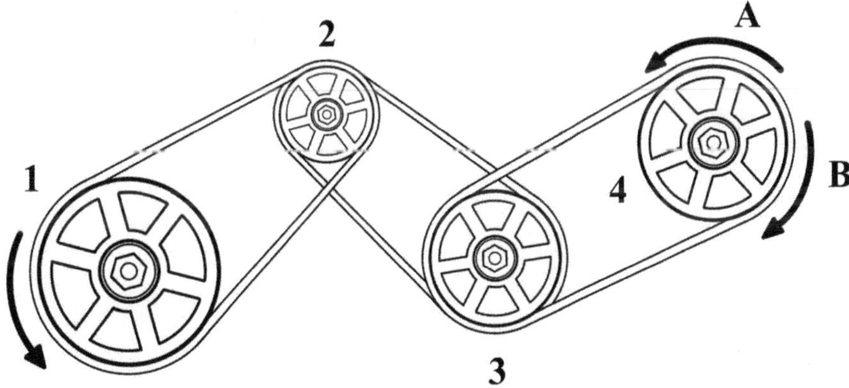

Practice Answers

1. C: Both paths are the same length. The first half of path A is identical to the second half of path B, and vice versa.

2. A: The force of the explosion will propel everything above it into the air.

3. A: Because these pulleys are connected by belts, they will all turn in the same direction.

Parts Assembly

What Are These Questions Testing?

These questions test your ability to assemble a larger object from two or more smaller objects.

What Is the Question Format?

The test will illustrate several parts, and each part will be labeled with one or more letters indicating how the parts might fit together. In addition, the test will show several possible answer choices with the parts assembled in a certain way. You will have to identify which of the assemblies could be formed from the parts.

A simple example will make this explanation clearer. In the illustration below, the top side of the rectangular block and the small face of the triangle are both marked with the letter "A," indicating that those two faces must contact each other. Which of the assemblies 1 through 3 could be built from the parts as specified?

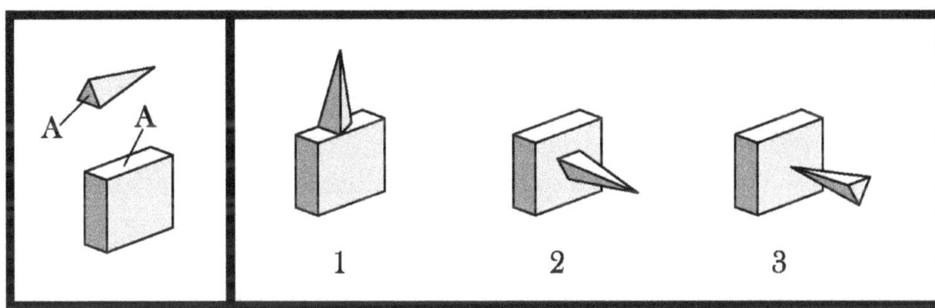

Answer: Assembly 1 is the only one in which the faces marked with "A" are connected. The other two assemblies are not arranged according to the specifications.

Note that the assemblies don't have to be functional, useful, or represent an object that actually exists in real life. The questions simply test your ability to arrange the parts according to the letters on the faces of the parts. Therefore, when you are arranging the parts, don't worry about the function or purpose of the assembly.

How Can I Answer These Questions More Effectively?

If two pieces of the assembly fit together in a very obvious way, you can sometimes eliminate answer choices in which those two pieces aren't arranged properly. This strategy works particularly well when the assembly contains pieces that are unusually shaped, or that fit together in an unusual way. For example, in the illustration below, which of the following assemblies could be put together from the parts as shown?

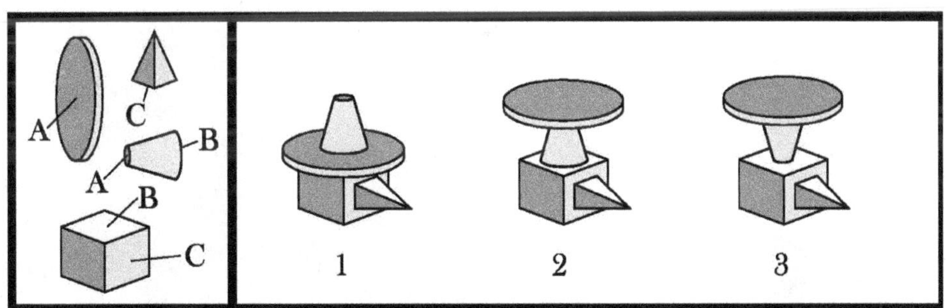

Answer: The coin-shaped piece must contact the narrow end of the cone-shaped piece. This fact eliminates assemblies 1 and 3 from consideration, even if you don't analyze how the pyramid and cube fit together.

Practice Questions

1. Which of the following assemblies can be formed from the given parts?

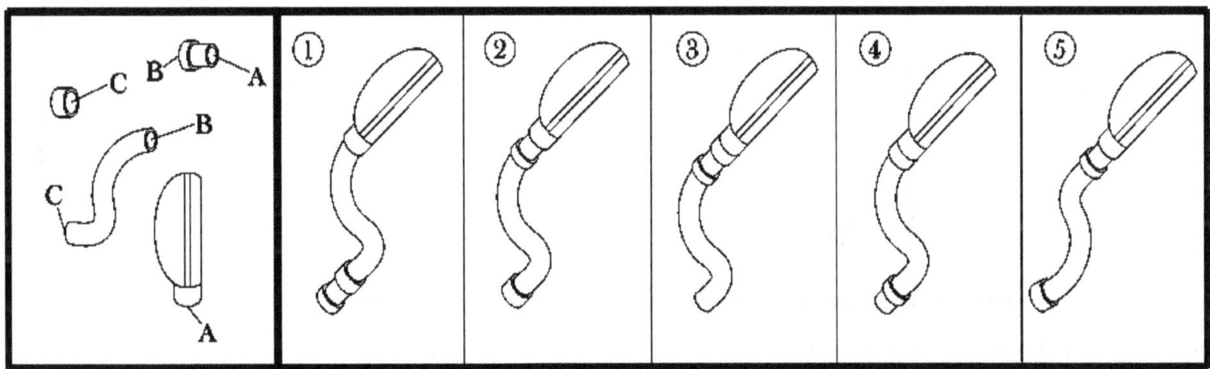

2. Which of the following assemblies can be formed from the given parts?

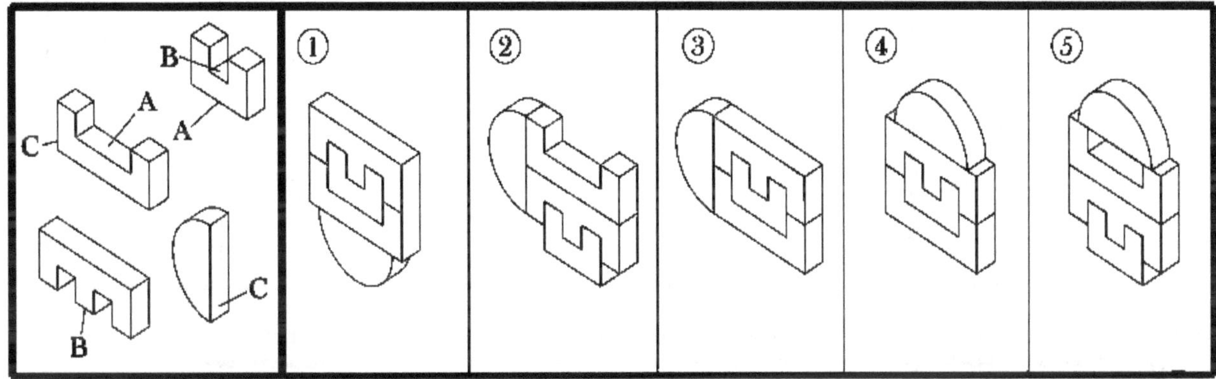

3. Which of the following assemblies can be formed from the given parts?

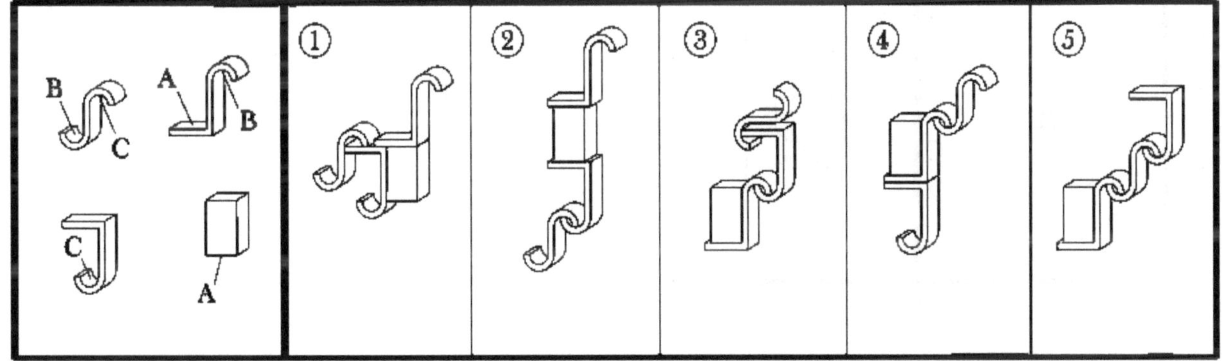

Parts Assembly

4. Which of the following assemblies can be formed from the given parts?

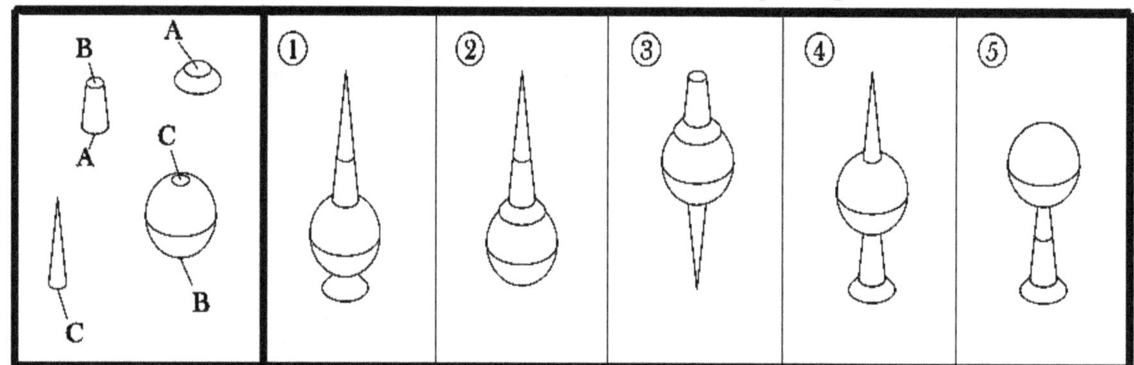

5. Which of the following assemblies can be formed from the given parts?

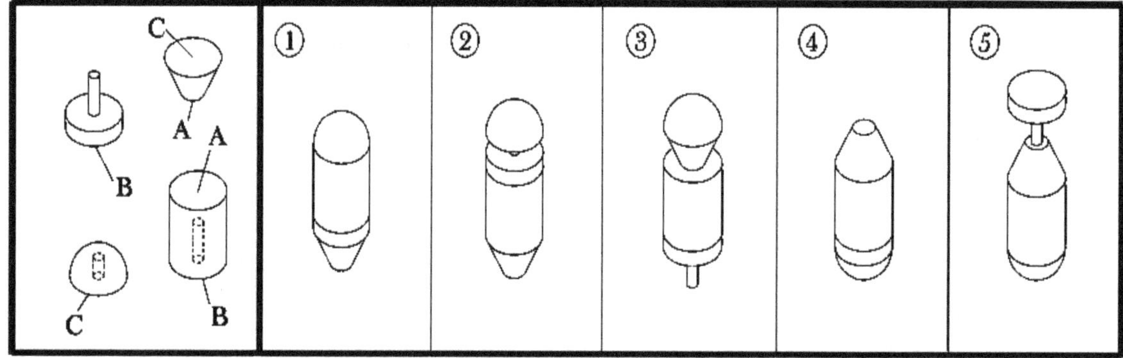

6. Which of the following assemblies can be formed from the given parts?

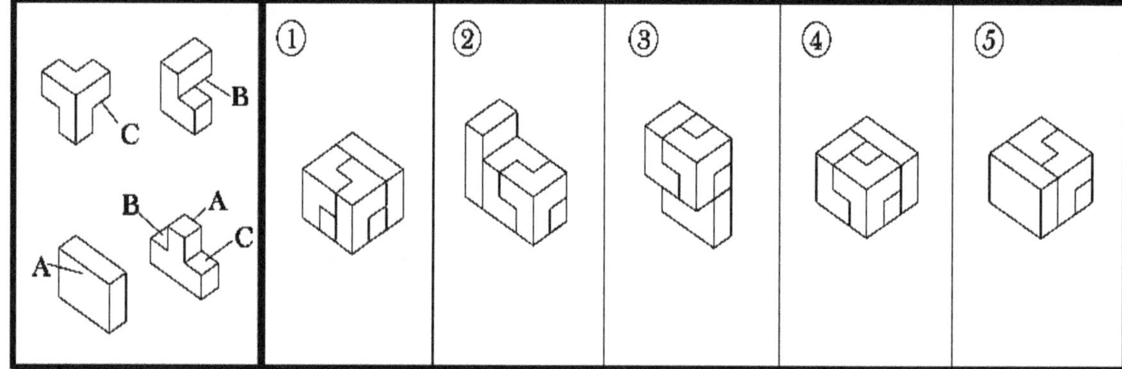

7. **Which of the following assemblies can be formed from the given parts?**

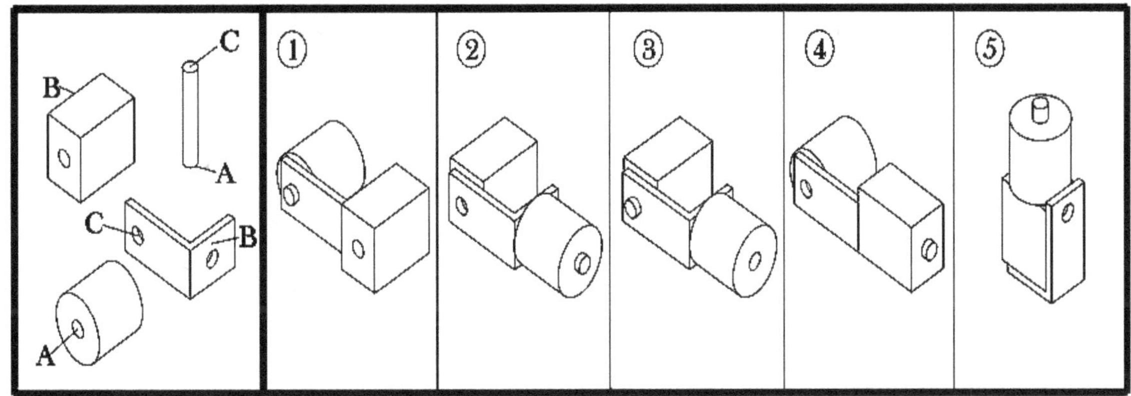

8. **Which of the following assemblies can be formed from the given parts?**

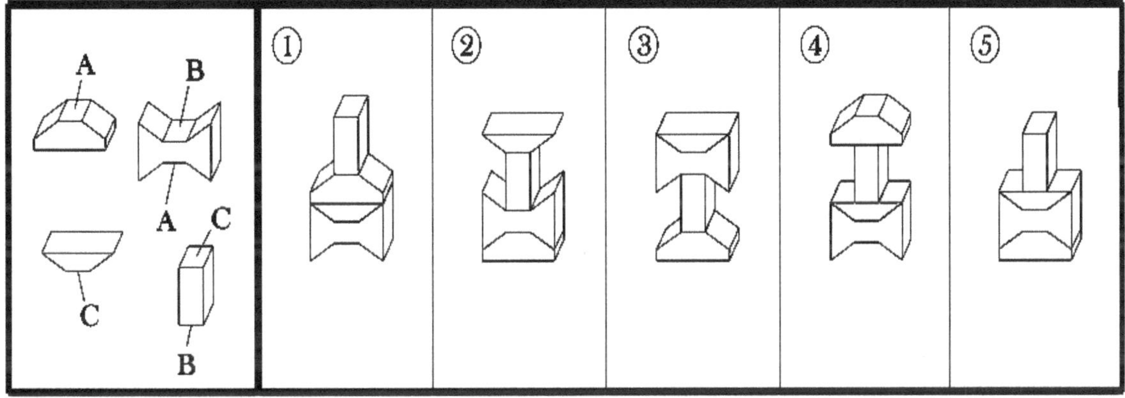

9. **Which of the following assemblies can be formed from the given parts?**

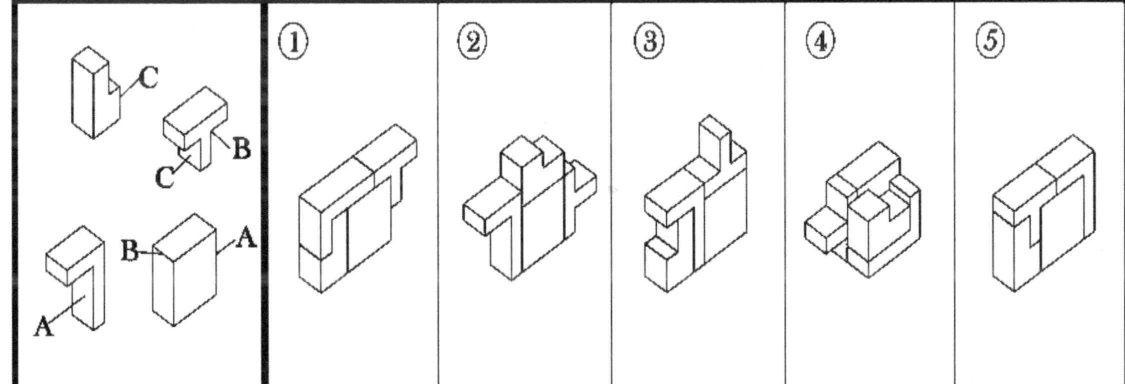

10. Which of the following assemblies can be formed from the given parts?

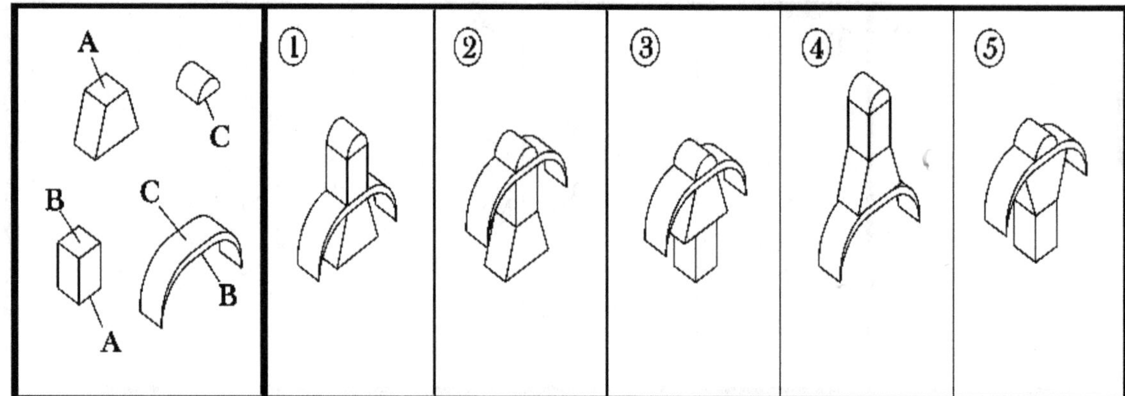

Practice Answers

1. The answer is 2. Because end C of the hose fits onto surface C of the nut, you can deduce that the lower end of the assembly must look like either choice 2 or choice 5. Therefore, you can eliminate answer choices 1, 3, and 4.

Choices 2 and 5 look similar, but notice that end C of the hose is closer to the bend than end B is. Because only assembly 2 fits this constraint, this is the correct answer.

2. The answer is 3. All the parts, except the semicircular part, must combine to form the rectangle shown in choices 1, 3, and 4. Therefore, you can eliminate choices 2 and 5. Out of the remaining choices, the flat end C of the semicircular piece must fit on side C of the rectangle, making 3 the only possible choice.

3. The answer is 5. The hooks form a "chain" of brackets that contact the block at surface A.

Note that although in this case, the parts incidentally form a functional chain of brackets that support the block, this is not the reason why answer 5 is correct. Answer 5 is correct because, and only because, the faces of each part in the assembly fit together as specified in the drawing. The functionality of the assemblies is irrelevant to choosing the correct answer.

4. The answer is 4. Note that each end of the sphere connects to another part, so you can eliminate answers 2 and 5. Out of the remaining choices, only 4 fits together according to the specifications.

5. The answer is 3. Notice that narrow end A of the cone-shaped piece fits to the cylinder. The only assembly that meets this specification is 3.

6. The answer is 4. Face A of the lower right piece must contact face A of the rectangular block. The other choices (1, 2, 3, and 5) are incorrect because they don't meet this requirement.

7. The answer is 1. The cylinder is connected to the long end of the bracket. Only choices 1 and 4 meet this requirement, so you can eliminate choices 2, 3, and 5. Of the remaining choices, only 1 shows the rod in the cylinder.

8. The answer is 2. The bowtie-shaped piece has the trapezoidal piece A on one side, and the long rectangular piece on the other side. Choice 2 is the only choice that fits these requirements.

9. The answer is 5. Inner face A of the lower left block must contact face A of the square block, so you can eliminate choices 2, 3, and 4 based on this information. Of the remaining choices, the upper-right block must contact the upper-left block, and only choice 5 shows this configuration.

10. The answer is 2. The concave face B of the curved part must contact the rectangular block. Only choice 2 shows such a configuration.

Paper Folding

What Are These Questions Testing?

These questions are designed to test your geometric and spatial abilities. In particular, the questions test your ability to form three-dimensional objects by folding a flat pattern.

What Is the Question Format?

The test will show a flat (two-dimensional) pattern with dotted fold lines, and several three-dimensional objects. You will have to identify which of the three-dimensional objects can be made by folding the two-dimensional pattern along the dotted lines.

How Do I Improve My Ability to Identify Which Objects Can Be Formed from the Patterns?

The paper folding questions are among the most difficult questions covered in this study guide, but there are a few tips that can help you.

First, it may help to count the number of faces in the pattern. Each region separated by dotted lines will form a separate face when the pattern is folded into a three-dimensional object.

For example, in the drawing below, the pattern has five separate regions. When the pattern is folded, it creates a wedge-shaped object that also has five faces. If you were to see this pattern on a test, you could immediately eliminate any objects that had greater or fewer than five faces.

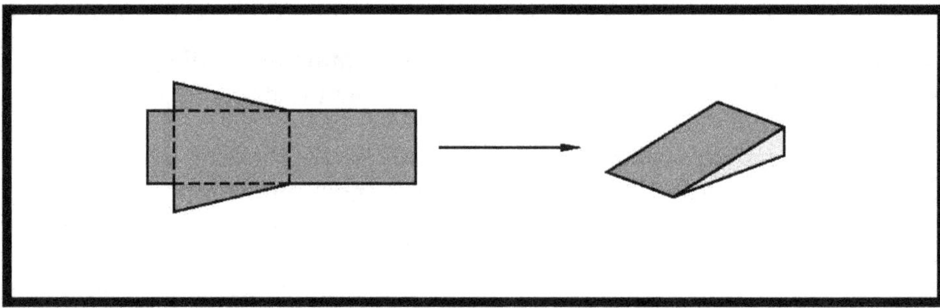

Second, you can sometimes mentally piece together part of the object, and eliminate answers that are obviously wrong.

In the figure below, try to determine which of the objects can be made from the pattern shown.

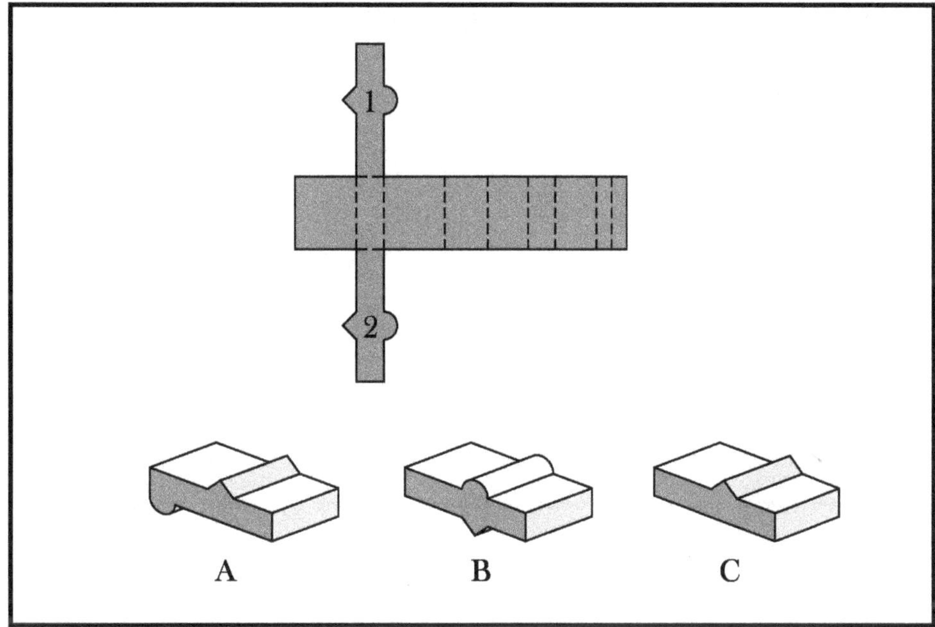

ANSWER: You can see that the pattern has two distinctively-shaped faces, 1 and 2. If you fold the pattern into a physical object, the object must include each of those distinctive faces. You can see that because answer choices A and C do not include two faces shaped like 1 and 2, these objects cannot be formed by folding the given pattern. Therefore, you can eliminate these answer choices, leaving choice B as the only possible answer.

If you are still having trouble with the practice problems in this section, it might help you to actually cut out the flat patterns in the practice section, and form them into shapes.

Practice Questions

1. Which shape can be formed by folding the given pattern?

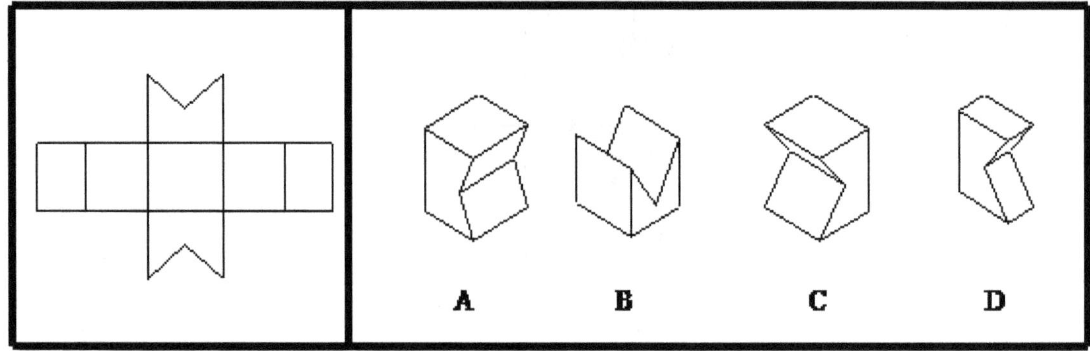

2. Which shape can be formed by folding the given pattern?

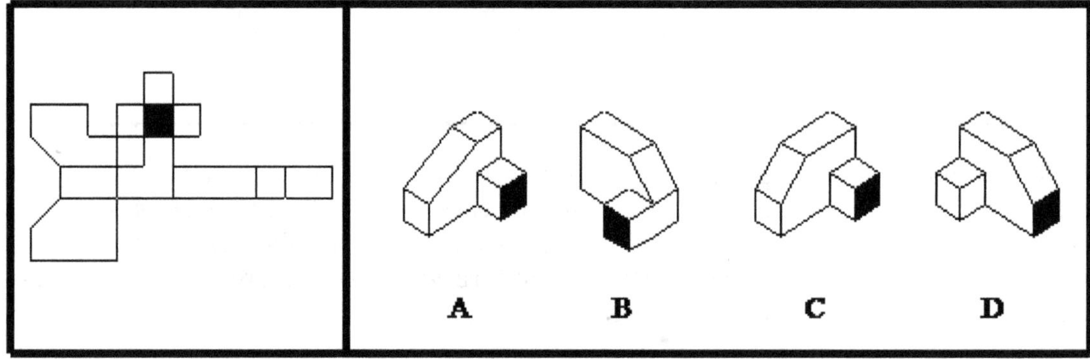

3. Which shape can be formed by folding the given pattern?

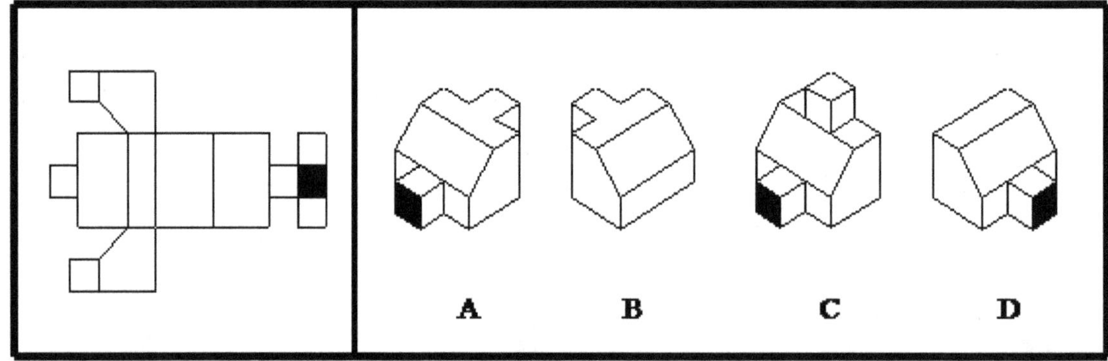

4. Which shape can be formed by folding the given pattern?

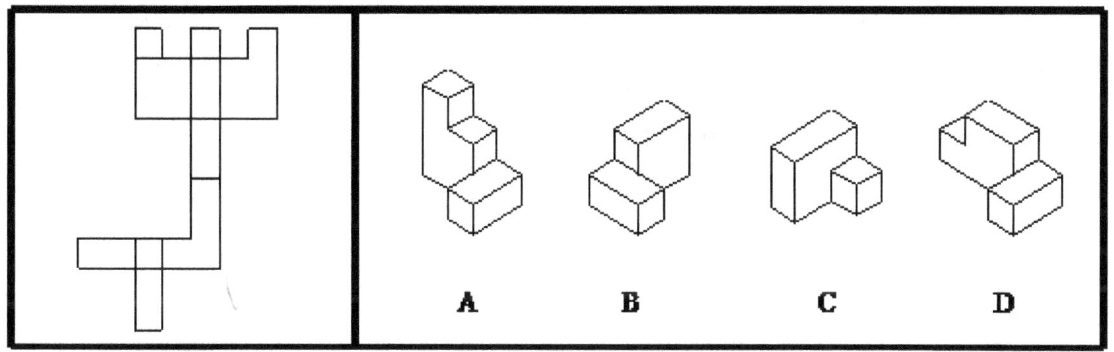

5. Which shape can be formed by folding the given pattern?

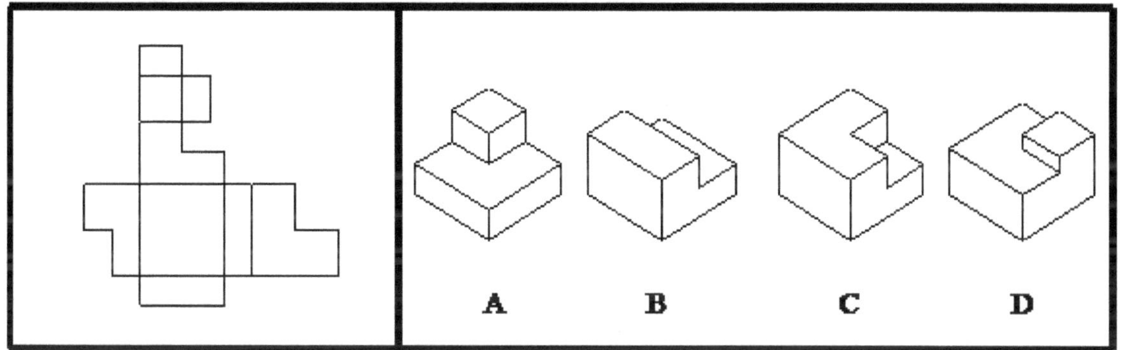

Practice Answers

1. Only C can be formed by folding the given pattern. You can eliminate choices A and B by examining the sawtooth-shaped face, and noticing that neither of the sawtooth-shaped faces in A or B matches the dimensions of the one given. Of the remaining answer choices, C is the correct one because D is much too thin to match the pattern.

2. The answer is C. The protrusion with the black square will form on the right, and the diagonal plane on choice A is too small.

3. The answer is D. D has enough paper to make only one cubical protrusion, not two.

4. The answer is B. When folded, the pattern will form two connected rectangular shapes.

5. The answer is A. When folded, the pattern will form a smaller box on top of a larger box. While choice D shows such an arrangement, the dimensions of the shape do not match those of the pattern.

Rotated Blocks

What Are These Questions Testing?

These questions are designed to test your spatial and geometric ability. In particular, they test your ability to recognize three-dimensional objects when the objects are shown from a different perspective.

What Is the Question Format?

The test will show a picture of a three-dimensional block, and several possible answer choices. One of the answer choices shows the same block as the original, but rotated. You will have to identify which of the answer choices is the same.

For example, in the picture below, which of the answer choices shows the same block as the original?

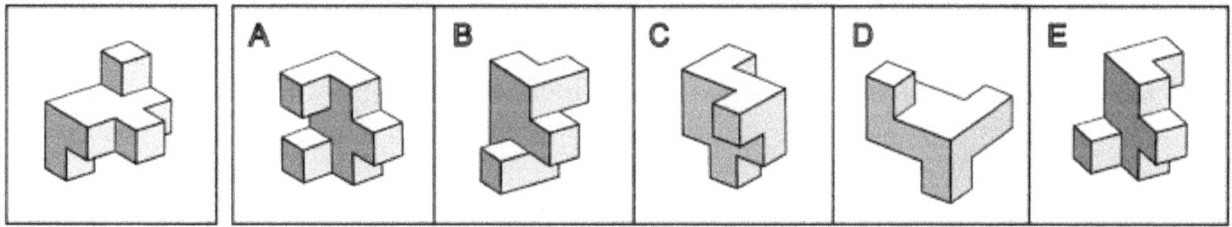

ANSWER: The answer is C. A is wrong because there are two protrusions on one side of the block, instead of one protrusion on each side like in the example block. B, D and E are also wrong because the protrusions are on the wrong part of the block.

How Do I Improve My Ability to Identify Which Blocks Are Rotated?

Due to the nature of these questions, there are very few tips or tricks that will help, and it is difficult to approach these questions methodically. However, if you are struggling with this section, it might be helpful to play a geometric puzzle game, such as Tetris. This will help you visualize how blocks can be rotated.

Practice Questions

1. Which of the answer choices shows the same block as the original?

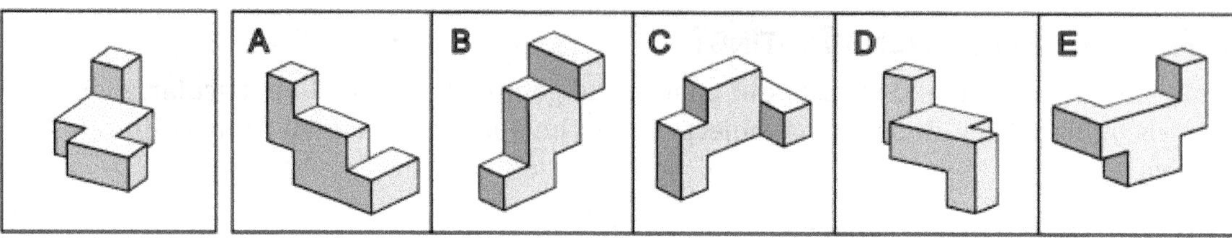

2. Which of the answer choices shows the same block as the original?

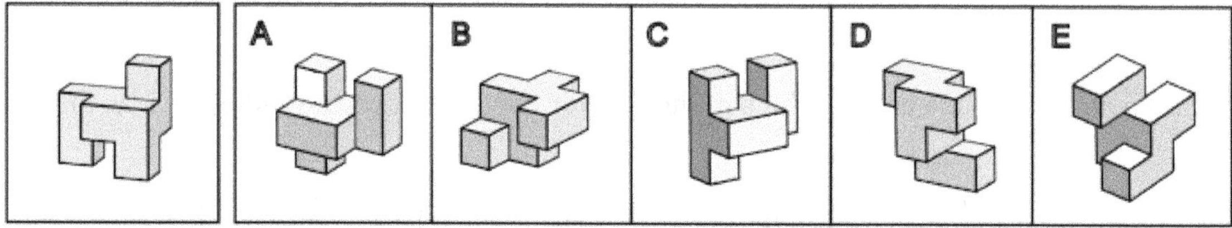

3. Which of the answer choices shows the same block as the original?

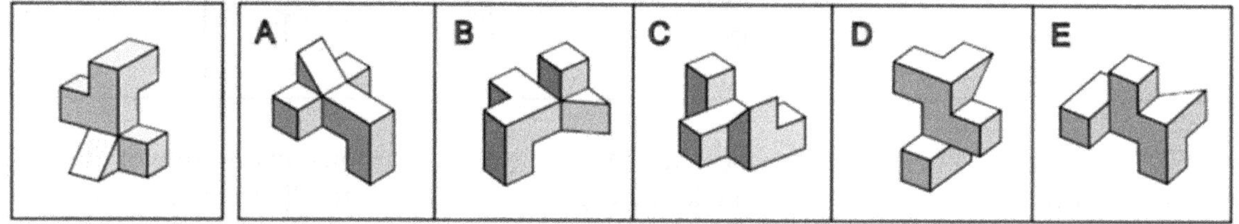

4. Which of the answer choices shows the same block as the original?

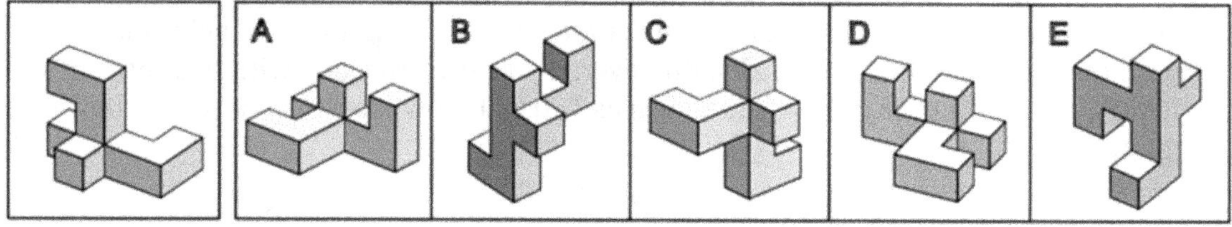

5. Which of the answer choices shows the same block as the original?

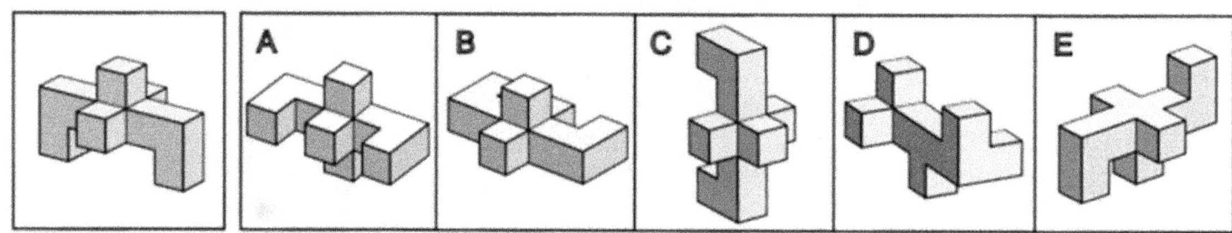

Practice Answers

1. A.

2. D

3. E

4. B

5. C

Apertures

What Are These Questions Testing?

These questions are designed to test your spatial abilities. In particular, these questions test your ability to fit three-dimensional objects through a two-dimensional aperture.

What Is the Question Format?

The test will show a picture of a three-dimensional object, and several two-dimensional openings. You will have to determine which of the openings the three-dimensional object can pass through.

To answer these questions correctly, there are two rules you need to know. First, you can rotate the object in any direction you wish before passing it through the opening. However, once the object starts passing through the opening, you are not allowed to rotate it. Second, if the cross-section of an object has the same shape as the opening, but is too large to fit, then that opening is not the correct one.

The example below shows a bracket with an angled protrusion in the center. Which of the following apertures could the object pass through?

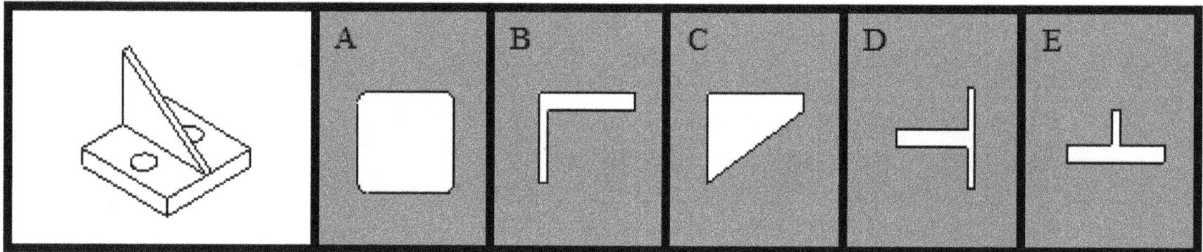

ANSWER: The answer is C. If you were to rotate the bracket into a side view, and flip it upside down, it could pass through the aperture in choice C. Answer D is close, but the thickness of the protrusion and base don't match the actual object, so the object would not pass through.

How Can I Improve My Ability to Answer These Questions?

If you are struggling with these questions, it might help to buy a mechanical drafting book and practice drawing front, top, and side view drawings of three-dimensional objects. This practice will help you develop your ability to visualize which objects can fit through which apertures.

Practice Questions

1. Which of the following apertures could the object pass through?

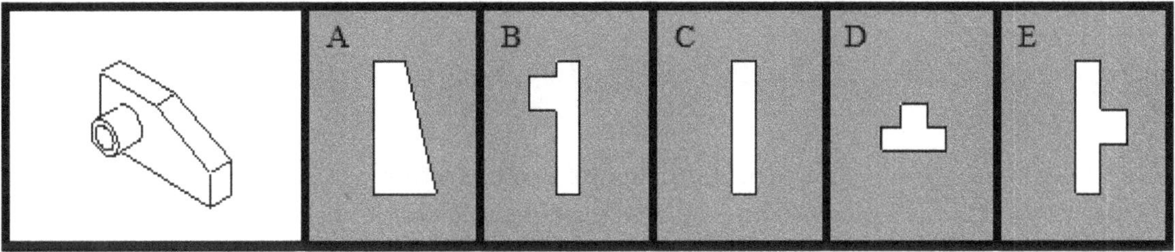

2. Which of the following apertures could the object pass through?

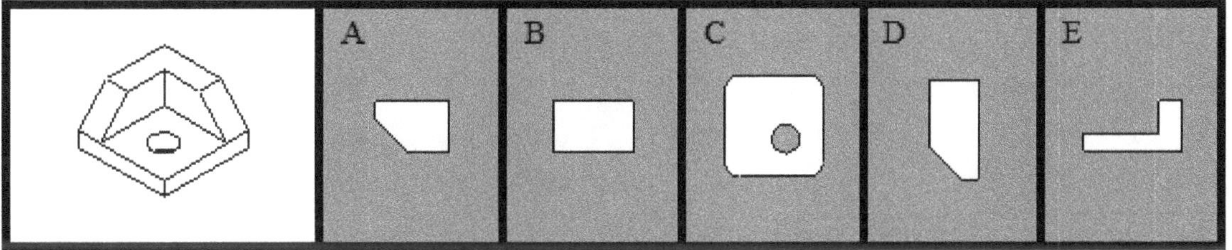

3. Which of the following apertures could the object pass through?

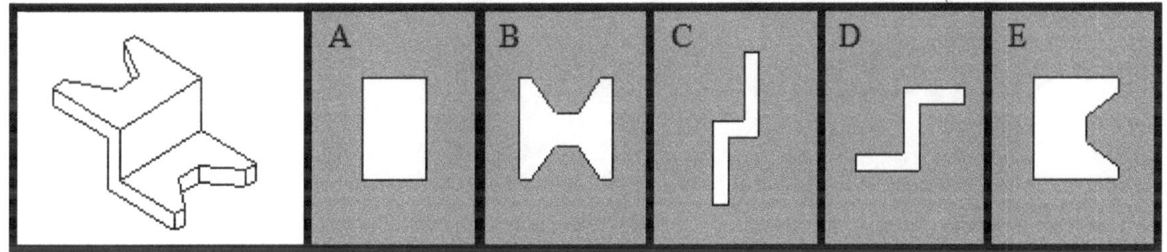

4. Which of the following apertures could the object pass through?

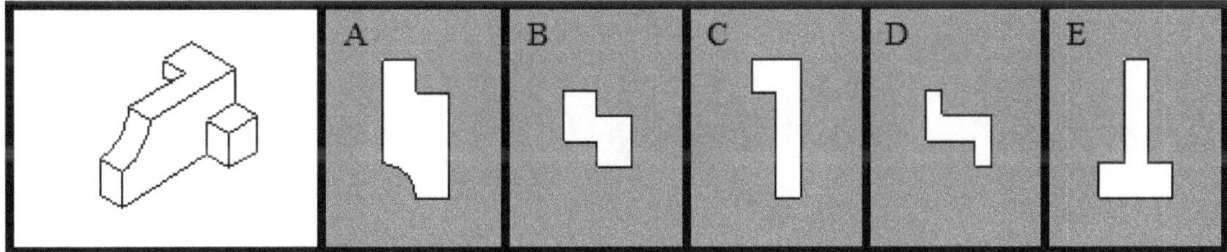

Practice Answers

1. The answer is B, which shows a top view of the object. E is close, but the area of the aperture that corresponds to the circular part of the object is in the wrong place.

2. The answer is D. Choice A is close, but the aperture is not big enough to accommodate the object.

3. The answer is A. If you view the object from the front and then rotate the object 90 degrees in a front view, the object's profile matches the aperture in choice A. Choices C and D are close to the object's side profile, but the dimensions don't exactly match.

4. The answer is E, which corresponds to a top view of the object. Choices B and D approximate a back view of the object, but the thicknesses don't match those of the actual object.

Perspective Visualization

What Are These Questions Testing?

The perspective visualization questions test your ability to determine what a particular perspective view of a particular three-dimensional object would look like.

The perspective visualization questions are similar to the aperture questions because they require you to understand the relationship between three-dimensional objects and perspective views. However, the aperture questions require you to determine a two-dimensional view given a three-dimensional object, while the perspective visualization questions require you to determine a two-dimensional view based on other two-dimensional views.

What Is the Question Format?

The test will show you two out of three perspective views of a three-dimensional object: a top, front, and end view. Based on the two views given, you will have to determine what the remaining view looks like. For example, if the test provides the top and end view of the object, you will have to determine what the end view looks like.

In the example below, the front and end views of the object are provided. Based on these views, what would the top view of the object look like?

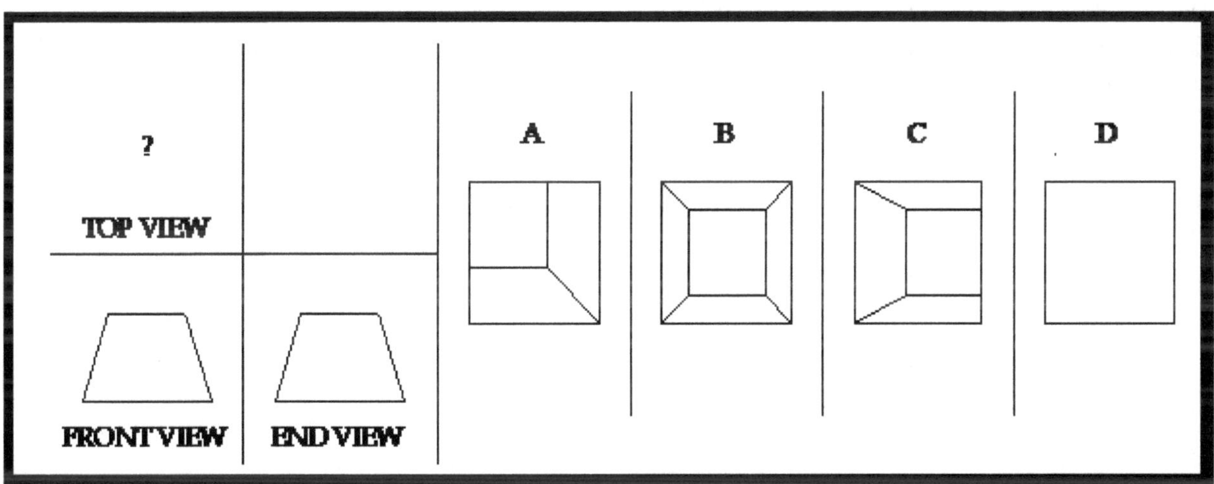

ANSWER: The answer is B. Because the front and end views both show an identical trapezoid, the figure must be tapered symmetrically on all sides. Thus, the top view will look like that shown in choice B.

Hidden vs. Visible Lines

The problems on this section of the test require you to distinguish between hidden and visible lines. A hidden line represents an edge that cannot be seen in a particular view of a part, while a visible line represents an edge that *can* be seen in a particular view. Hidden lines are depicted as dashed lines, while visible lines are depicted as solid lines.

A simple example will make this concept clearer. In the drawing below, a part is shown in a three-dimensional view, front view, and side view with edges A, B, C, and D labeled. When the part is viewed from the front, edges B, C, and D remain visible. However, edge A is obscured by a front face of the part. Therefore, edge A is a hidden line in the front view, so it is depicted with a dashed line.

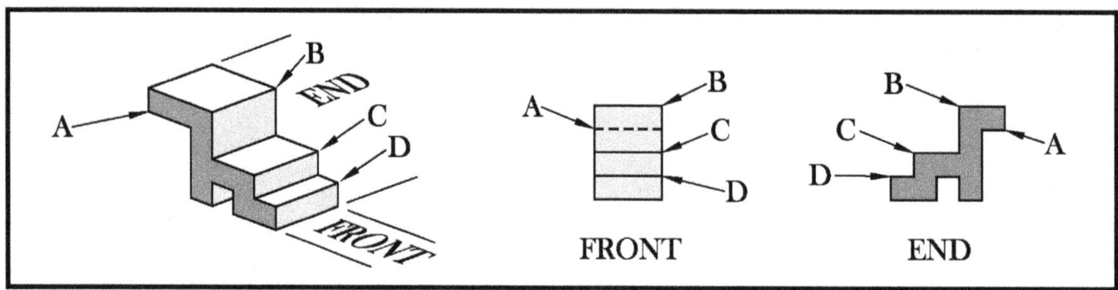

Hidden lines are not only used to represent straight edges. They can also to indicate a hole or bore that goes through the part. In such cases, the dashed lines are drawn along the maximum width of the hole or bore.

How Can I Improve My Ability to Answer These Questions Correctly?

The best way to approach these problems is to look at the two views you are given, and try to recreate the three-dimensional object from those views. Once you understand what the object looks like, it should be easy to determine what the third view looks like. If you have trouble recreating the object mentally, it might help to sketch the object on paper.

Besides doing the practice questions in this section, you might consider buying a mechanical drafting book and doing the problems in that book. This practice will help you understand how the top, front, and end views relate to each other.

Practice Questions

1. Which one of the following answer choices shows the end view of the object?

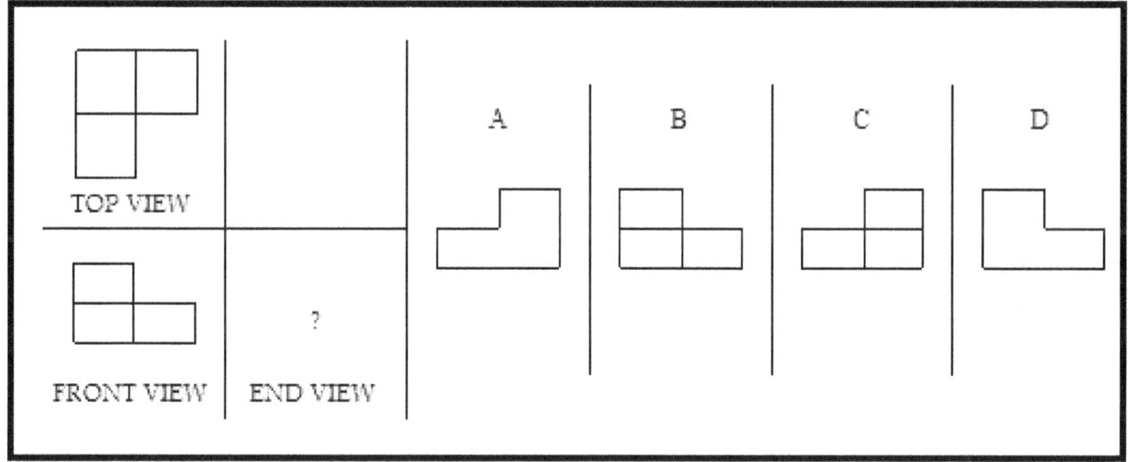

2. Which of the following answer choices shows the top view of the object?

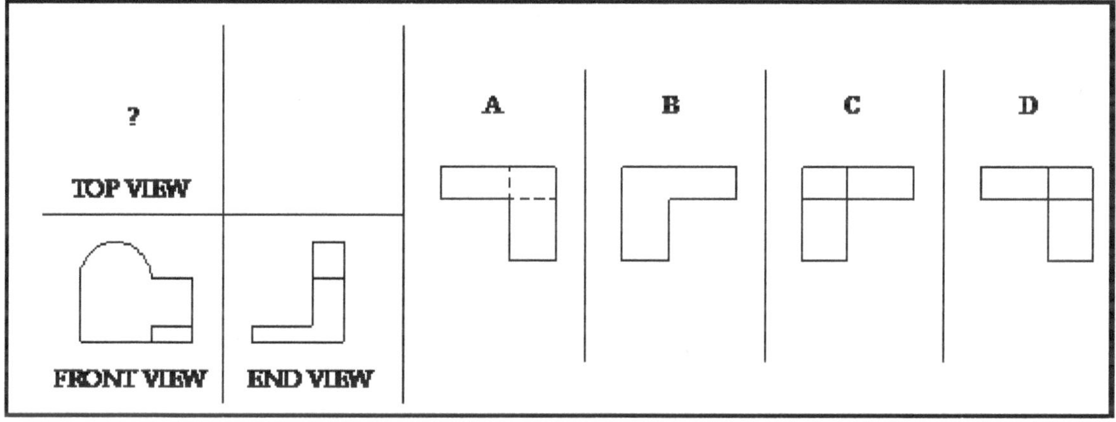

3. Which of the following answer choices shows the front view of the object?

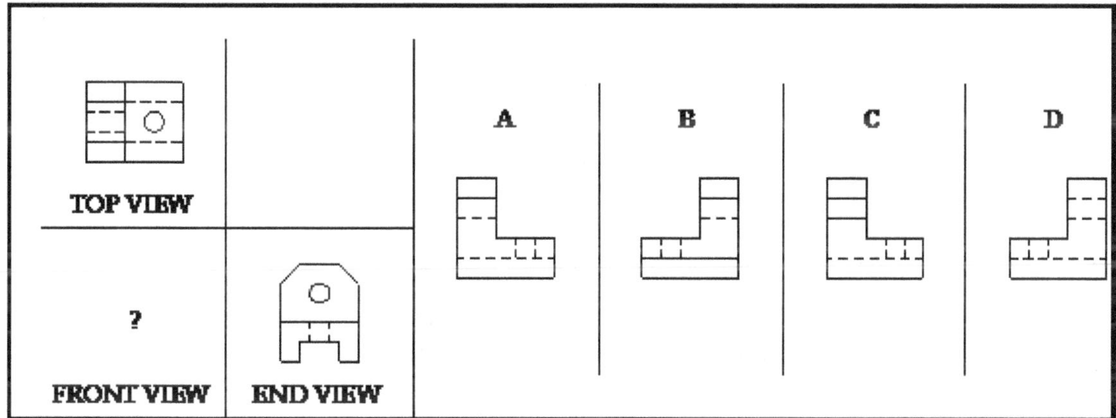

4. Which of the following answer choices shows the end view of the object?

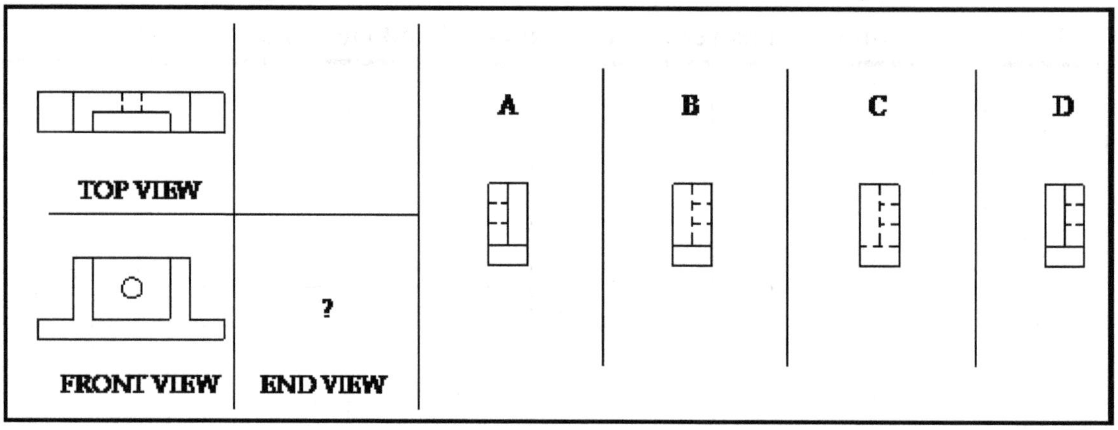

TOP VIEW

FRONT VIEW

?

END VIEW

A

B

C

D

Practice Answers

1. The answer is C. Based on the top view and the front view, you can tell that the object consists of four blocks, with one of the stacks having two blocks. In the front view, one of the stacks on the left is two blocks high. When viewed in the end view, the stack with two blocks will appear to be on the right, so the answer is C.

2. The answer is D. Note that the interior lines in the top view represent the junction between the rounded part and the flat top ledge, and the junction between the main body of the object and the protrusion sticking out toward the front. Neither of these lines are hidden, so they must be solid instead of dotted lines, which eliminates choices A and B. The protrusion is on the right side rather than on the left, which leaves choice D as the only possible option.

3. The answer is A. From the parallel sets of dashed lines in the top view and the end view, you can determine that there are two holes through the object: a vertical hole and a horizontal hole. Furthermore, you can also determine that the object has a protrusion that juts out toward the right (i.e., out of the page in the end view perspective).

These constraints eliminate choices B and D because the protrusion in these options juts toward the left rather than the right. Of the two remaining choices, A is the correct one because only A has a dashed line to indicate the horizontal hole. (One of the dashed lines in A coincides with a solid line, so this dashed line is not shown.)

4. The answer is B. From the top and front views, you can tell that there is a hole, indicated by the parallel dashed lines, through the back part of the object. This eliminates choice A, in which the hole is shown going through the front of the object. Of the remaining choices, only B shows a dashed line for the interior ledge and a solid line for the exterior protrusions.

Painted Blocks

WHAT ARE THESE QUESTIONS TESTING?

These questions are designed to test your geometric abilities. In particular, the questions test your ability to identify how many blocks in an arrangement have a certain number of exposed sides.

WHAT IS THE QUESTION FORMAT?

The test will show an arrangement of blocks of identical sizes. The blocks have been glued or cemented together as shown, and each exterior surface of the block has been painted except the base. You will have to determine how many blocks in the arrangement have a given number of painted sides.

For example, in the arrangement below, how many cubes have one side painted?

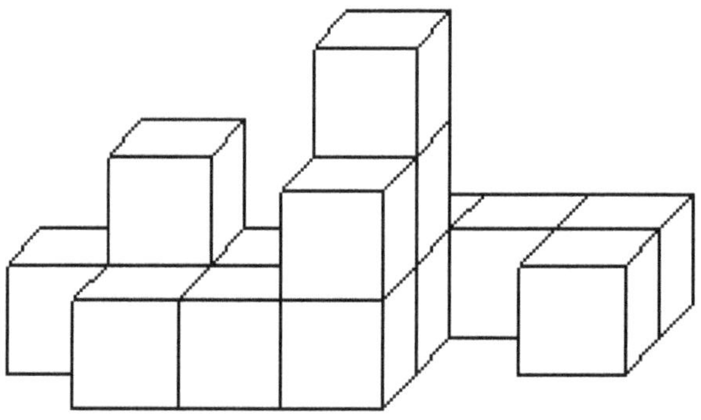

Figure A

ANSWER: The answer is two. There are two cubes that have only one side painted: the bottom block in the two-block-high stack on the left, and the bottom block in the three-block-high stack on the right.

Practice Questions

1. In the figure shown here, how many cubes have two sides painted?

2. In the figure shown here, how many cubes have three sides painted?

3. In the figure shown here, how many cubes have four sides painted?

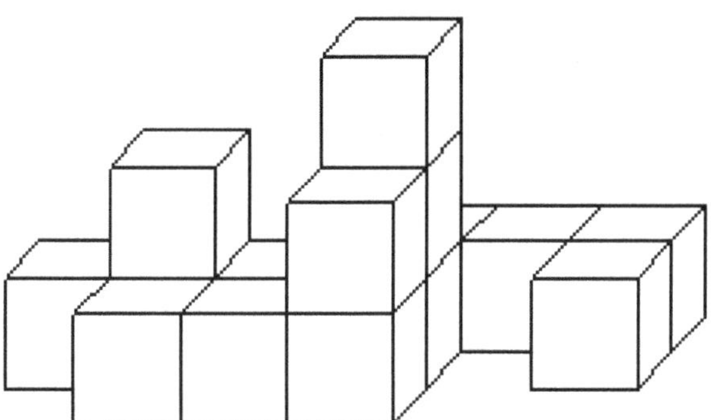

Practice Answers

1. The answer is three. There are two cubes in the front row, and one cube in the middle row.

2. The answer is five. There is one block with three painted sides in the front row, one in the middle row, and three in the back row.

3. The answer is three. There is one block with four painted sides in the front row, and two in the back.

Instrument Comprehension

What Are These Questions Testing?

These questions are designed to test your familiarity with and understanding of common instruments.

What Is the Question Format?

The question format will vary depending on the types of instruments that the test covers. This section of the book will focus on the compass and the artificial horizon, two instruments commonly used in airplanes. Test questions related to these instruments will illustrate a compass and an artificial horizon inside an airplane cockpit. Based on the readings of both of these instruments, you will have to determine the position and orientation of the airplane.

How Do I Read the Compass and Artificial Horizon Instruments?

The compass, a relatively intuitive instrument with which many people are familiar, shows which direction a person or vehicle is facing. When a person is facing north, for example, the needle on the compass points toward the "N." If the person is facing a direction between south and southeast, the needle will point between "S" and "SE."

The artificial horizon is an instrument that shows how the nose and wings of a plane are tilted. For most people, the artificial horizon is less intuitive and less familiar than the compass. However, if you imagine yourself actually flying in a plane, the artificial horizon becomes easier to read and understand. The artificial horizon has two components that illustrate how the nose of an airplane is tilted with respect to the ground: the miniature wings and the horizon bar. The miniature wings represent the actual wings of the aircraft, and the horizon bar represents the horizon, the imaginary line that divides the ground and the sky from the pilot's point of view. When the miniature wings are level with the horizon bar, the plane is level. When the miniature wings are above the horizon bar, the plane is tilted upward, and when the miniature wings are below the horizon bar, the plane is tilted downward. These categories of nose tilt are shown in the drawing below.

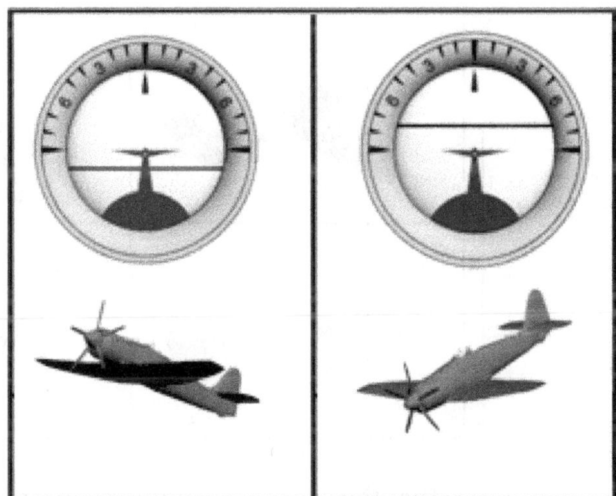

To illustrate how the wings are tilted from side to side, the artificial horizon instrument also has a dial with degree marks representing the bank angle. A needle on the dial indicates the exact bank angle, and the horizon bar is tilted accordingly, as shown in the picture below. If the left wing of the plane is tilted downward, the needle will be to the right of the center of the dial; if the right wing is tilted downward; the needle will be to the left of the center. Note that the tilted horizon bar reflects the pilot's point of view: if the left wing of the plane is tilted downward, the horizon will appear to be tilted in the opposite direction.

To answer the questions on this test, you will have to use information from both the compass and artificial horizon to determine how the plane is oriented. If the plane is flying north, it will appear to fly into the page in the illustrations.

For example, based on the compass and artificial horizon shown below, which of the answer choices represents the orientation of the plane?

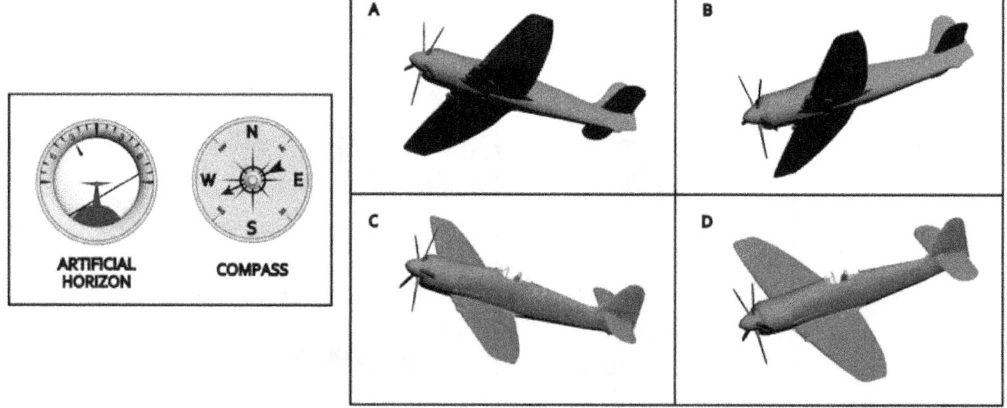

ANSWER: The answer is A. First, notice that the compass is pointing in a west-southwest direction. If a north-flying plane is facing into the page, then a westbound plane will be facing left. The compass indicates that the plane is flying somewhere between west and southwest, so the illustration will show a plane that appears to be facing left and just slightly out of the page.

Second, notice that the miniature wings in the artificial horizon are above the horizon line, and the needle on the dial is to the left of the center. From this information, you know that 1) the nose of the plane is tilted upward, and 2) the left wing of the plane is tilted upward, and the right wing is tilted downward. Because only the plane illustrated in choice A fits this description, it is the correct answer.

How Can I Improve My Ability to Read the Compass and Artificial Horizon?

Most people don't encounter these instruments on an everyday basis, so the best way to improve your ability to read them is simply to do the practice question in this section. However, although the artificial horizon is not commonly found outside of aircraft, you might want to practice using a real compass if you are still having trouble with these questions. You can find a reasonably-priced compass at most outdoor or sporting goods stores.

Practice Questions

1. Which of the answer choices represents the orientation of the plane?

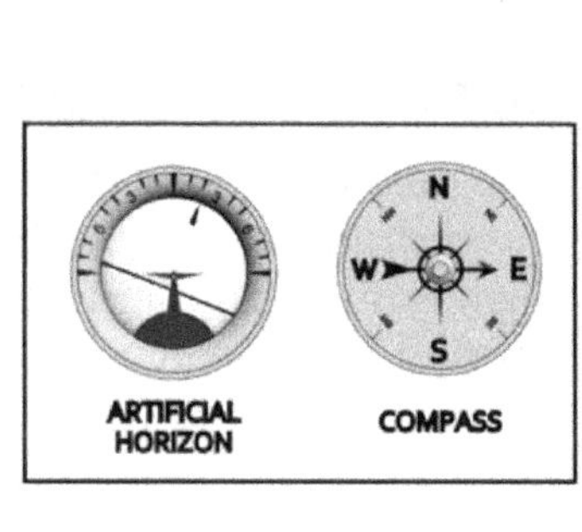

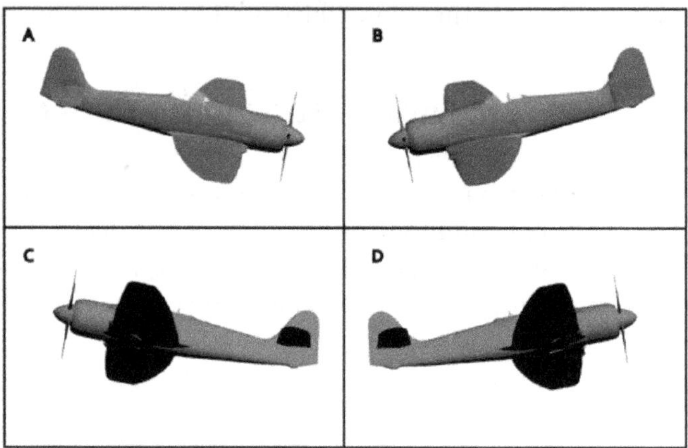

2. Which of the answer choices represents the orientation of the plane?

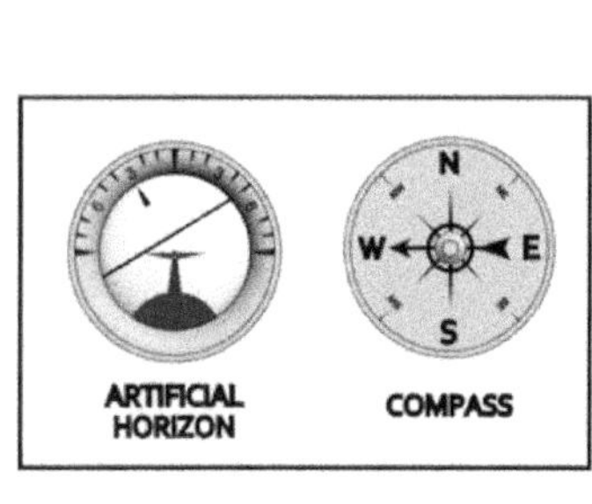

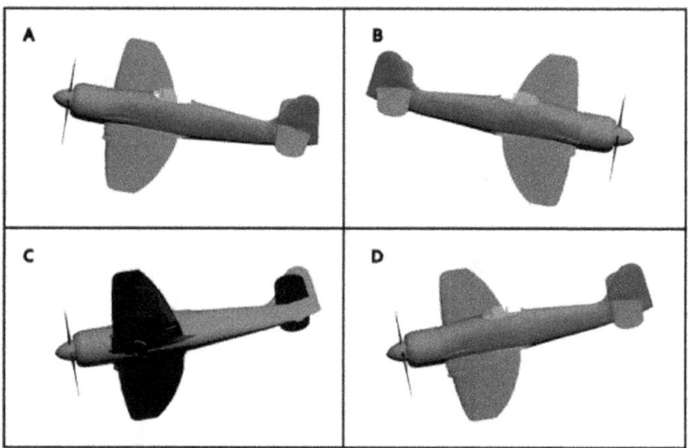

3. Which of the answer choices represents the orientation of the plane?

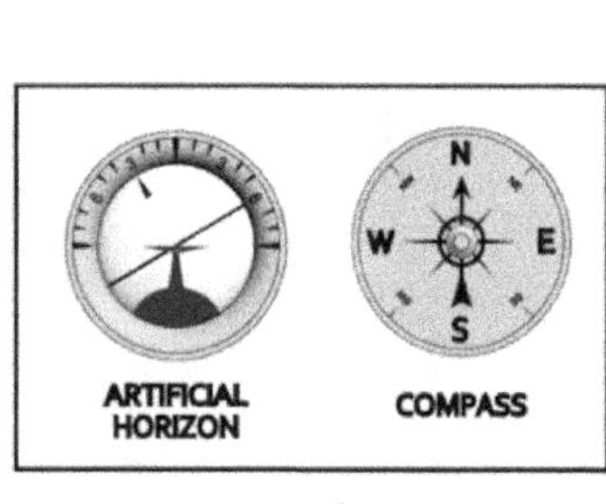

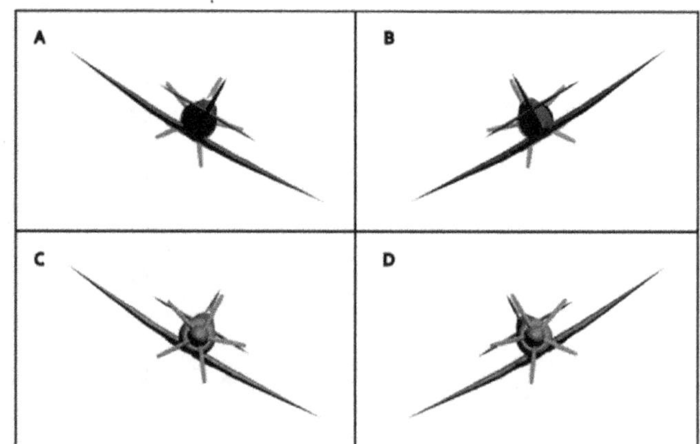

4. Which of the answer choices represents the orientation of the plane?

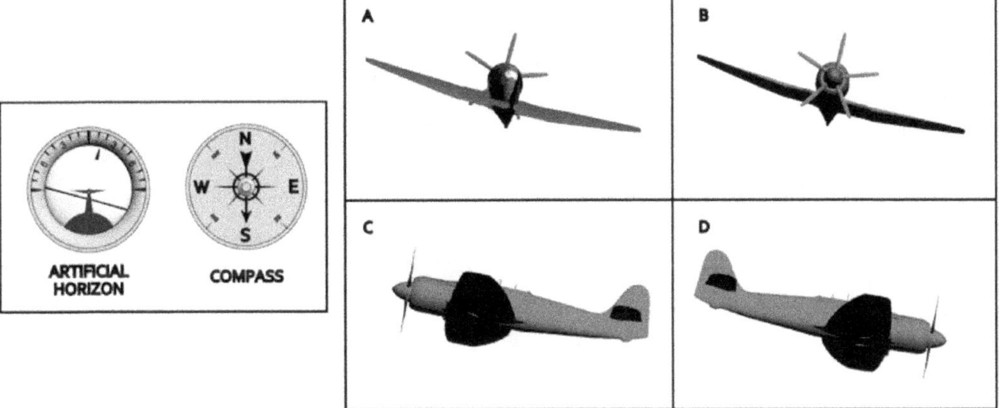

5. Which of the answer choices represents the orientation of the plane?

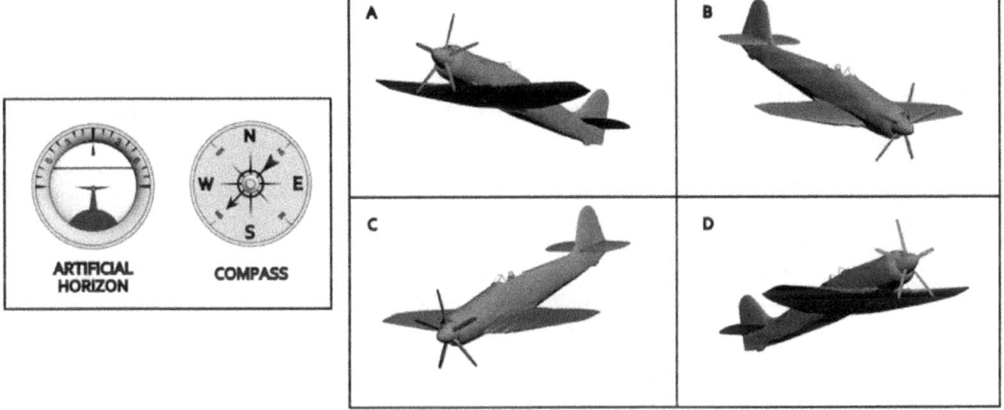

6. Which of the answer choices represents the orientation of the plane?

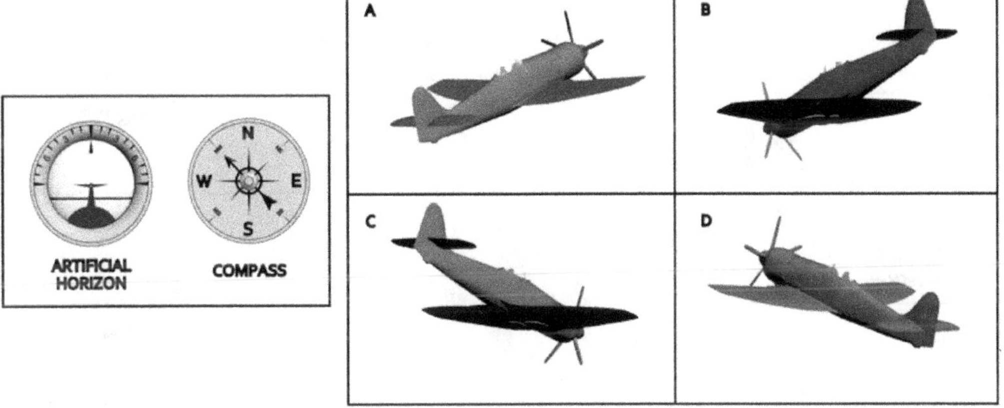

7. **Which of the answer choices represents the orientation of the plane?**

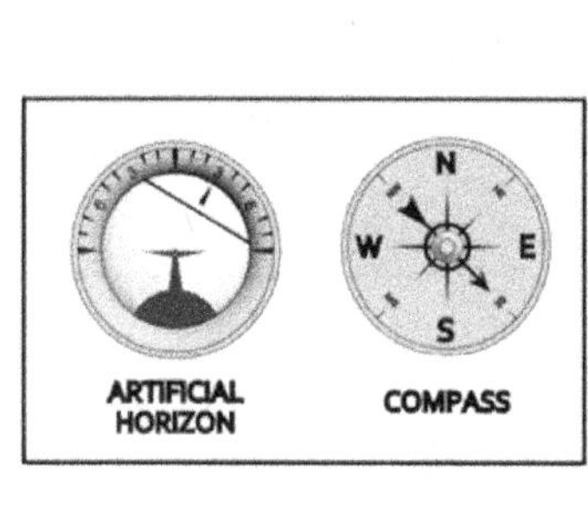

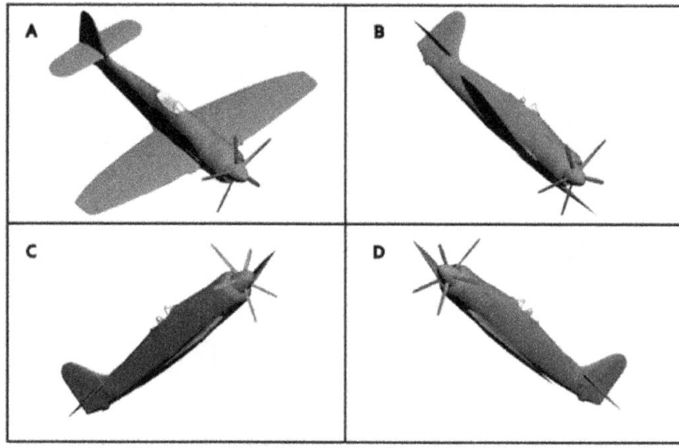

8. **Which of the answer choices represents the orientation of the plane?**

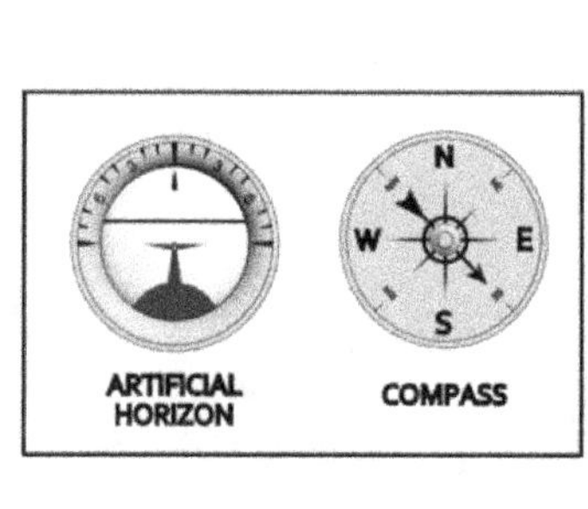

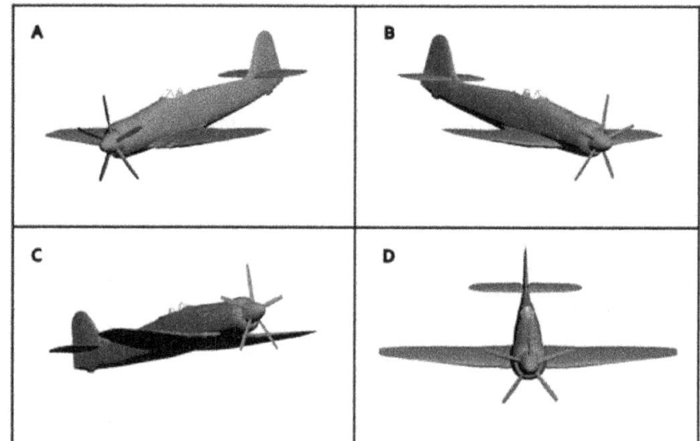

9. **Which of the answer choices represents the orientation of the plane?**

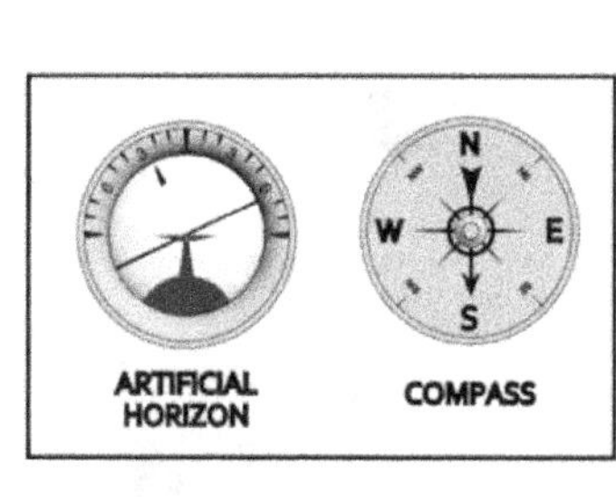

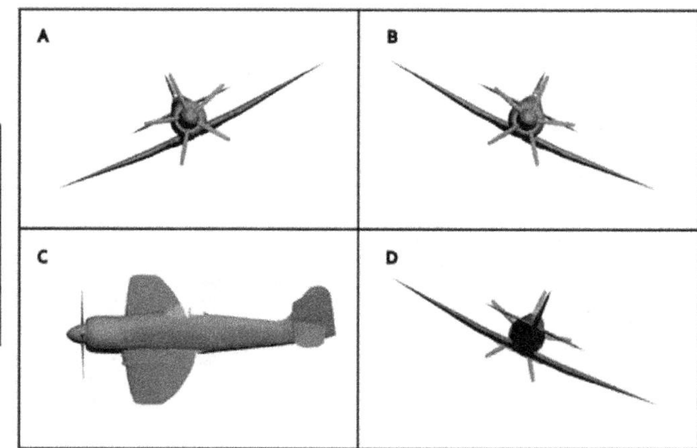

10. Which of the answer choices represents the orientation of the plane?

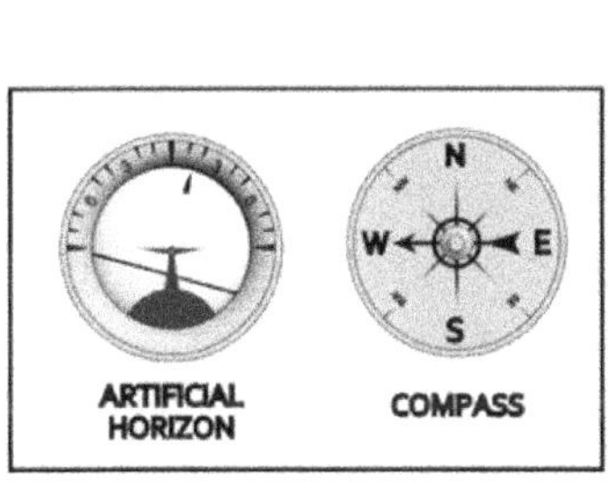

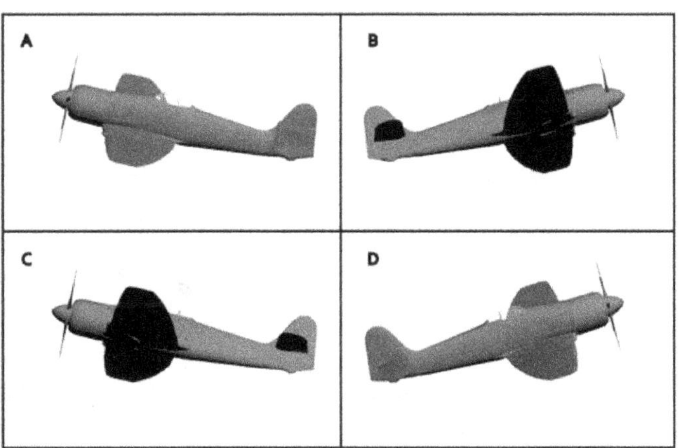

Practice Answers

1. The answer is D. The plane is flying east, which eliminates choices B and C. The artificial horizon indicates that the right wing of the plane is tilted upward. Only choice D meets this requirement.

2. The answer is C. The plane is facing west, which eliminates choice B. The artificial horizon indicates that the left wing of the plane is facing upward, so the answer is choice C.

3. The answer is A. The plane is facing north, which eliminates choices C and D. The artificial horizon indicates that the left wing is tilted upward, so the answer is choice A.

4. The answer is B because this is the only answer choice in which the plane is facing south.

5. The answer is C. The miniature wings indicate that the nose is tilted downward, which eliminates choices A and D. Of the two remaining choices, the answer must be C because the plane is flying southwest.

6. The answer is D. The artificial horizon indicates that the nose is tilted upward, which eliminates choices B and C. In addition, the compass is pointing northwest. Only choice D meets both requirements.

7. The answer is B. The compass shows that the plane is flying southeast, so you can eliminate choice D. In addition, the artificial horizon indicates that the nose of the plane is tilted downward, and the right wing of the plane is tilted upward. The only choice that meets both requirements is B.

8. The answer is B. The miniature wings in the artificial horizon are below the horizon bar, so the nose of the plane is tilted downward. As explained earlier, a plane that is traveling north is facing into the page. Therefore, a plane that is going southeast will have the orientation shown in choice B.

9. The answer is A. Because the compass is pointing south, the plane must appear to fly out of the page, so you can eliminate choices C and D. In addition, the artificial horizon indicates that the plane's left wing is tilted upward. Thus, A is the correct answer.

10. The answer is A. The compass indicates that the plane is flying west, which eliminates choices B and D. Also, the artificial horizon indicates that the right wing of the plane is tilted upward. Thus, A is the correct answer.

Hole Punching

What Are These Questions Testing?

These questions are designed to test your logical and visualization abilities.

What Is the Question Format?

The test will illustrate a piece of paper folded in a particular way. After the imaginary paper has been folded, the test will then illustrate a number of holes punched through the folded paper. Based on the given information, you will have to determine the number and locations of holes when the imaginary paper is unfolded.

How Do I Answer These Questions?

The best way to answer these questions is to first determine the number of holes, then determine their locations. To determine the number of holes, remember that for each hole punched in the folded paper, there will be one hole for each layer of paper when the paper is fully unfolded. In the example illustrated below, how many holes will there be when the paper is unfolded?

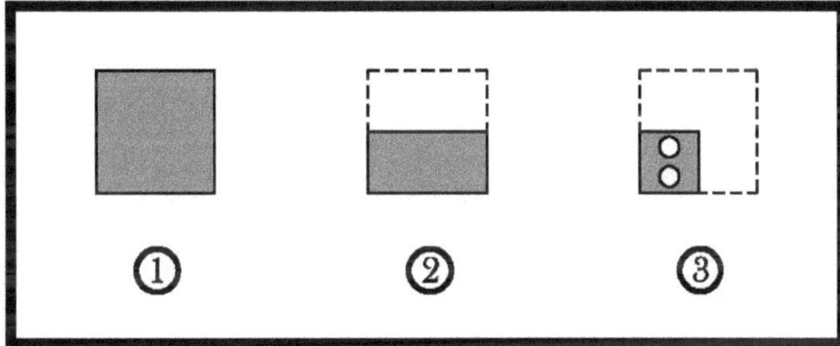

ANSWER: The paper is folded in half twice, and there are four layers of paper. There are two holes punched through the four layers of paper, so the unfolded paper will have a total of eight holes.

After determining the number of holes, you can determine the locations of the holes by working backward, unfolding the paper in your mind. The holes will be symmetrical with respect to the fold line. For example, when the paper above is unfolded once, two new holes will be revealed. These two new holes are the same distance from the fold line as the original holes.

When the paper is unfolded a second time, as shown below, four new holes are revealed. The four new holes are the same distance from the fold line as the respective original holes.

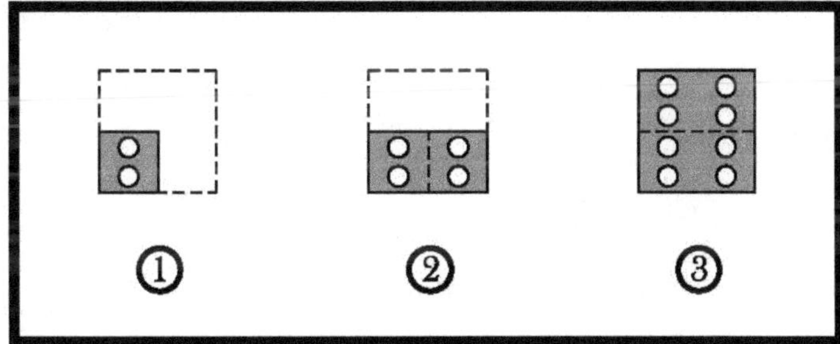

After you have finished unfolding the paper in your mind, pick the answer choice with the correct number and position of holes. Some tests will have no answer choices, and will require you to mark the locations of the holes on a grid.

How Can I Improve My Ability to Visualize the Holes?

If you are having trouble with the practice problems, it might help you to cut rectangular pieces of paper and fold and punch them as shown in the practice problems. After punching the holes, unfold the paper in the opposite order from which you folded them, noting the location of each newly revealed hole. By practicing with physical pieces of paper, you will be able to more easily visualize the imaginary paper and holes on the actual test.

Practice Questions

1. How will the holes appear when the paper is unfolded?

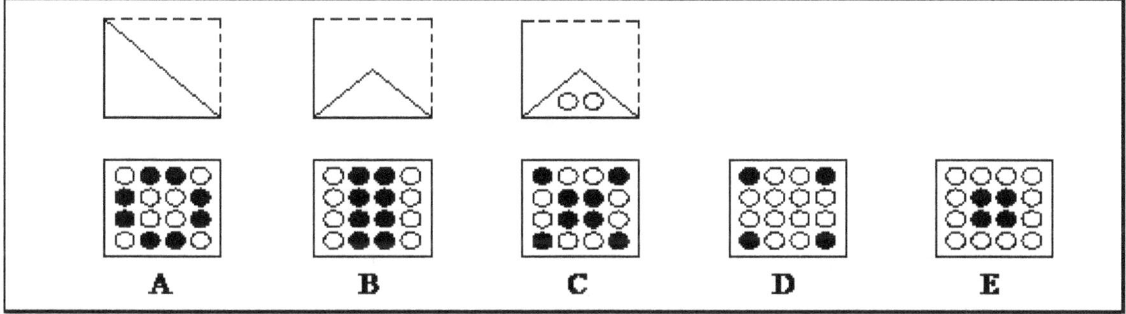

2. How will the holes appear when the paper is unfolded?

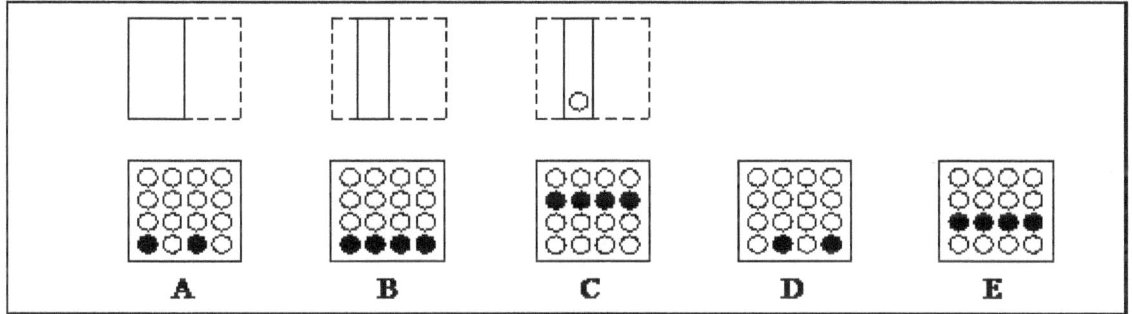

3. How will the holes appear when the paper is unfolded?

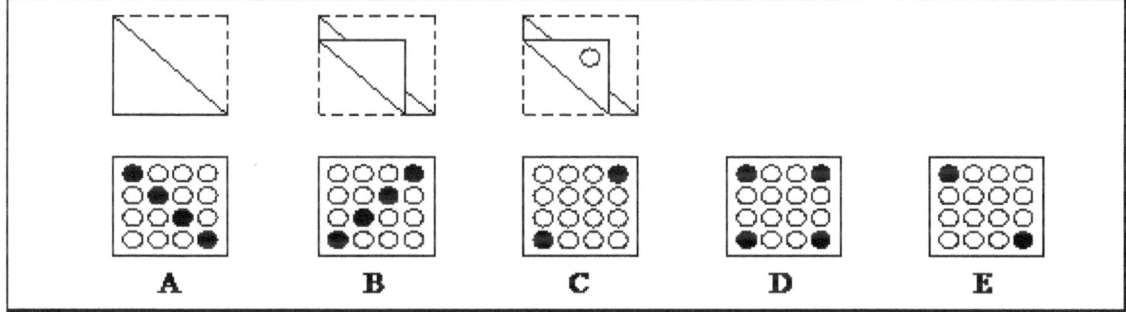

4. How will the holes appear when the paper is unfolded?

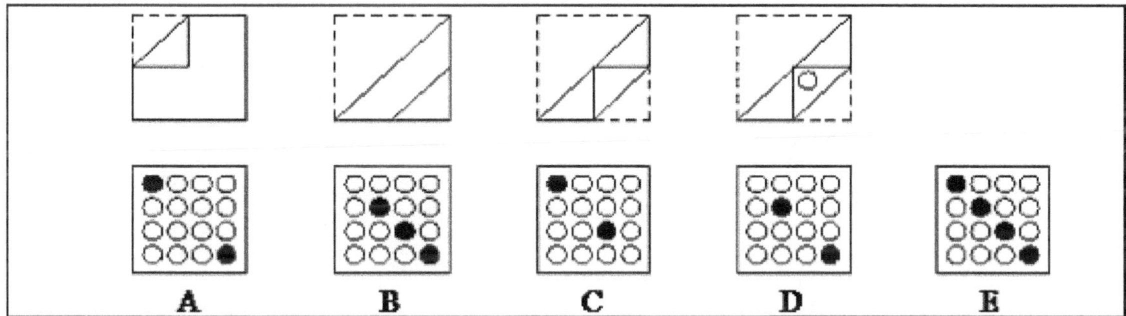

5. How will the holes appear when the paper is unfolded?

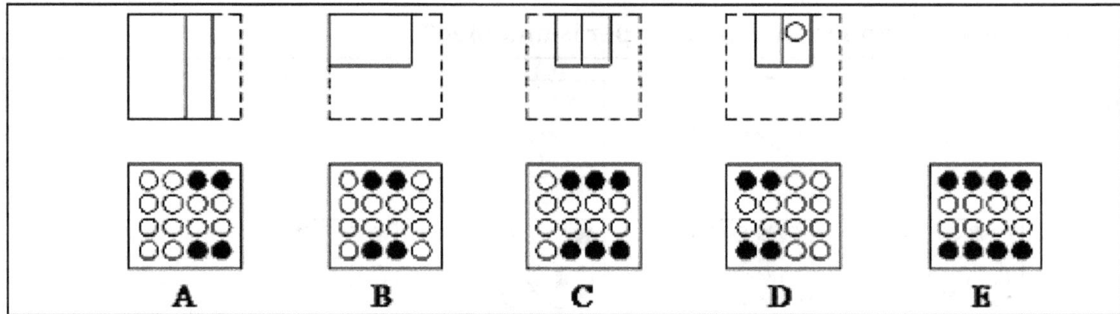

Practice Answers

1. The answer is A. When the sheet is unfolded the first time, it will reveal two additional vertical holes. When the sheet is unfolded a second time, the vertical and horizontal holes will be "mirrored" across the diagonal fold line, so there will be a total of eight holes in the positions shown in choice A.

2. The answer is B. When the sheet is unfolded the first time, another hole will appear along the bottom of the sheet. When the sheet is unfolded a second time, two more holes will appear near the bottom of the sheet.

3. The answer is C. Note that the sheet is first folded diagonally, then it is folded again in the opposite direction. However, the hole is only punched through two layers of paper, not four, so there will only be two holes.

When the paper is unfolded the first time, one hole (through two layers of paper) will appear in the bottom left corner. When the paper is unfolded a second time, a second hole will appear in the upper right corner.

4. The answer is E. When the sheet is unfolded the first time, there will be two holes, each through two layers of paper, that appear in the bottom right quadrant. After the sheet is unfolded a second time, another two holes appear across the diagonal fold line.

5. The answer is A. Note that although the sheet is folded three times, the hole is only punched through four layers of paper, so there will be four holes.

When the paper is unfolded the first time, no new holes appear because there are no holes through these layers of paper. When the paper is unfolded a second time, one new hole appears on the opposite side of the horizontal fold line. Finally, when the paper is unfolded a third time, two new holes appear on the opposite side of the vertical fold line.

Hidden Blocks

What Are These Questions Testing?

These questions are designed to test your spatial, geometric, and logical abilities.

What Is the Question Format?

The test will show a drawing of a three-dimensional arrangement of blocks, and ask you to identify how many blocks are in the arrangement. Typically, the blocks are arranged in irregular shapes, and some of the blocks are hidden. You will have to use spatial intuition and reasoning to determine the number of blocks.

If Some of the Blocks Are Hidden, How Do I Know How Many Blocks There Are?

There are two rules you can use to help you determine the number of blocks.

The first and most important rule to remember is that blocks can't be suspended in midair. That is, if a block isn't on the bottom level of the arrangement, it must be supported by another block, even if the supporting block can't be seen. We'll explain this concept

For example, try to figure out how many blocks there are in the arrangement below.

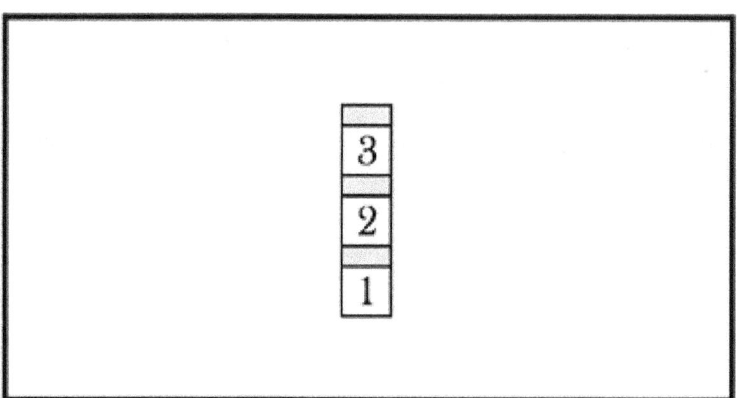

Answer: In this arrangement, the only blocks you can see directly are blocks 1, 2, and 3. However, it's clear that these three blocks can't be directly on top of each other, so blocks 2 and 3 must be supported by additional blocks. Because block 2 is one level higher than block 1, it must be supported by one extra block, and because block 3 is two levels higher than block 1, it must be supported by two extra blocks.

Therefore, the total number of blocks in the arrangement is six—three visible blocks and three invisible blocks.

The picture below is a side view of the arrangement, with the hidden blocks shaded.

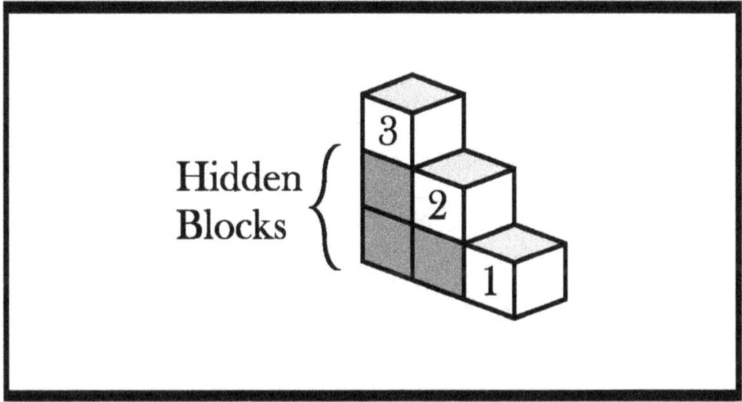

Now, try a more complex example. How many blocks are in the arrangement below?

Answer: You can see blocks 1 through 11 directly. However, there must be two hidden blocks supporting block 9, and one hidden block supporting block 7. Therefore, the arrangement contains a total of fourteen blocks: ten visible and three hidden.

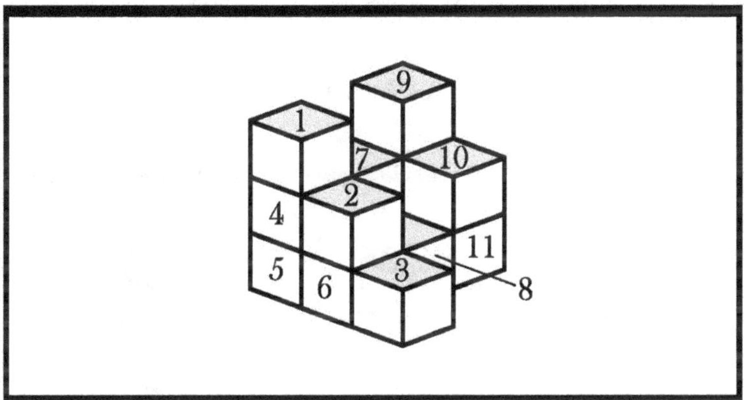

To better display the hidden blocks, the picture below shows an exploded view of the arrangement, with the hidden blocks shaded.

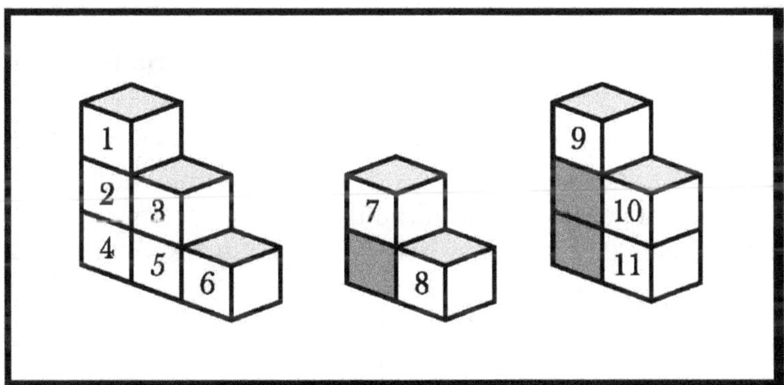

The second rule is: When dealing with very large, complex block arrangements, try to separate the arrangement into vertical "slivers" from left to right, similar to those shown in the exploded view above. By counting the number of blocks in each sliver, you can more effectively keep track of how many blocks are in the arrangement.

Look at the example below. How many blocks are in this arrangement?

Answer: The arrangement is five blocks wide, so it can be broken into five vertical slivers. The first vertical sliver on the left contains one block, the second sliver has three, the third sliver has five, and so on. By counting the number of blocks in each sliver, you can see that there are a total of seventeen blocks in the arrangement.

The drawing below shows an exploded view of the arrangement, broken into slivers. The hidden blocks are shaded.

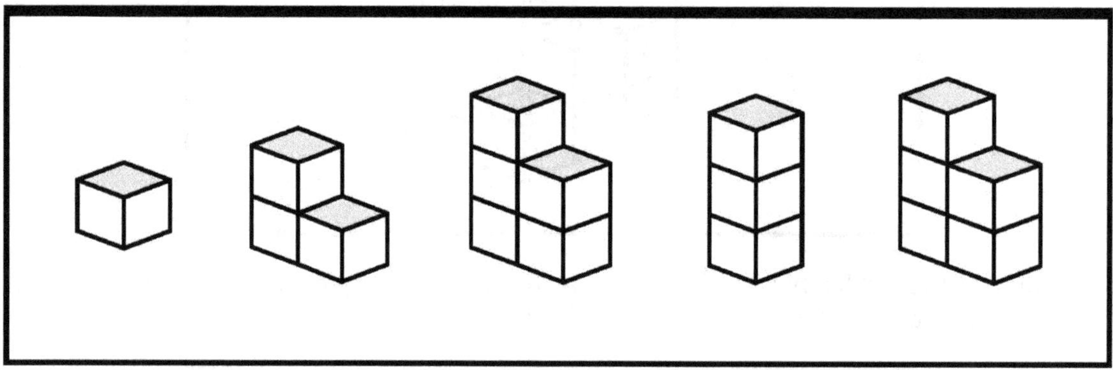

Is There Any Way to Improve My Ability to Determine the Number of Blocks in Each Arrangement?

The best way to develop this ability is by doing the exercises in this section. If you are still having difficulty with this section, it might help to buy a set of children's blocks and try to recreate the block arrangements in the practice problems. Although this may seem silly or simplistic, working hands-on with three-dimensional objects may help you gain more spatial intuition.

Practice Questions

1. How many blocks are in the arrangement below?

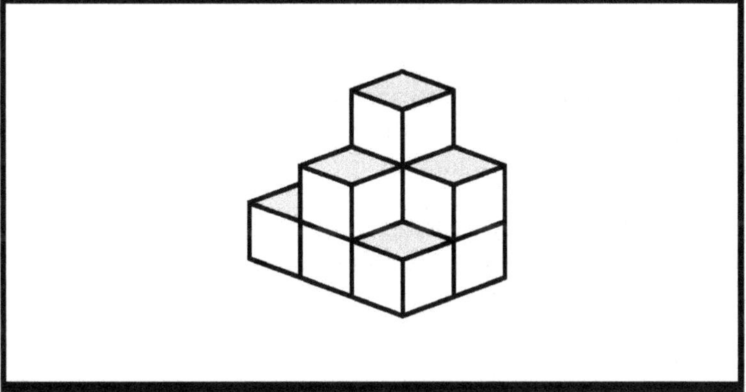

2. How many blocks are in the arrangement below?

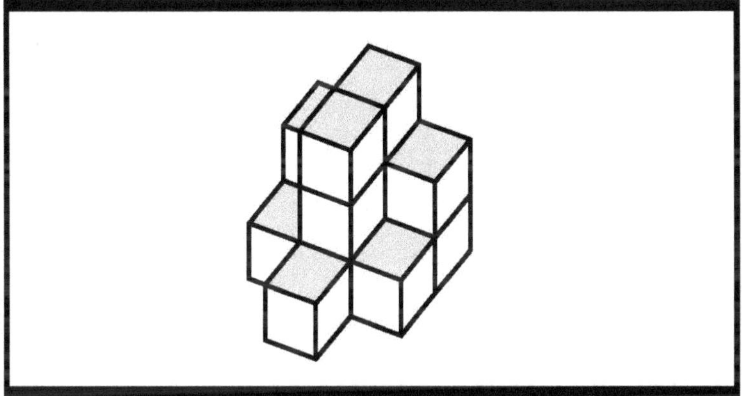

3. How many blocks are in the arrangement below?

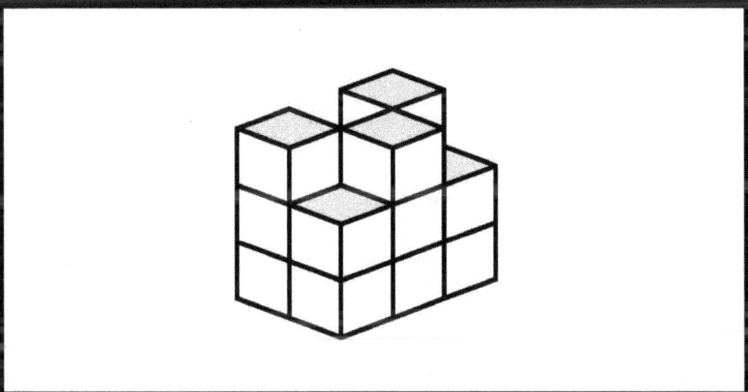

Practice Answers

1. There are a total of nine blocks in the arrangement. Although there are only seven blocks visible in the perspective below, there must be two hidden blocks in the three-block high stack in the middle.

2. There are a total of thirteen blocks in the arrangement: three blocks in the leftmost vertical sliver, seven blocks in the middle, and three in the right sliver. Note that three blocks in the middle sliver and one block in the right sliver are hidden.

3. There are a total of thirteen blocks in the arrangement: five blocks in the leftmost vertical sliver, three blocks in the middle vertical sliver, and five blocks in the rightmost sliver.

Counting Touching Blocks

WHAT ARE THESE QUESTIONS TESTING?

These questions are designed to test your spatial, geometric, and logical abilities.

WHAT IS THE QUESTION FORMAT?

The test will show a drawing of a three-dimensional arrangement of blocks with the same size and shape, and ask you to identify how many other blocks a particular block is touching. Typically, the blocks are arranged in irregular shapes, and some of the blocks are hidden. You will have to use spatial intuition and reasoning to determine how many blocks are touching the block in question.

HOW DO I KNOW HOW MANY BLOCKS ARE TOUCHING THE PARTICULAR BLOCK?

First, it is important to know which blocks qualify as "touching" the other block. If at least part of a face of one block touches at least part of a face of another block, those blocks are considered to touch each other. However, if a block shares only a corner or an edge with another block, the two blocks do not touch.

The example below illustrates the difference between touching and non-touching blocks. Block A is touching blocks 1, 2, and 3 because part of a face of block A is touching each of these blocks. However, blocks 4 and 5 do *not* touch block A because they only contact block A at an edge; that is, they share no area with any faces of block A. Therefore, block A is touching three blocks in this picture.

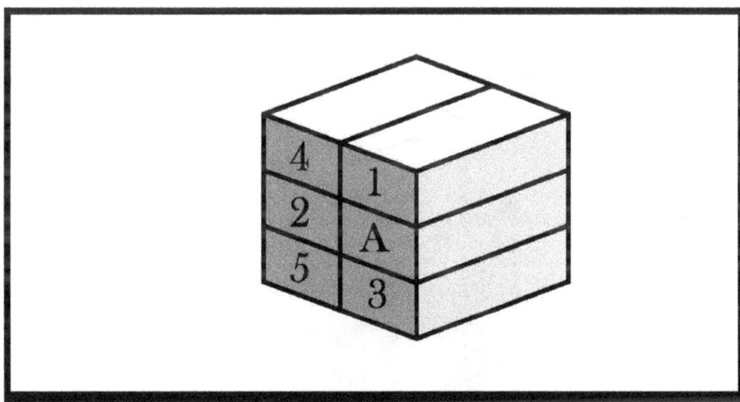

Sometimes, the blocks may be positioned so that certain blocks are hidden from view. In these cases, you will have to use basic spatial intuition and logic to determine the number of blocks touching a particular block.

In the example below, try to figure out how many blocks are touching block A.

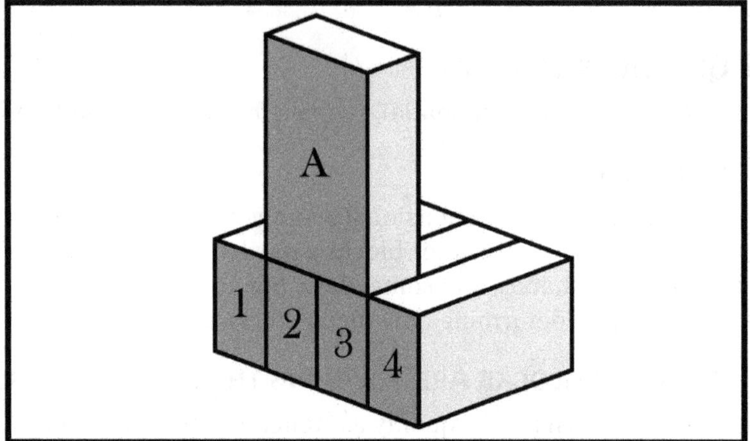

Answer: There are two blocks touching block A. Even though blocks 1 and 4 each share an edge with block A, they do not "touch" block A, as the word is used in the context of the test. Only blocks 2 and 3 actually touch a face of block A, so block A is only touching two blocks.

ARE THERE ANY WAYS TO MAKE IT EASIER TO COUNT THE NUMBER OF TOUCHING BLOCKS?

Remember that for a block to count as "touching," it much contact a face of that block. Therefore, it might help to count the number of blocks that are touching each face of the block in question.

Try to apply this strategy to the example below, in order to count the number of blocks touching block A.

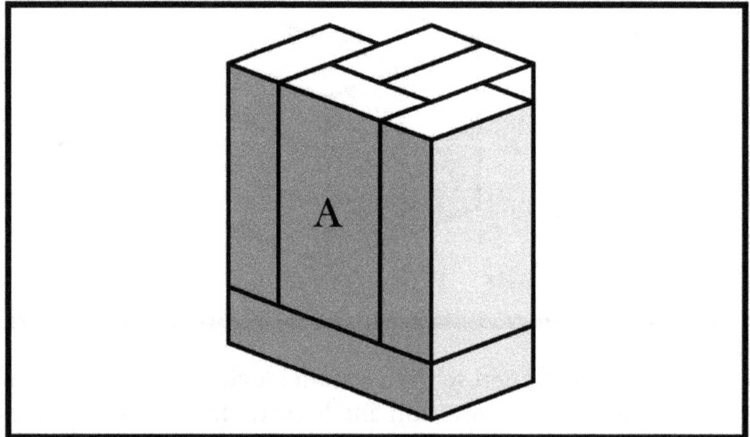

Answer: The back face of block A is touching two blocks. The left face of block A is touching one block, as is the right side. The bottom face is touching one block. Therefore, block A is touching a total of five blocks.

If you are still having trouble with the practice questions, it might help to try to re-create the example problems with a set of rectangular blocks. Practicing with physical blocks will make it easier to visualize hidden blocks when the blocks are drawn on paper.

Practice Questions

The explanations to these problems use terms like "top," "left," and "front" to refer to the faces of the blocks. Because this terminology can be confusing due to the angled view of the block arrangements, the illustration below is provided to help you keep these terms straight.

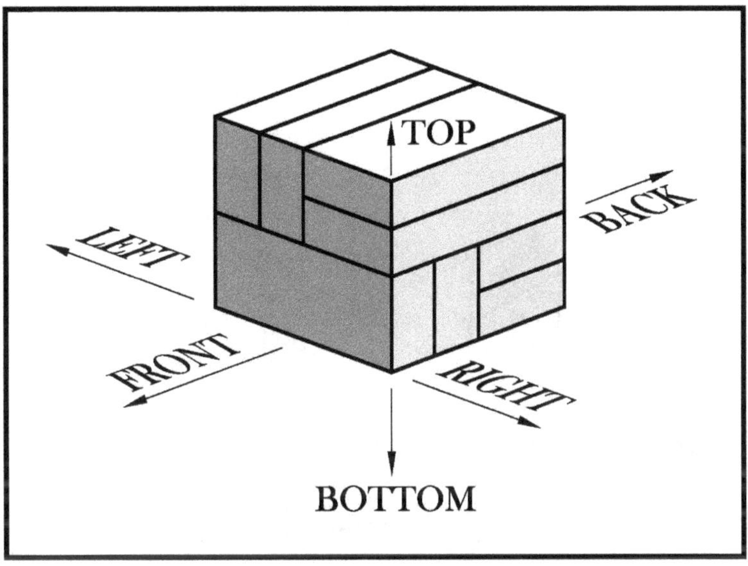

Once you understand these terms, proceed to the practice problems below.

1. How many blocks are touching block 1 in the arrangement below?

2. How many blocks are touching block 2 in the arrangement below?

3. How many blocks are touching block 8 in the arrangement below?

4. How many blocks are touching block 14 in the arrangement below?

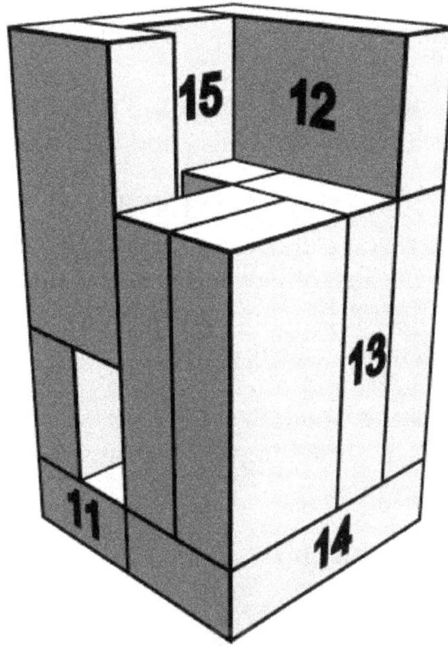

5. How many blocks are touching block 18 in the arrangement below?

Practice Answers

1. There are a total of six blocks touching block 1. One block (block #4) is touching the top face of block 1, two blocks are touching the left face, and three blocks are touching the bottom face.

2. There are a total of seven blocks touching block 2. Two blocks are touching the left face of block 2, one block (block 4) is touching the right face, and four blocks are touching the bottom face.

Note that the picture only directly shows two blocks (block 5 and the block in front of it) touching the bottom face of block 2. However, you can deduce from the picture that block 3 and the block in front of it must also touch block 2. Because the width of each block is twice the thickness, the width of block 3 and the block next to it must extend underneath block 5. Therefore, block 5 touches both of these blocks, even if it isn't explicitly shown in the picture.

3. A total of eight blocks are touching block 8. One block is touching the left face, one block is touching the right face, three blocks are touching the bottom face, one block is touching the top face, and two blocks are touching the back face.

4. A total of five blocks are touching block 14. One block (block 11) is touching the left face, and four blocks are touching the top face.

5. A total of nine blocks are touching block 18. Four blocks, including blocks 19 and 17, are touching the front face of block 18; four blocks are touching the back face; and one block is touching the bottom face.

Cut-Ups

What Are These Questions Testing?

These questions are designed to test your ability to identify what shapes can be formed by combining two or more smaller shapes.

What Is the Question Format?

The test will show two or more pieces, and one larger shape for each of the answer choices. You will have to select which of the larger shapes in the answer choices can be formed by combining the small pieces. Some problems will require you to rotate one or more of the pieces.

For example, the drawing below shows two pieces. Which of the answer choices A through D can be formed by combining the pieces?

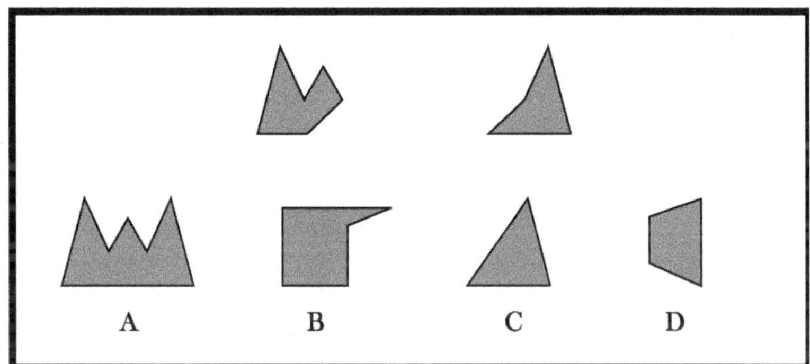

ANSWER: A can be formed by simply sliding the left piece and the right piece together. The pieces can't be arranged in such a way as to form any of the other answer choices.

How Do I Know Which Shapes Can Be Formed from the Pieces?

Unfortunately, cut-up problems require a large amount of geometric intuition, so it can be difficult to apply a consistent methodology in order to solve them. However, you can often start by eliminating answers that are obviously wrong. Frequently, it will be clear that one or more of the answer choices can't be formed by combining the pieces. By eliminating the obviously wrong answers, you can increase your chances of guessing correctly even if you're not sure of the exact answer.

In addition, it may help to rotate the test page and examine the pieces from a different angle. The shapes in the answer choices are not always oriented in the same way as the given pieces, so a different viewpoint might help you see what shapes the pieces can form.

Is There Any Way to Develop My Ability to See Geometric Shapes?

Besides doing the practice problems in this section, buying a puzzle that requires you to form shapes out of triangle pieces can be helpful. In addition, crafts or hobbies that involve geometry, such as woodworking or origami, can help improve your geometric intuition.

Practice Questions

1. Which of the shapes below can be formed from the given pieces?

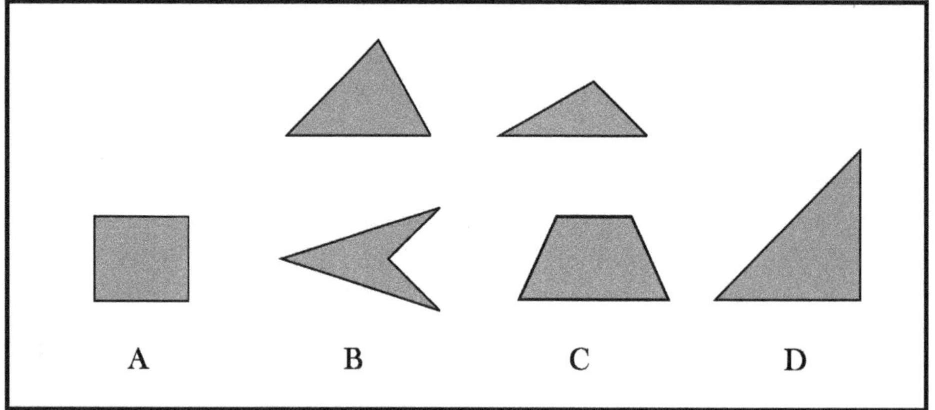

2. Which of the shapes below can be formed from the given pieces?

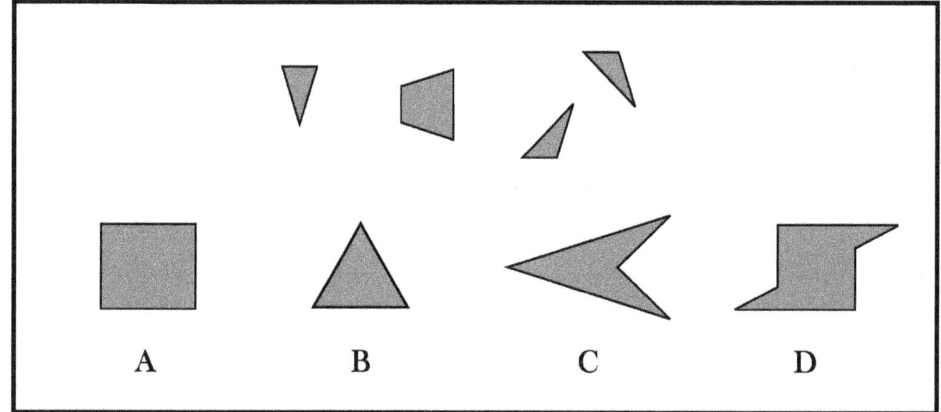

3. Which of the shapes below can be formed from the given pieces?

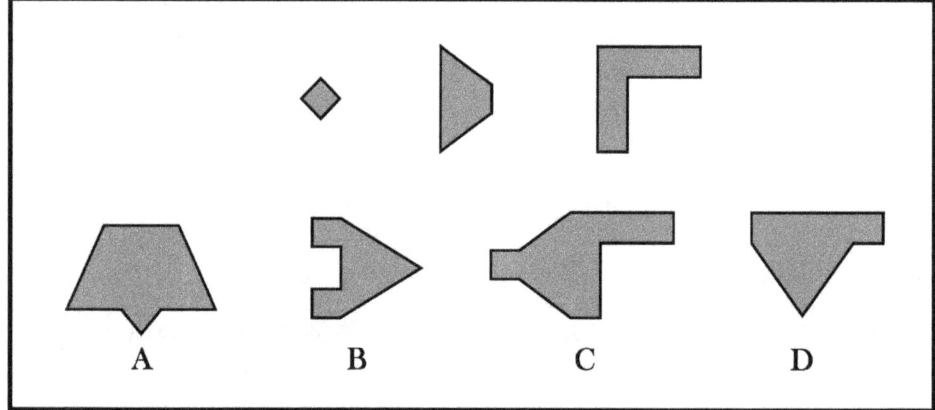

Practice Answers

1. Only D can be formed by combining the two pieces. The piece on the right must be rotated 90 degrees to form the triangle in D.

2. Only C can be formed by combining the pieces. The piece on the left and the two pieces on the right must be rotated to form the shape shown in C.

3. Only C can be formed by combining the pieces. The pieces on the left and in the center must be rotated to form the shape.

Hidden Figures

What Are These Questions Testing?

These questions test your ability to identify particular two-dimensional shapes with a complicated arrangement of shapes.

What Is the Question Format?

The test will show five complex arrangements of geometrical shapes, where each arrangement looks much like a puzzle that has been put together. In addition, the test will show five different figures. Each one of the figures is hidden in a different one of the arrangement of shapes. You will have to determine which figure is in which shape arrangement.

On the next page is an example of a hidden figures question set.

Practice Questions

Instructions: For each question, select the answer letter of the figure at the top of the page that appears within the image shown. The figure that appears within the image will have the same size and orientation as the figure shown at the top of the page.

a.

b.

c.

d.

e.

1. 

2. 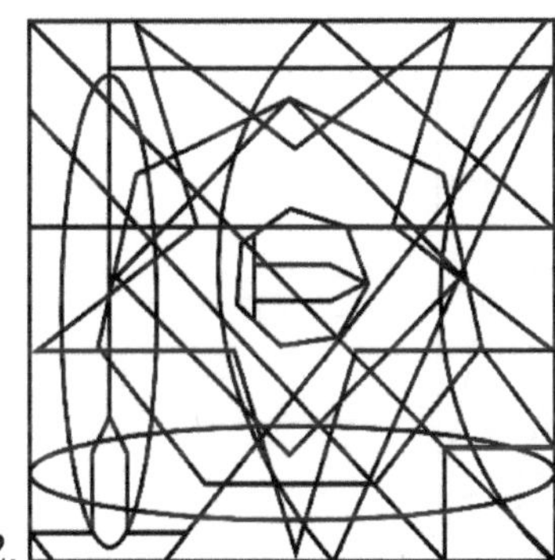

3. 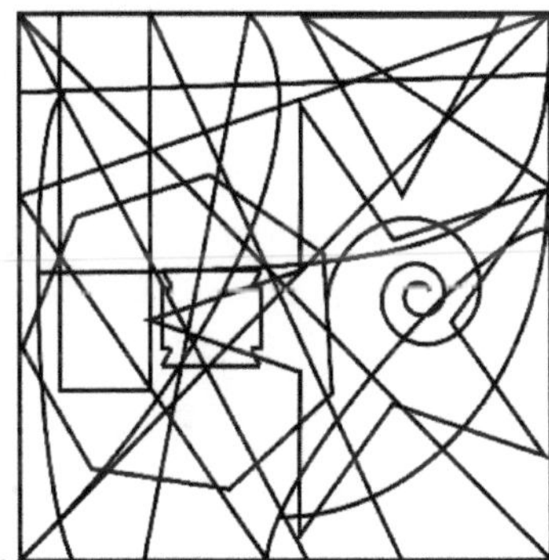

4. 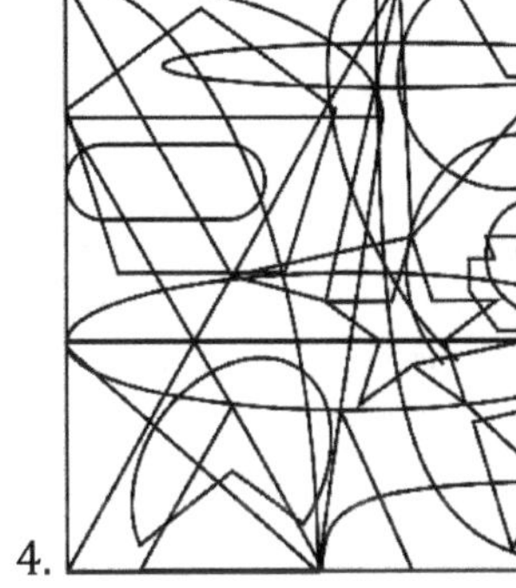

5. 

Practice Answers

a.

b.

c.

d.

e.

1. D:

4. B:

2. E:

5. A:

3. C:

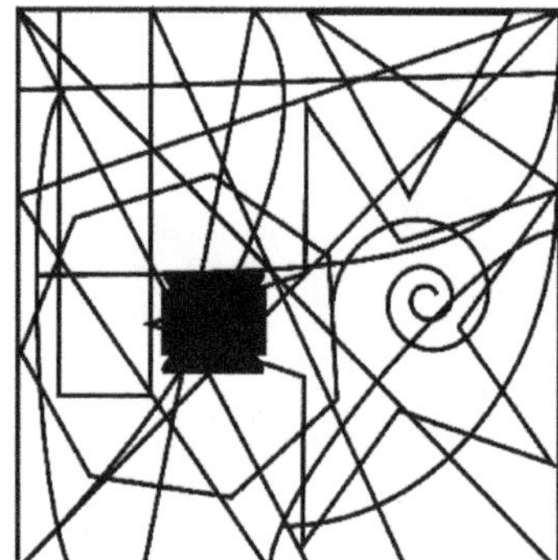

Mechanical Aptitude Practice Test

Pulleys

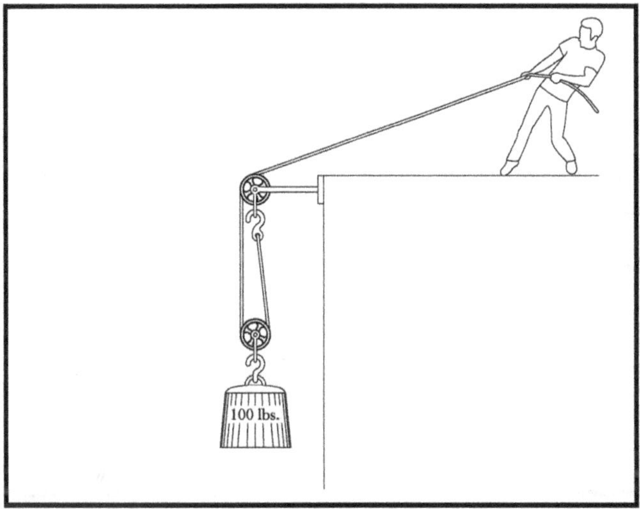

1. In the figure above, about how much force does the man have to pull with to raise the 100 lb weight?

a. 200 pounds
b. 100 pounds
c. 50 pounds
d. 25 pounds

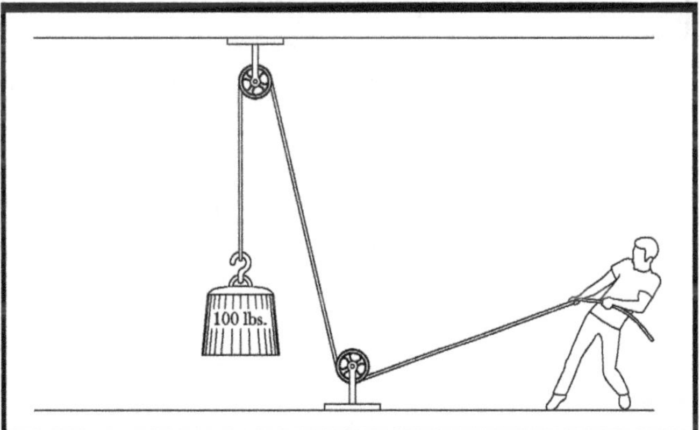

2. In the figure above, about how much force does the man have to pull with to raise the 100 lb weight?

a. 200 pounds
b. 100 pounds
c. 50 pounds
d. 25 pounds

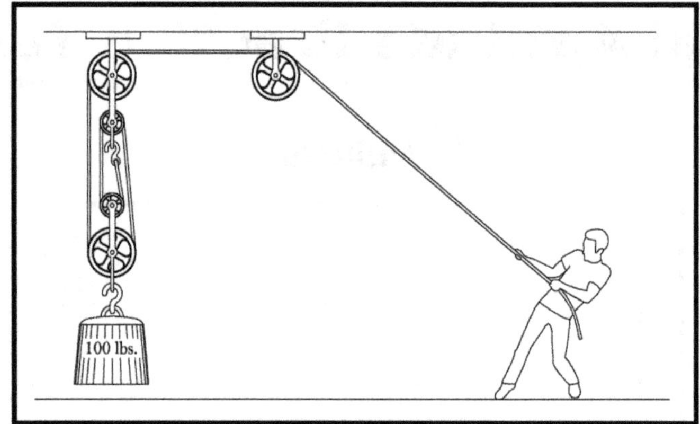

3. In the figure above, about how much force does the man have to pull with to raise the 100 lb weight?

a. 100 pounds
b. 50 pounds
c. 33 pounds
d. 25 pounds

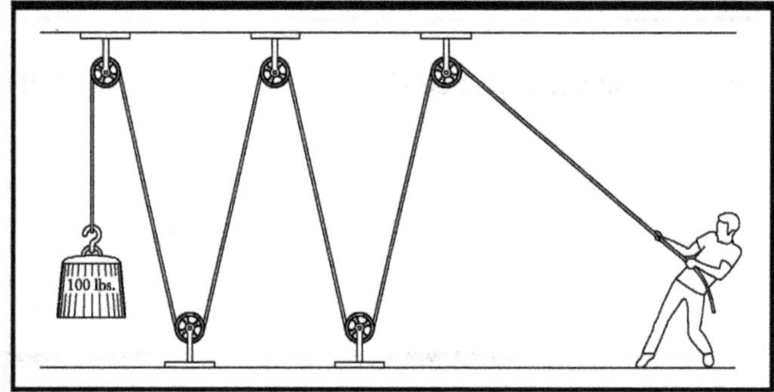

4. In the figure above, about how much force does the man have to pull with to raise the 100 lb weight?

a. 100 pounds
b. 50 pounds
c. 20 pounds
d. 17 pounds

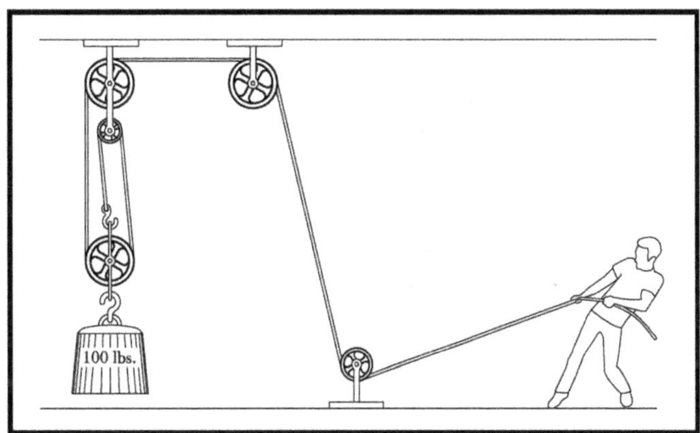

5. In the figure above, about how much force does the man have to pull with to raise the 100 lb weight?

a. 100 pounds
b. 50 pounds
c. 33 pounds
d. 25 pounds

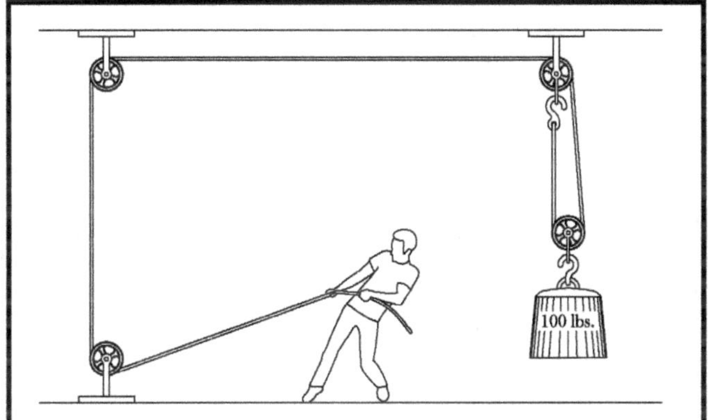

6. In the figure above, about how much force does the man have to pull with to raise the 100 lb weight?

a. 200 pounds
b. 100 pounds
c. 50 pounds
d. 25 pounds

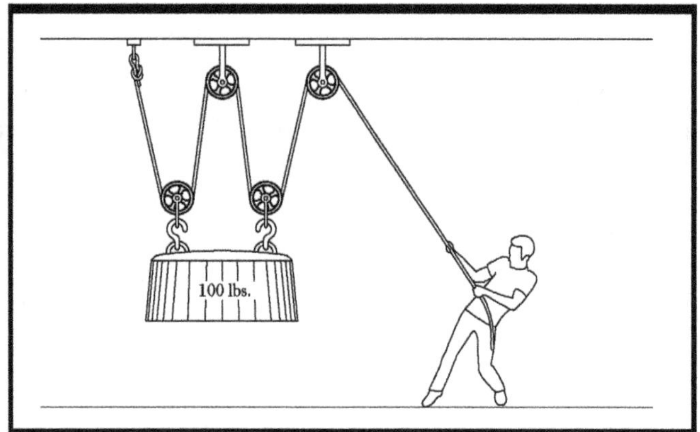

7. In the figure above, about how much force does the man have to pull with to raise the 100 lb weight?

a. 100 pounds
b. 50 pounds
c. 33 pounds
d. 25 pounds

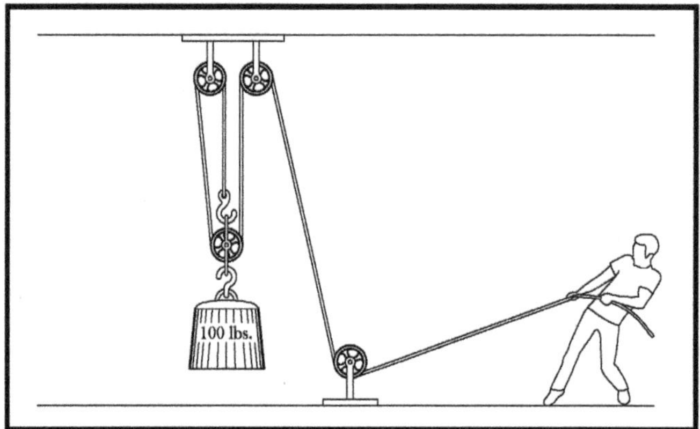

8. In the figure above, about how much force does the man have to pull with to raise the 100 lb weight?

a. 100 pounds
b. 50 pounds
c. 33 pounds
d. 25 pounds

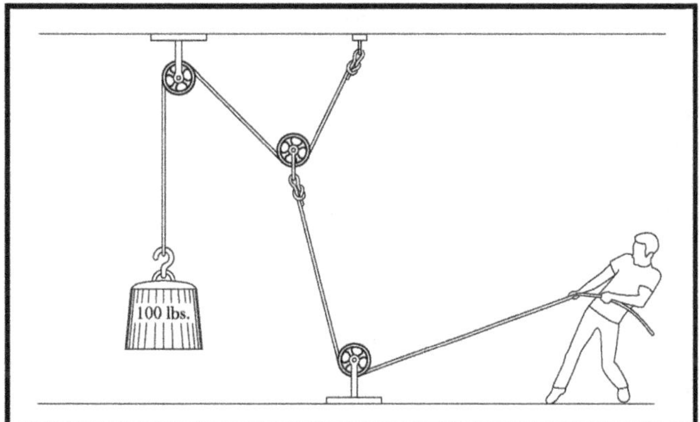

9. In the figure above, about how much force does the man have to pull with to raise the 100 lb weight?

a. 200 pounds
b. 100 pounds
c. 50 pounds
d. 25 pounds

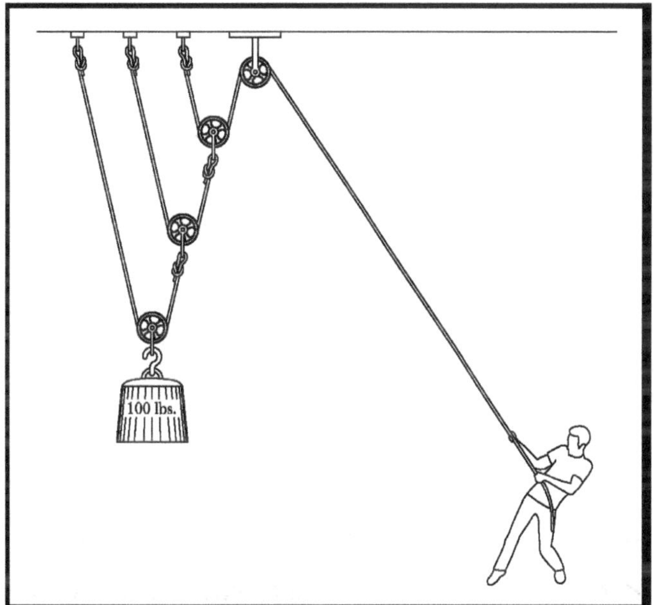

10. In the figure above, about how much force does the man have to pull with to raise the 100 lb weight?

a. 100 pounds
b. 33 pounds
c. 25 pounds
d. 13 pounds

Gears

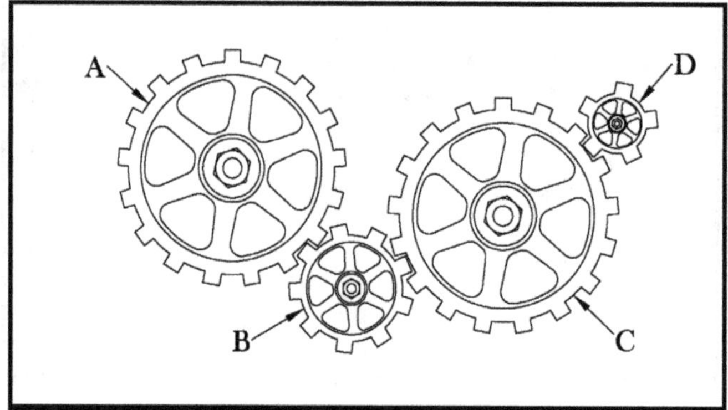

1. In the figure above, if gear D is turning clockwise, which direction is gear A turning?

a. Clockwise
b. Counterclockwise

2. In the figure above, if gear C is turning at 100 RPM, which of the following is the best estimate for how fast gear B is turning?

a. 30 RPM
b. 50 RPM
c. 100 RPM
d. 200 RPM

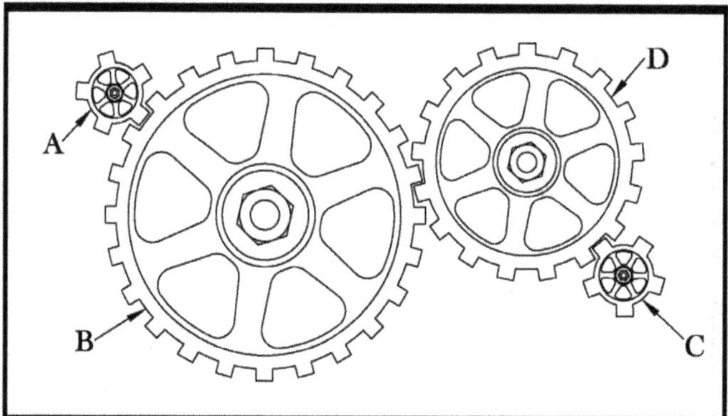

3. In the figure above, if gear B is turning clockwise, which direction is gear D turning?

a. Clockwise
b. Counterclockwise

4. In the figure above, if gear C is turning at 100 RPM, which of the following is the best estimate for how fast gear A is turning?

a. 30 RPM
b. 50 RPM
c. 100 RPM
d. 200 RPM

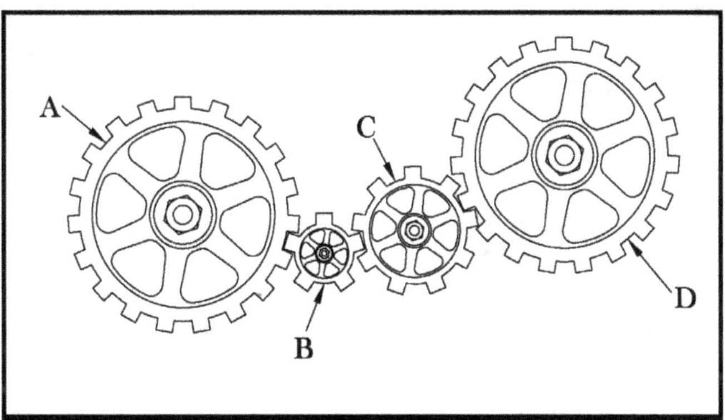

5. In the figure above, if gear B is turning clockwise, which direction is gear D turning?

a. Clockwise
b. Counterclockwise

6. In the figure above, if gear B is turning at 100 RPM, which of the following is the best estimate for how fast gear A is turning?

a. 30 RPM
b. 50 RPM
c. 100 RPM
d. 200 RPM

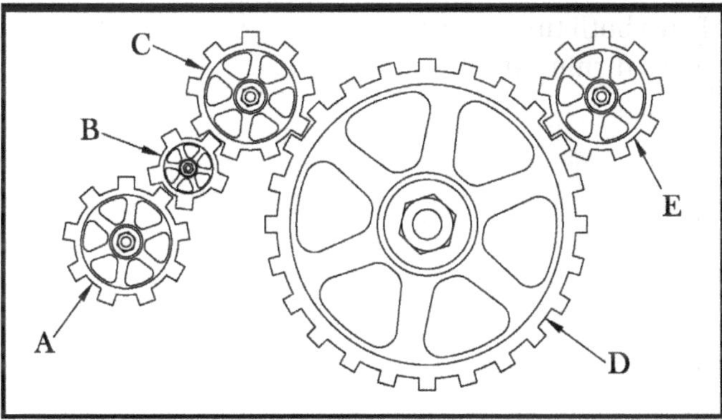

7. Given the gear system shown in the figure above, which of the following statements cannot be true?

a. Gear A and gear E are both turning counterclockwise.
b. Gear B is turning clockwise, while gear C is turning counterclockwise.
c. Gear E and gear B are both turning clockwise.
d. Gear D is turning counterclockwise, while gear A is turning clockwise.

8. Given the gear system shown in the figure above, which of the following statements cannot be true?

a. Gear A is turning about 100 RPM, while gear B is turning about 200 RPM.
b. Gear B is turning about 100 RPM, while gear D is turning about 20 RPM.
c. Gear D is turning about 100 RPM, while gear A is turning about 250 RPM.
d. Gear A is turning about 100 RPM, while gear E is turning about 50 RPM

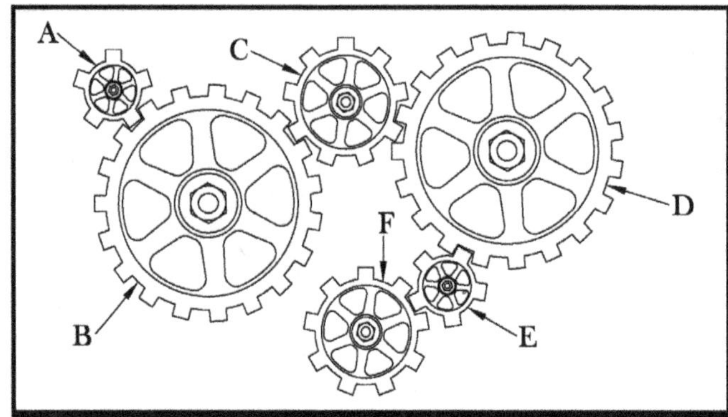

9. Given the gear system shown in the figure above, which of the following statements cannot be true?

a. Gear A and gear E are both turning about 100 RPM.
b. Gear B is turning clockwise, while gear D is turning counterclockwise.
c. Gear C is turning about 100 RPM while gear E is turning about 200 RPM.
d. Gear A and gear F are turning opposite directions.

10. Given the gear system shown in the figure above, which of the following statements cannot be true?

a. Gear C and gear F are both turning clockwise about 100 RPM.
b. Gear B and gear D are both turning clockwise at about 100 RPM.
c. Gear A and gear E are both turning clockwise at about 100 RPM.
d. Gear A and gear F are turning at different speeds.

Mechanical Concepts

This is a test of your ability to understand mechanical concepts. Each question has a picture, a question and three possible answers. Read each question carefully, study the picture, and decide which answer is correct.

1. Objects 1 and 2 are submerged in separate tanks, both filled with water. In which tank (A or B) will the water level be the highest? (If equal, mark C)

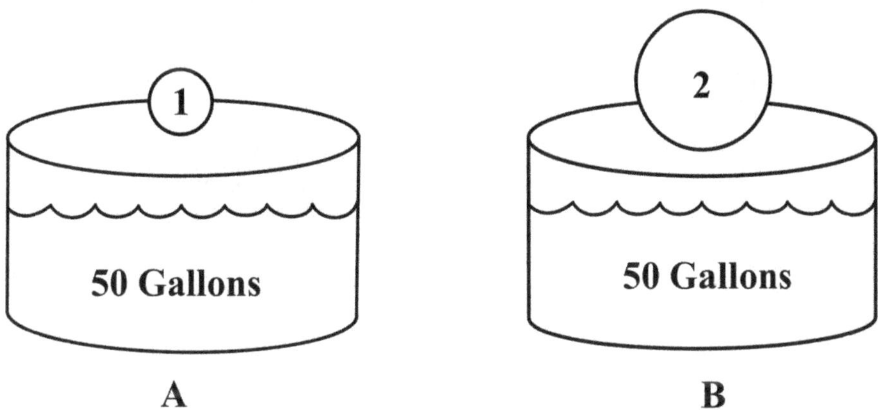

2. If ball 1 and ball 2 are of equal weight and moving at the same speed, in which direction (A, B or C) will ball 1 tend to go when it collides with ball 2 at point X?

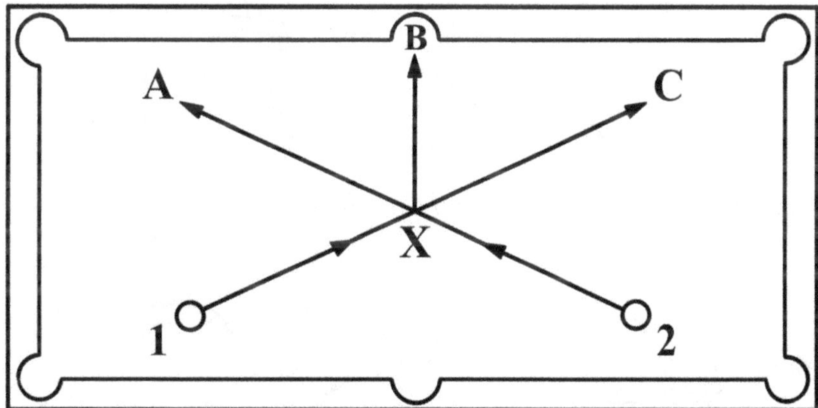

3. In which direction (A or B) will gear 5 spin if gear 1 is spinning counter-clockwise? (If both, mark C)

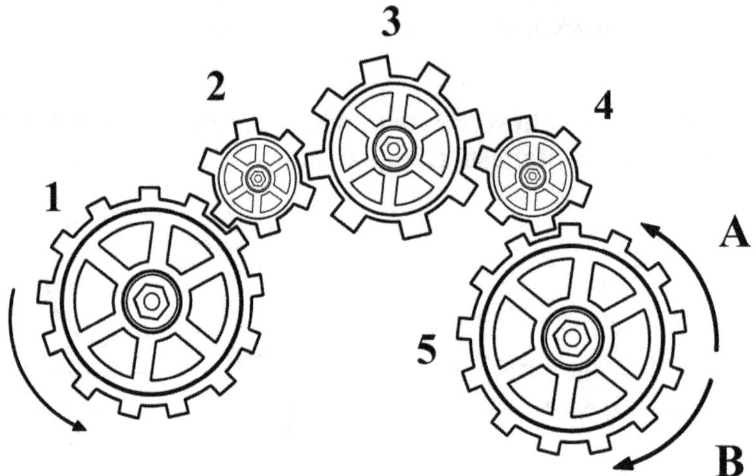

4. Which of the two identical objects (A or B) will launch a higher distance when the springs are released? (If equal, mark C)

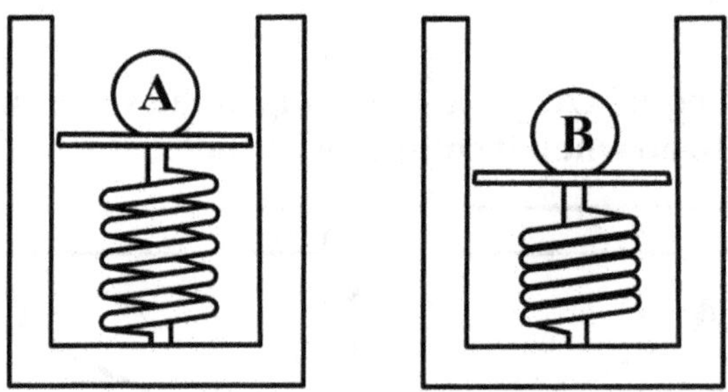

5. A watering can is filled with water. Which of the pictures (A or B) shows a more accurate representation of how the water will rest?

6. Among this arrangement of three pulleys, which pulley (A, B or C) turns fastest?

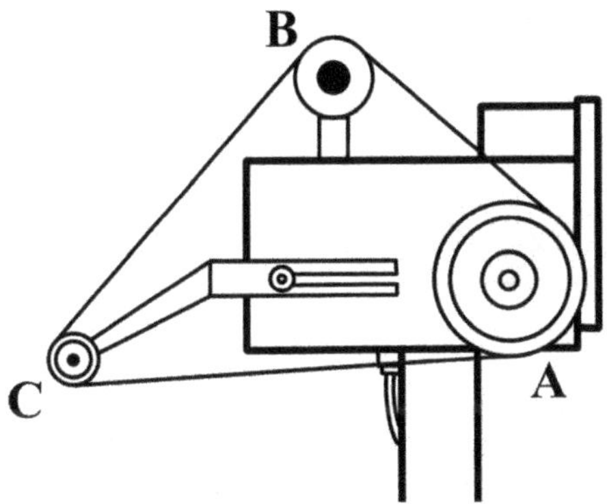

7. Which of the two scenarios (A or B) requires more effort to pull the weight up off the ground? (If equal, mark C)

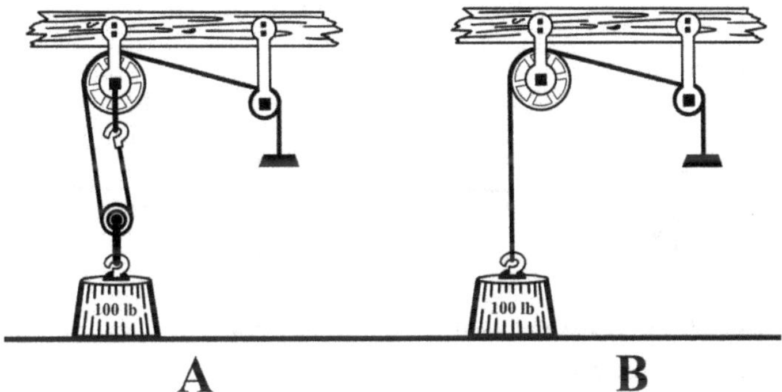

8. Which switch (A, B or C) should be closed in order to start the pump motor?

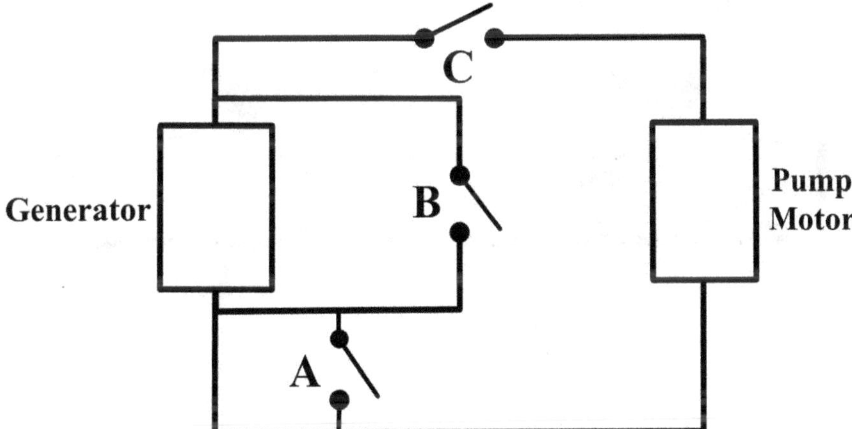

9. **If both ramps are 5 feet tall, which situation (A or B) requires more force to peddle the bicycle up the ramp? (If equal, mark C)**

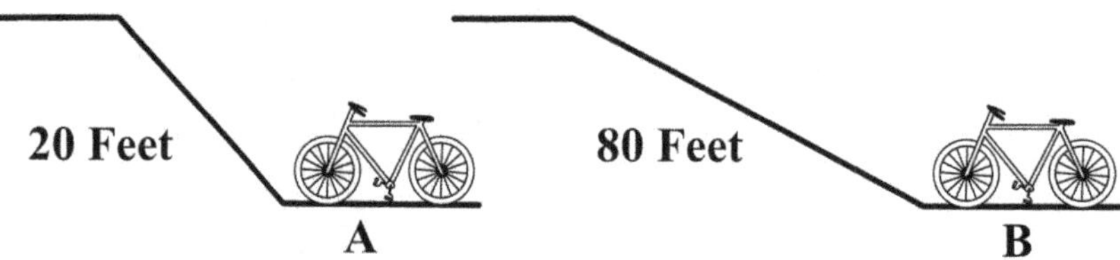

10. **When the spring is released, the ball travels away from the spring to its highest point (A) and then begins to travel back towards its place of origin. At which point (A, B or C) will the ball travel to after it hits the spring a second time?**

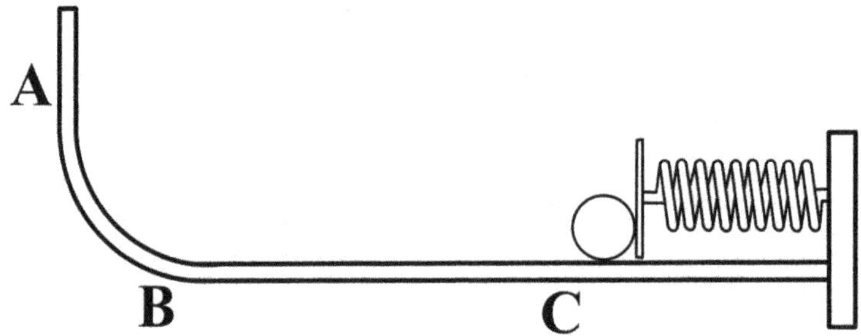

11. **Which of the two boulders of equal weight (A or B) requires more force to push up the same length of hill? (If equal, mark C)**

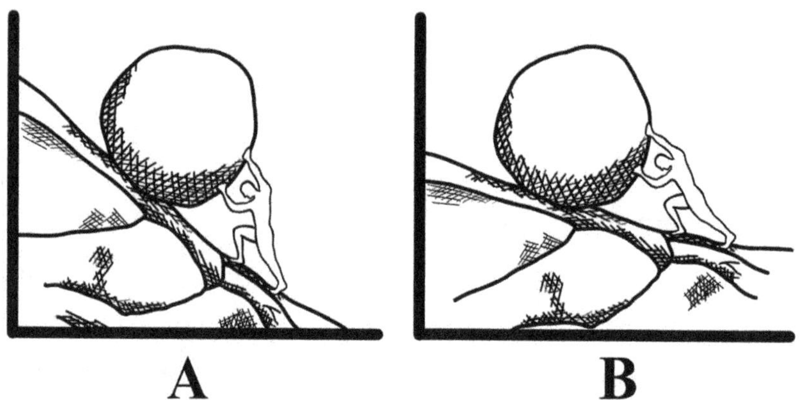

12. At which point (A, B or C) will the cannonball be traveling the slowest?

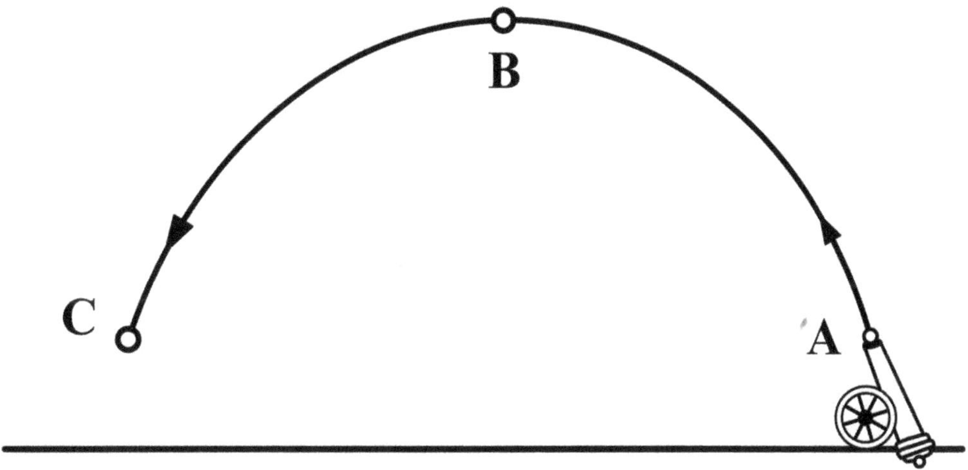

13. On which side of the pipe (A or B) would the water speed be slower? (If equal, mark C)

14. In which of the two figures (A or B) is the person bearing more weight? (If equal, mark C)

15. Which of the two lift trucks (A or B) carrying the same amount of weight is more likely to tip over? (If equal, mark C)

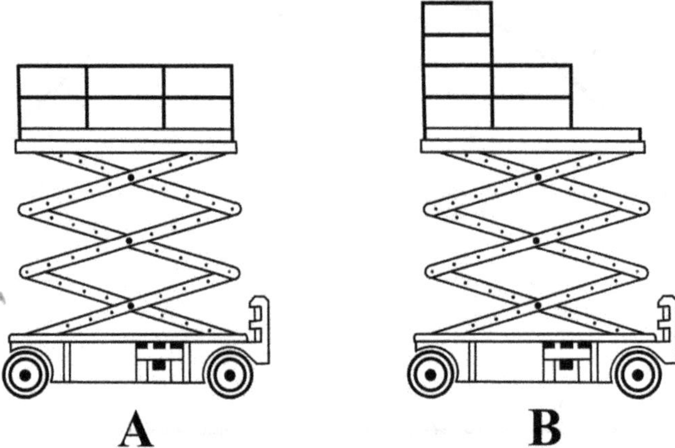

16. The weight of the boxes is being carried by the two men shown below. Which of the two men (A or B) is carrying more weight? (If equal, mark C)

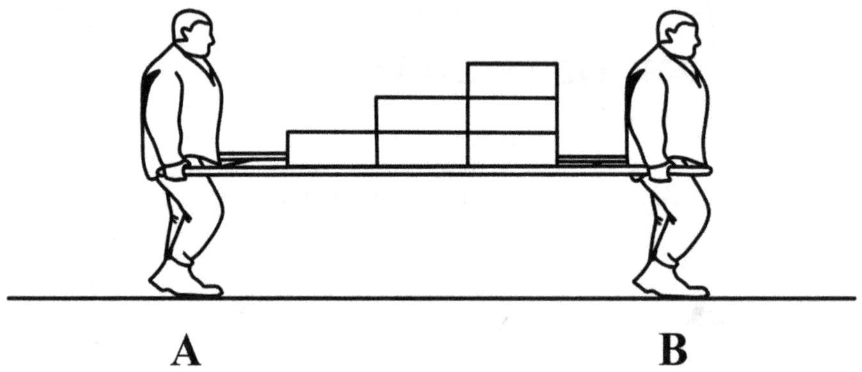

17. In the pictures below, which of the angles (A or B) is braced more solidly? (If equal, mark C)

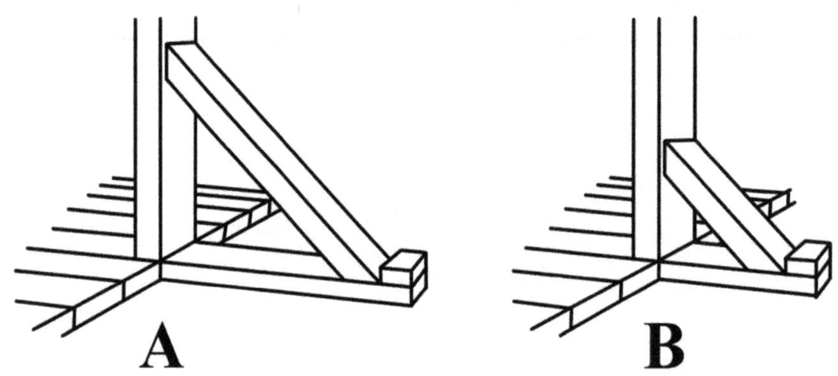

18. Given two birds sitting on branches of a tree at different elevations. Both drop objects of identical size and weight. Which object (A or B) will hit the ground with bigger force? (If equal, mark C)

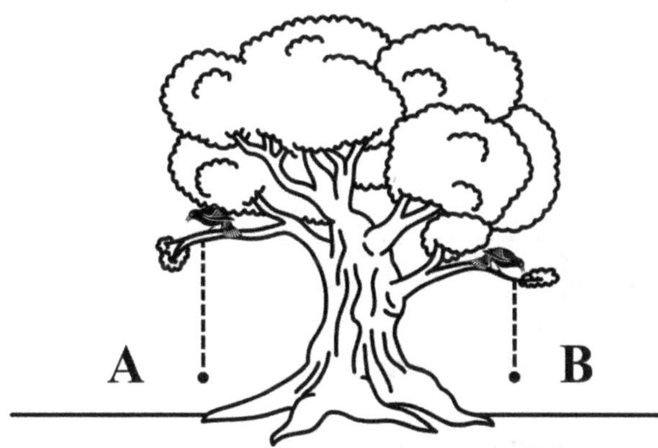

19. A wagon is pulled up two hills of equal slope and height. For which hill (A or B) did the wagon require less effort to reach the top? (If equal, mark C)

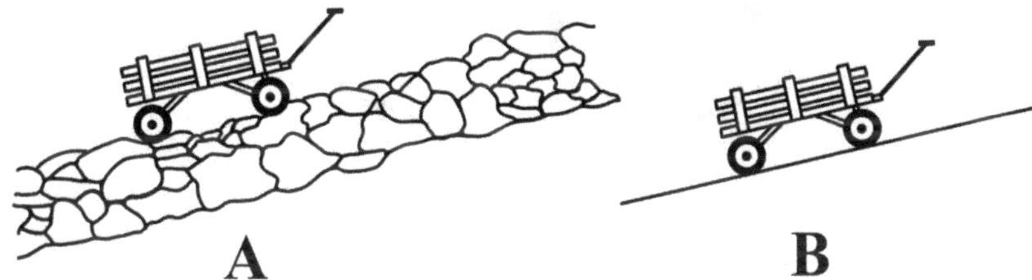

20. In which of the three positions (A, B or C) will it be easiest to accurately measure the amount of liquid in the graduated cylinder?

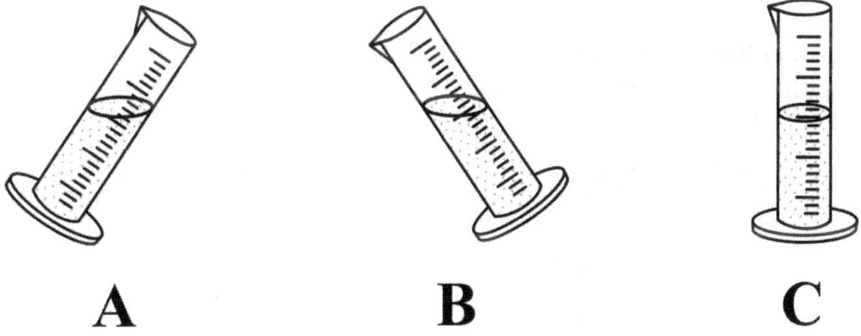

21. In which of the two figures (A or B) will the person require less force to lift a 100-pound weight? (If equal, mark C)

22. Which switch (A, B or C) should be closed to give power to the light?

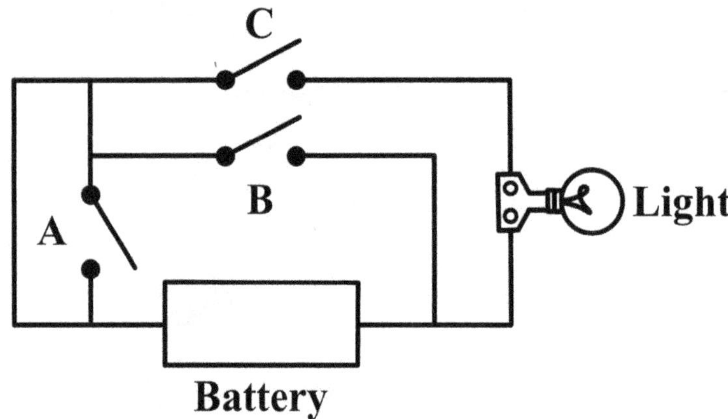

23. If the baseball and bowling ball are moving at the same speed, in which direction will the bowling ball tend to go when it collides with the baseball at point X?

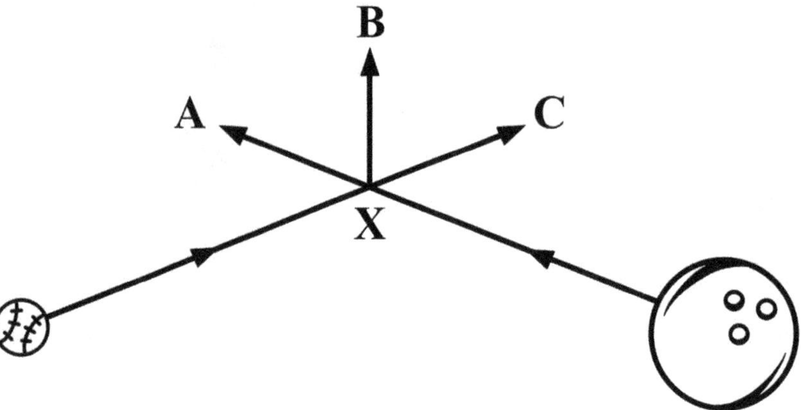

24. Which of the two rolls of paper towels (A or B) will undergo more revolutions if the ends of each roll were pulled downward with the same amount of force? (If equal, mark C)

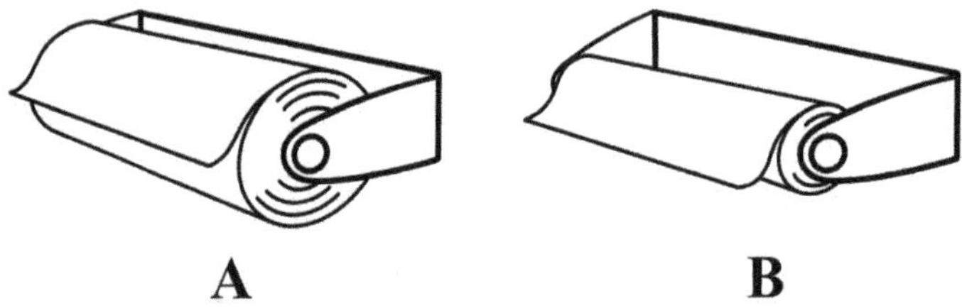

25. In which of the two containers (A or B) will water that is boiled to the same temperature cool more slowly? (If equal, mark C)

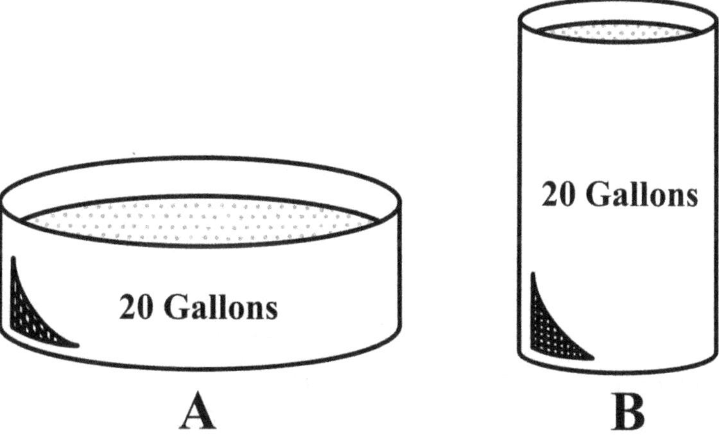

26. Salt is mixed into the water inside container A until it reaches a 50% solution. No salt is added to the water in container B. In which of the two containers (A or B) is an egg more likely to float? (If equal, mark C)

27. Which reflector (A or B) on the bicycle wheel is going to be traveling a greater distance when the wheel turns? (If equal, mark C)

28. A javelin is thrown into the air. At which point (A, B or C) will the javelin be traveling the fastest?

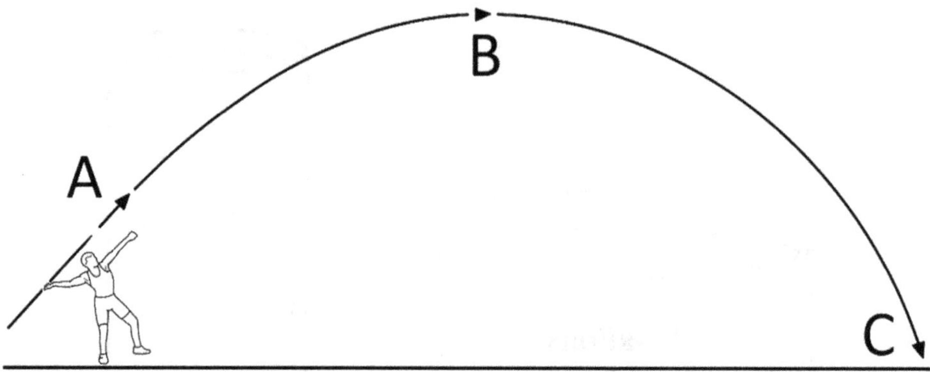

29. A child is released on the seat of a swing set at the position shown. To which point (A, B or C) will the child travel before he/she begins to return back to the point of origin?

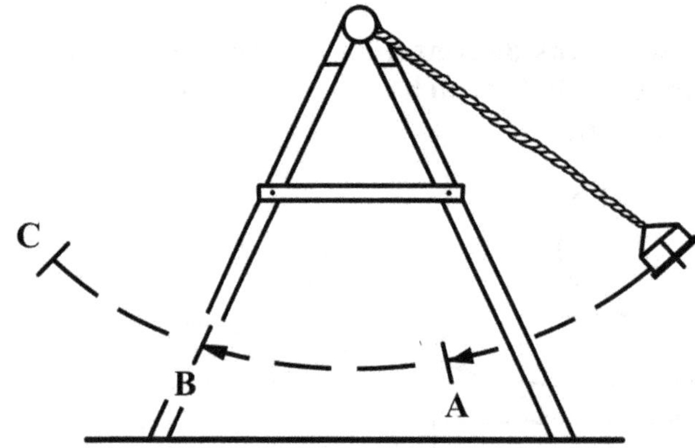

30. On which side of the pipe (A or B) would the water speed be slower? (If equal, mark C)

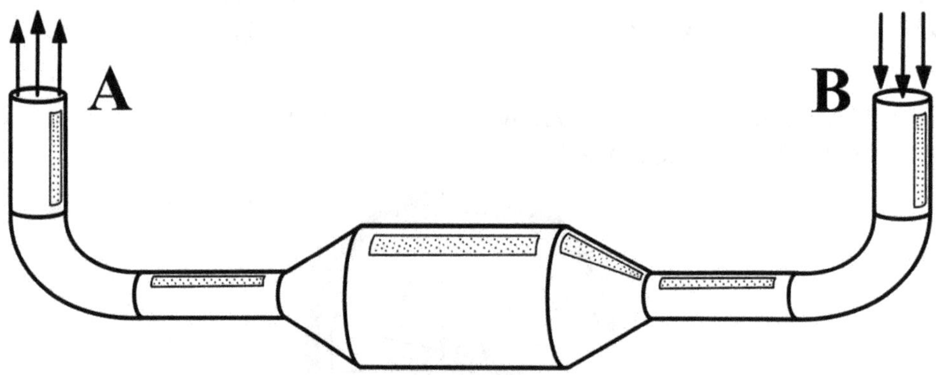

31. Given two objects shown below that are dropped from an elevation of 100 feet. Neglecting air resistance, which object (A or B) will fall at a faster rate? (If equal, mark C)

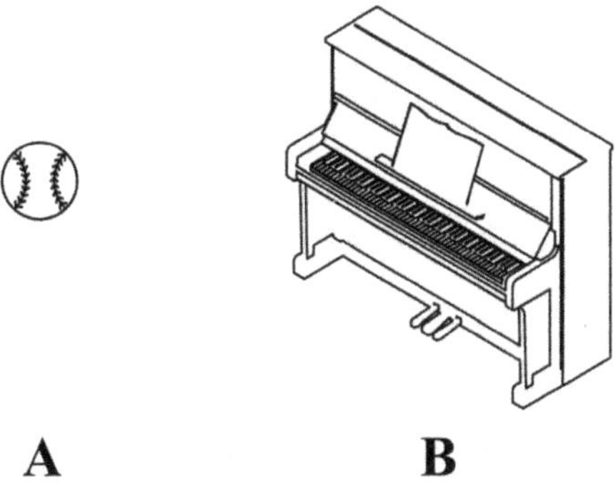

32. An athlete is holding a heavy metal ball attached to a wire and is rotating in the circular motion shown below. In which direction (A, B or C) would the ball travel when it is released at point X?

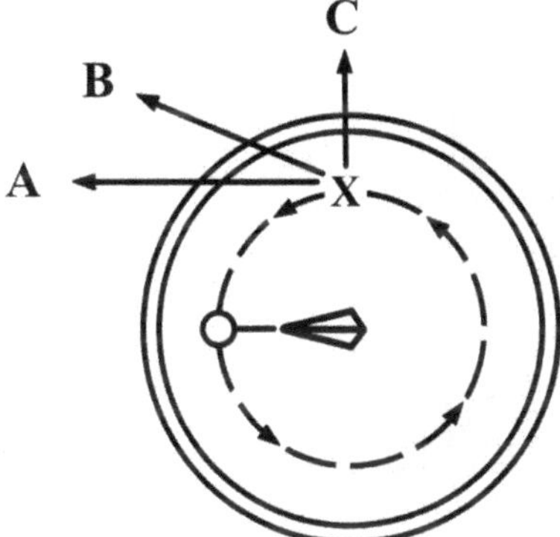

33. Which of the two wheels (A or B) will allow you to travel a further distance given the same rotational speed? (If equal, mark C)

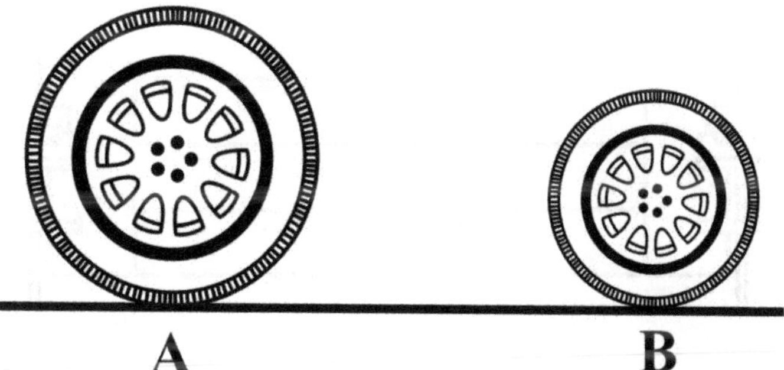

34. Two tanks with different capacities contain the same amount of gas, 50 kg. In which of the given tanks (A or B) will the gas pressure be greater? (If equal, mark C)

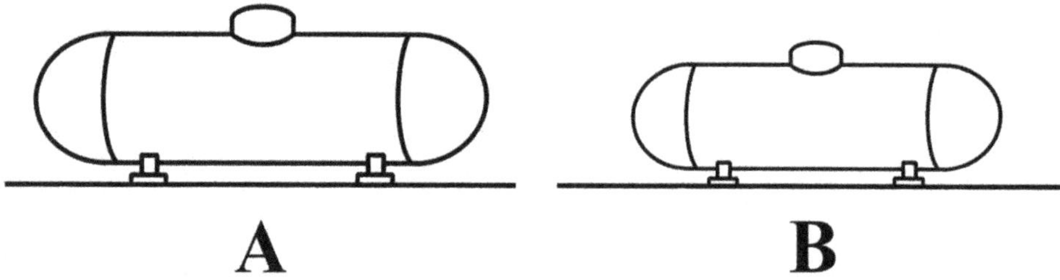

35. Given two water towers with identical tanks and identical amounts of water in each tank, which tower (A or B) will have greater water pressure coming out of the hose? Tank A is 80 feet tall and tank B is 180 feet tall. (If equal, mark C)

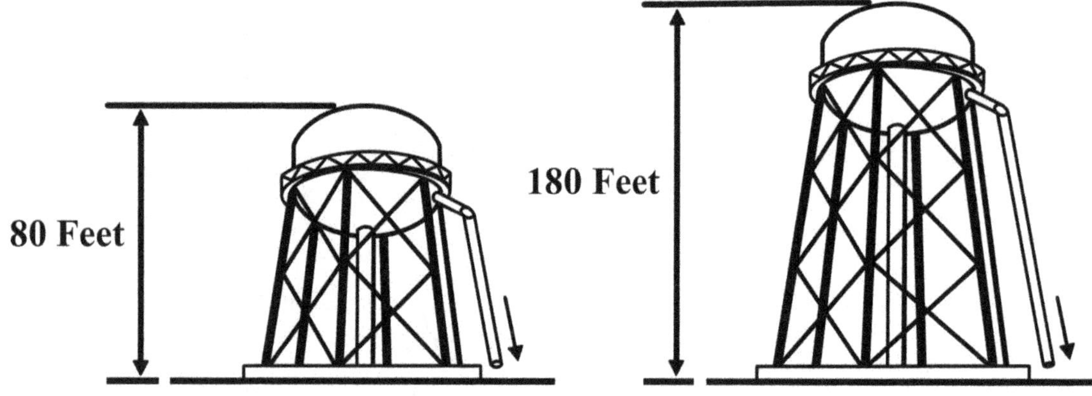

36. The weight of the boxes is resting on a platform suspended in the air by two ropes. Which of the two ropes (A or B) is supporting more of the weight? (If equal, mark C)

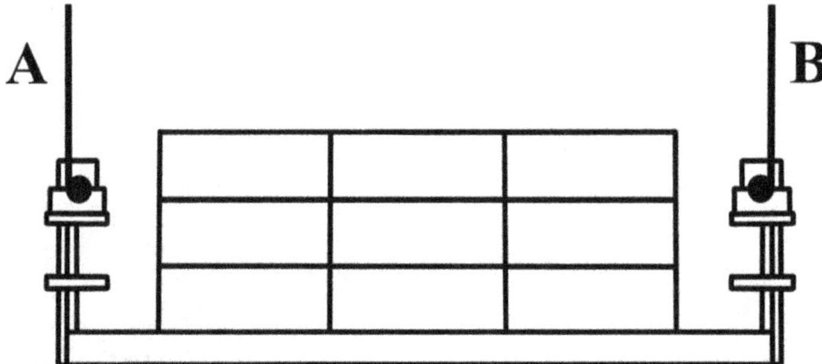

37. Container A contains 100 mL pure water and container B contains 100 mL oil. Assume two identical objects are thrown into the two containers; in which of these two containers is the object more likely to float? (If equally likely, mark C)

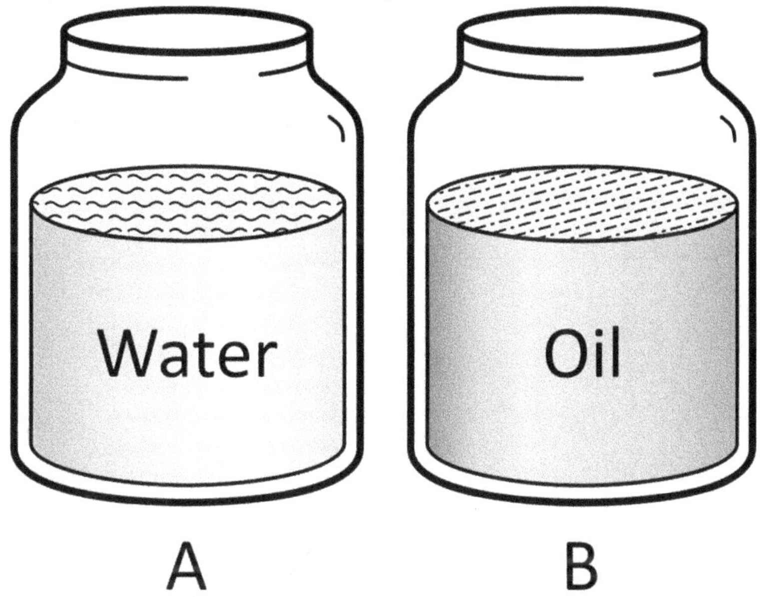

38. Which of the two scenarios (A or B) requires less effort to pull the weight up off the ground? (If equal, mark C)

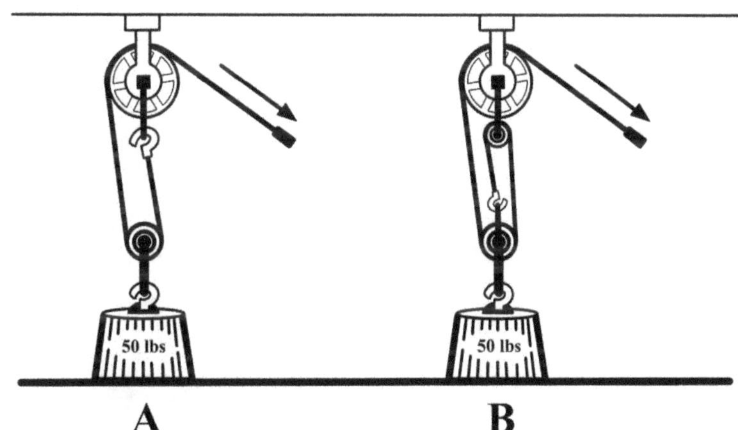

39. It takes a ball 1.25 seconds to reach the bottom of ramp A and 2.50 seconds to reach the bottom of ramp B. For which ramp (A or B) does the ball have more potential energy? (If equal, mark C)

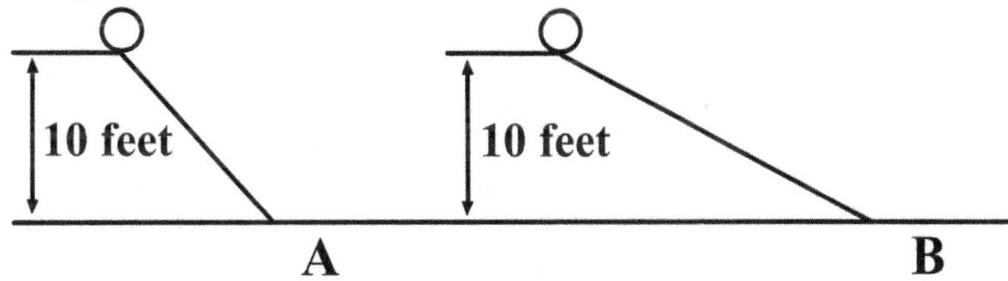

40. Container A holds 1 qt of water and container B holds 1 qt of motor oil. Assume each container is poured down a funnel at the same time. Which of the two contents will reach the bottom of the funnel more quickly? (If equal, mark C)

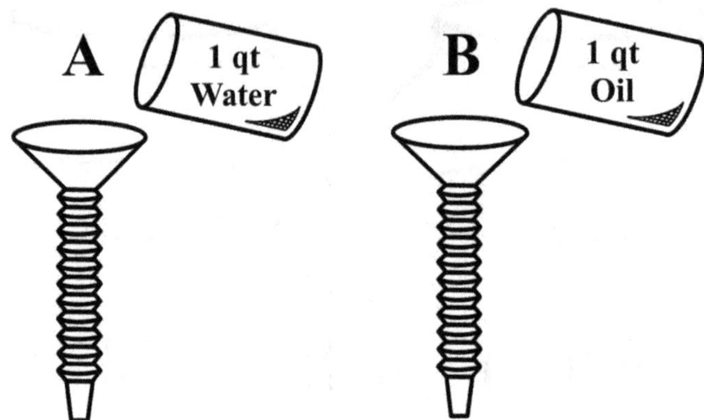

Parts Assembly

1. Which of the follow assemblies can be formed from the given parts?

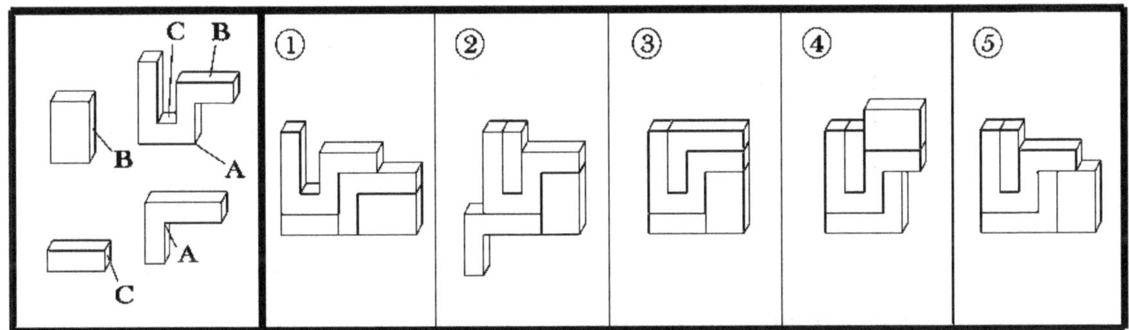

2. Which of the follow assemblies can be formed from the given parts?

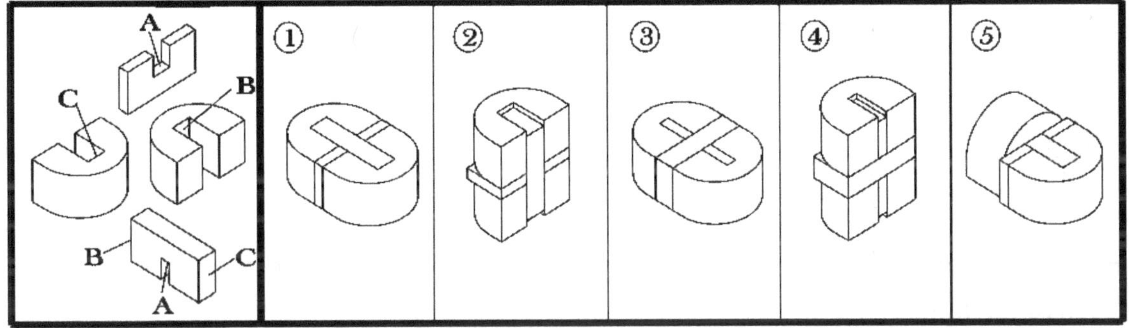

3. Which of the follow assemblies can be formed from the given parts?

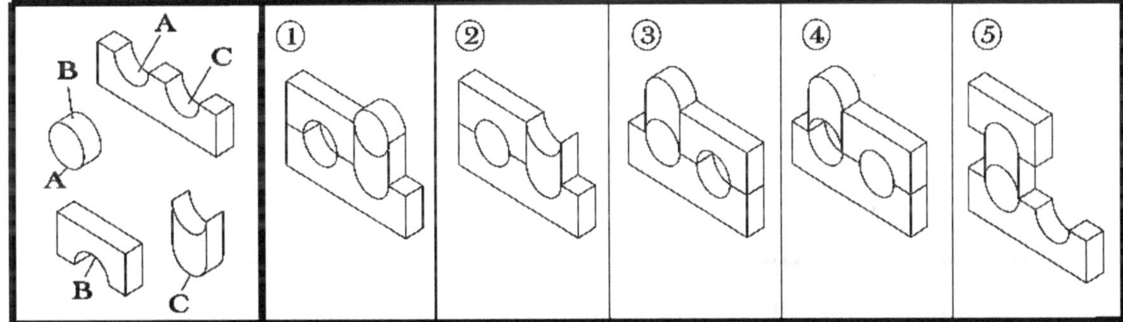

4. Which of the follow assemblies can be formed from the given parts?

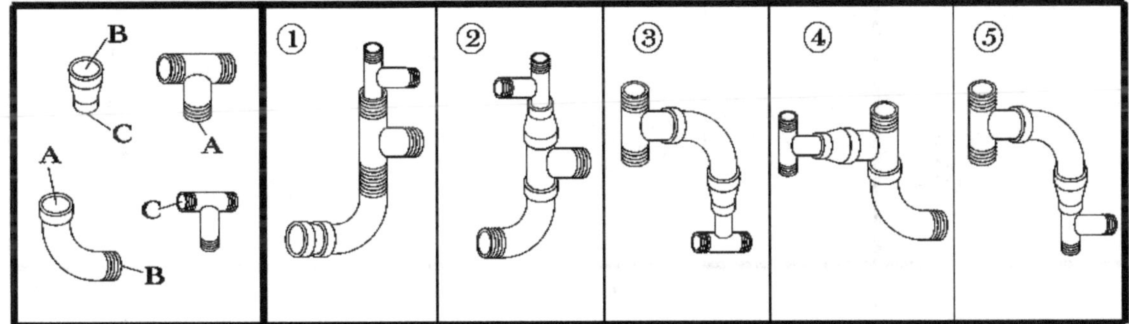

5. Which of the follow assemblies can be formed from the given parts?

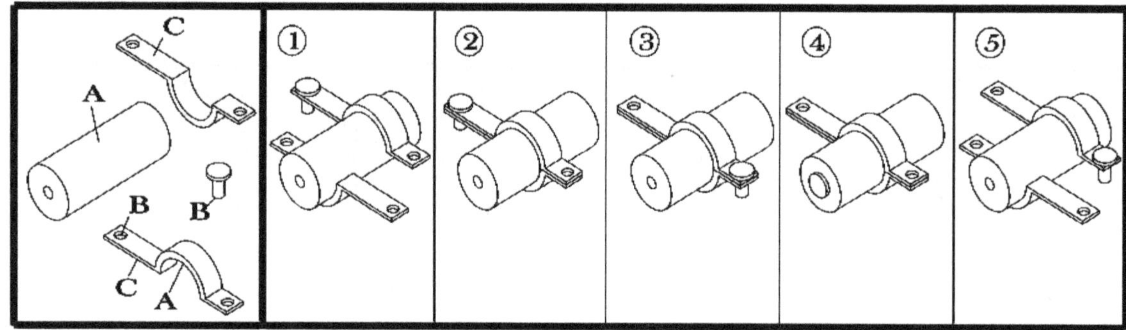

6. Which of the follow assemblies can be formed from the given parts?

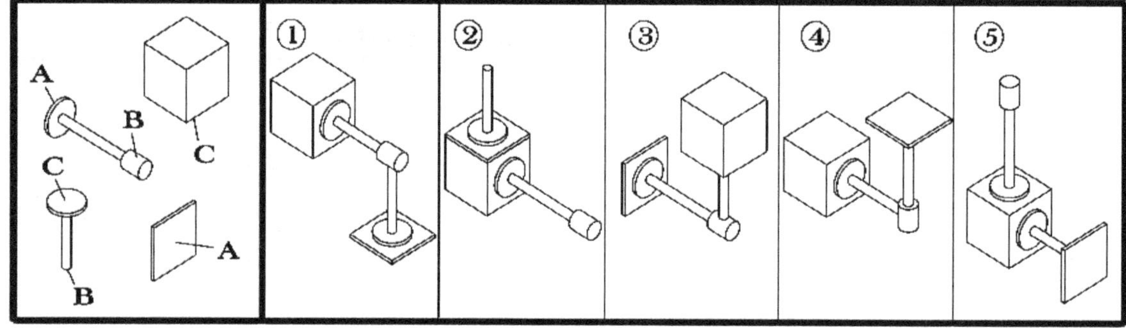

7. Which of the follow assemblies can be formed from the given parts?

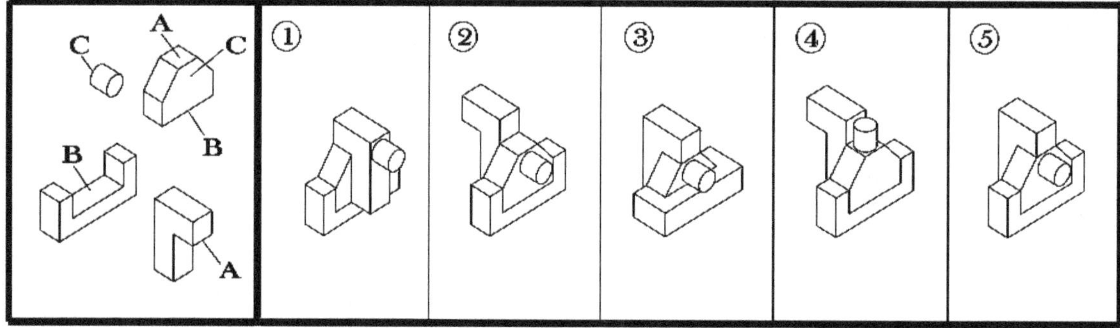

8. Which of the follow assemblies can be formed from the given parts?

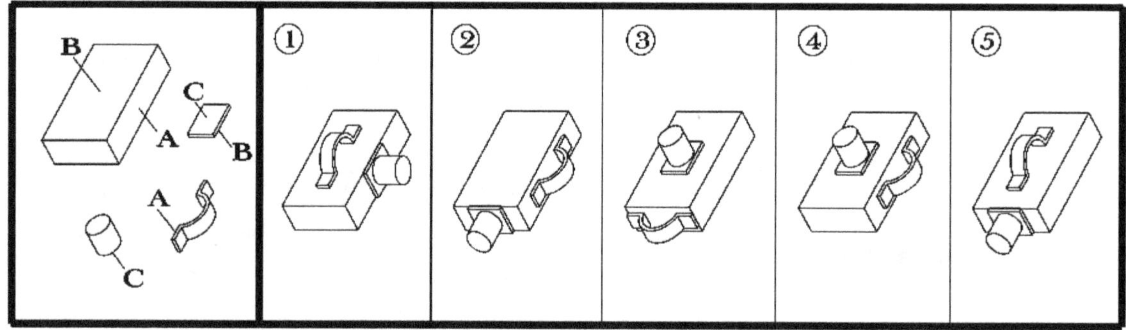

Parts Assembly

1. Which of the follow assemblies can be formed from the given parts?

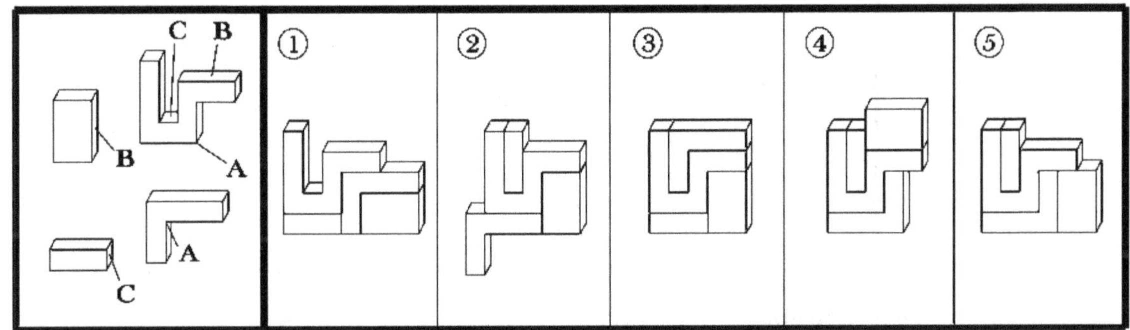

2. Which of the follow assemblies can be formed from the given parts?

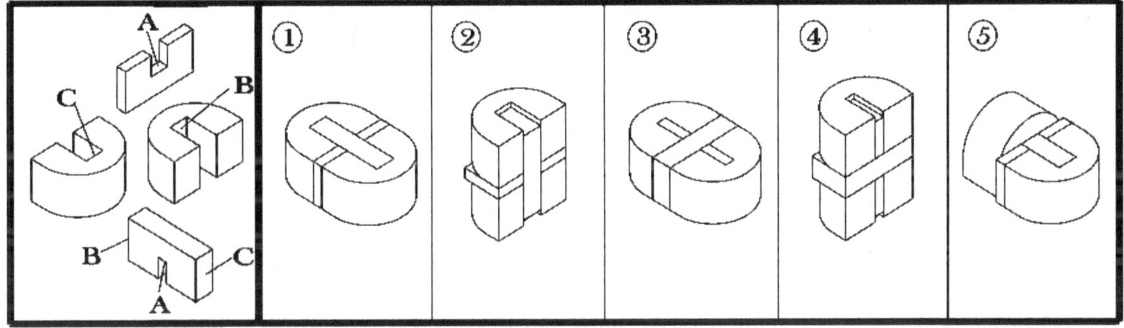

3. Which of the follow assemblies can be formed from the given parts?

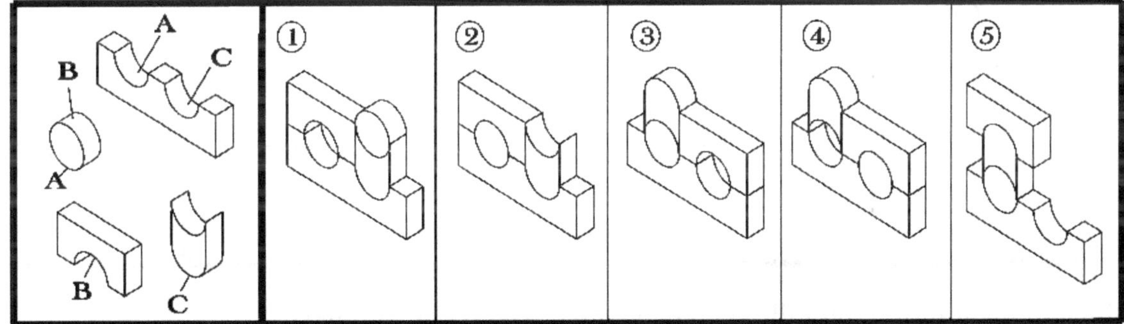

4. Which of the follow assemblies can be formed from the given parts?

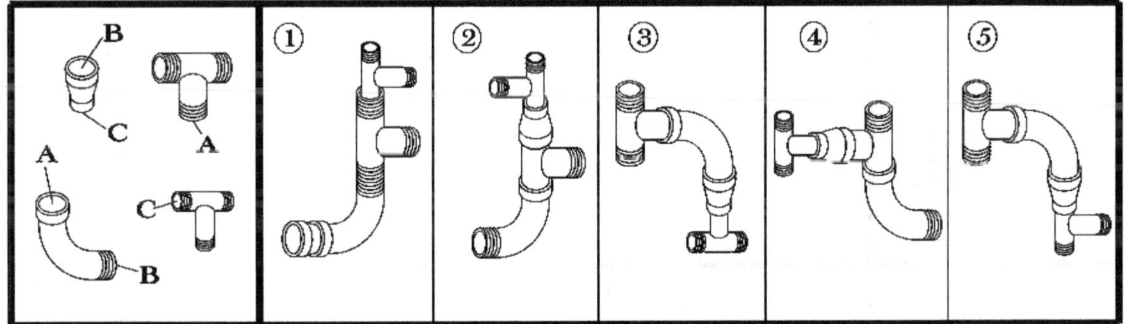

5. Which of the follow assemblies can be formed from the given parts?

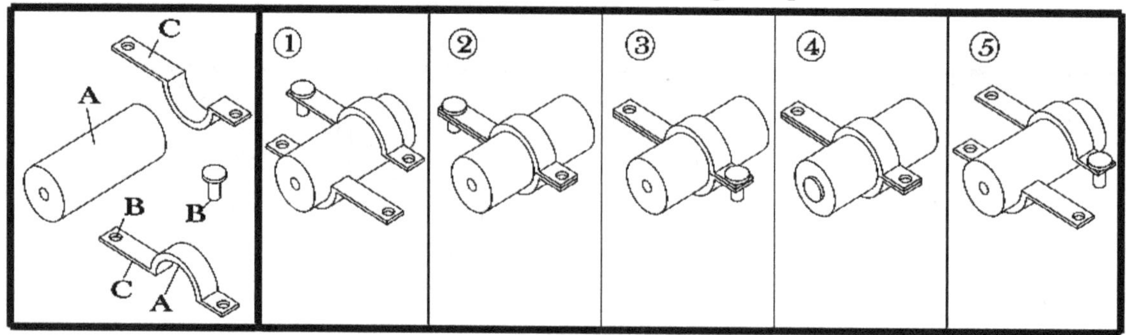

6. Which of the follow assemblies can be formed from the given parts?

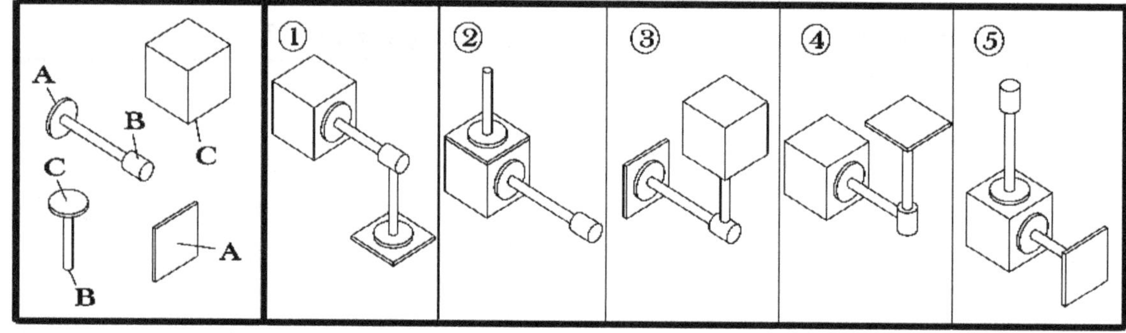

7. Which of the follow assemblies can be formed from the given parts?

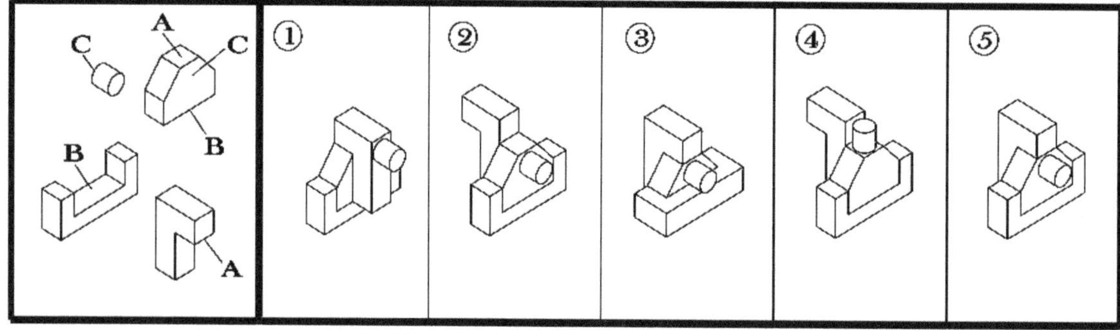

8. Which of the follow assemblies can be formed from the given parts?

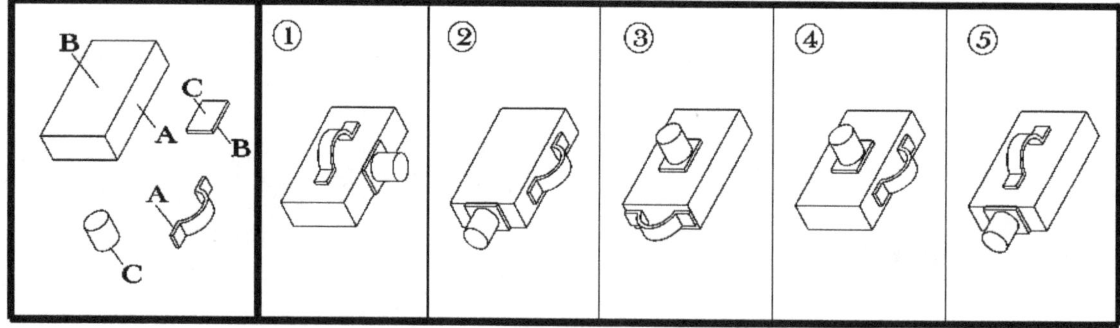

9. Which of the follow assemblies can be formed from the given parts?

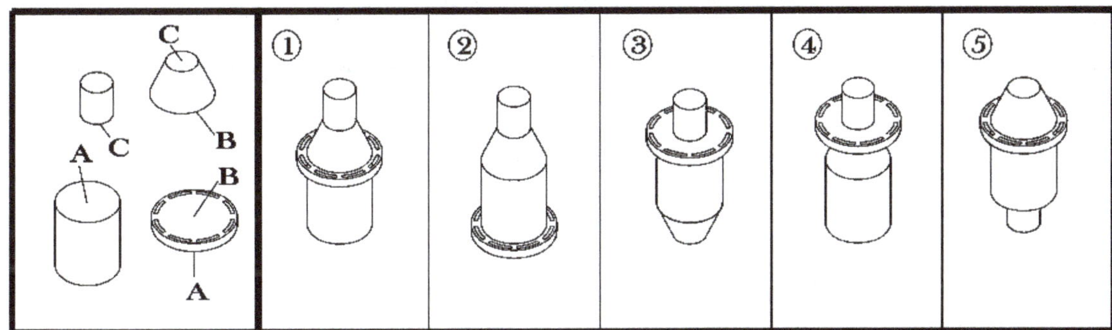

10. Which of the follow assemblies can be formed from the given parts?

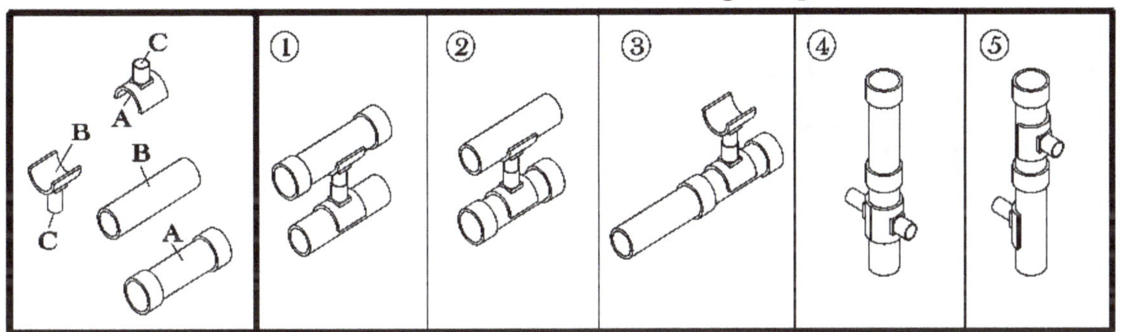

Paper Folding

1. Which shape can be formed by folding the given pattern?

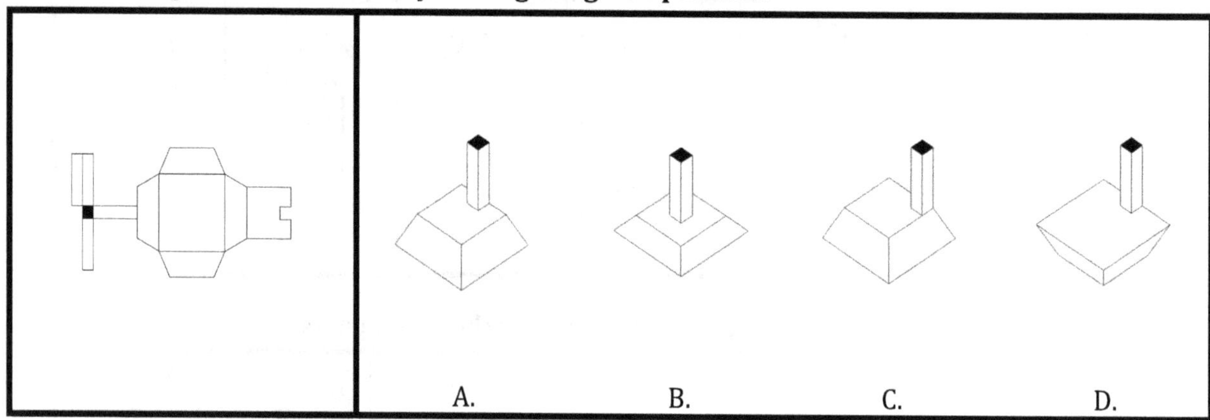

2. Which shape can be formed by folding the given pattern?

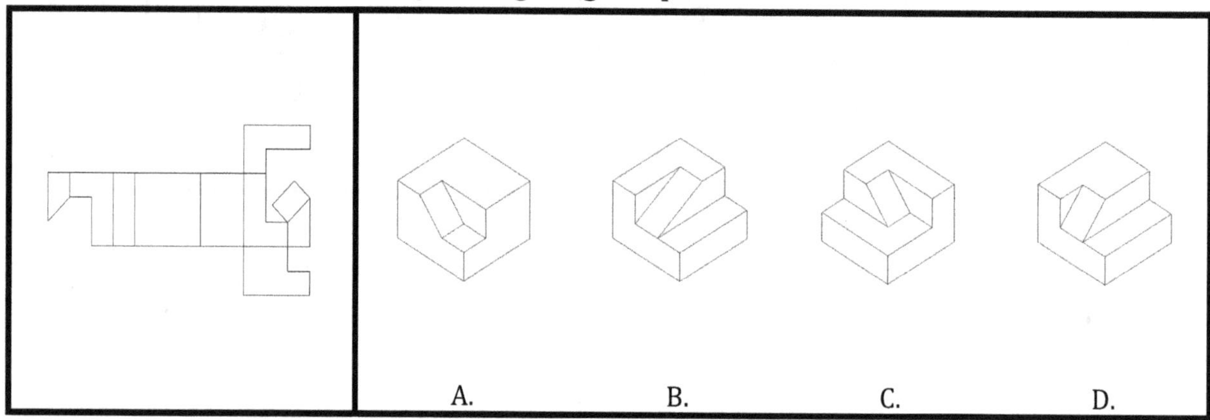

3. Which shape can be formed by folding the given pattern?

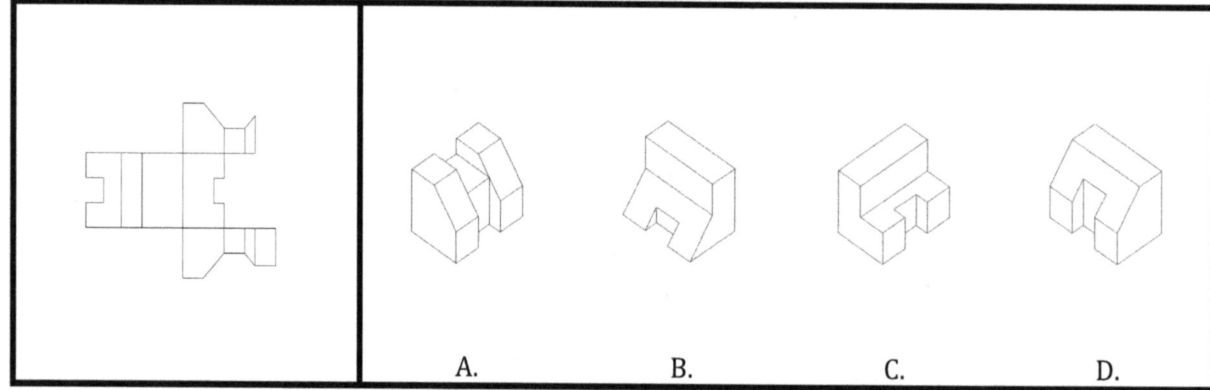

4. Which shape can be formed by folding the given pattern?

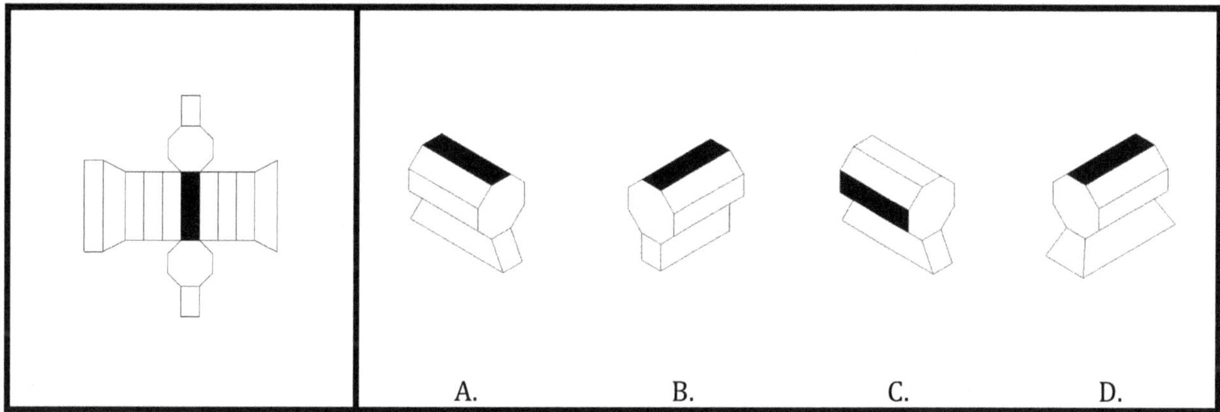

5. Which shape can be formed by folding the given pattern?

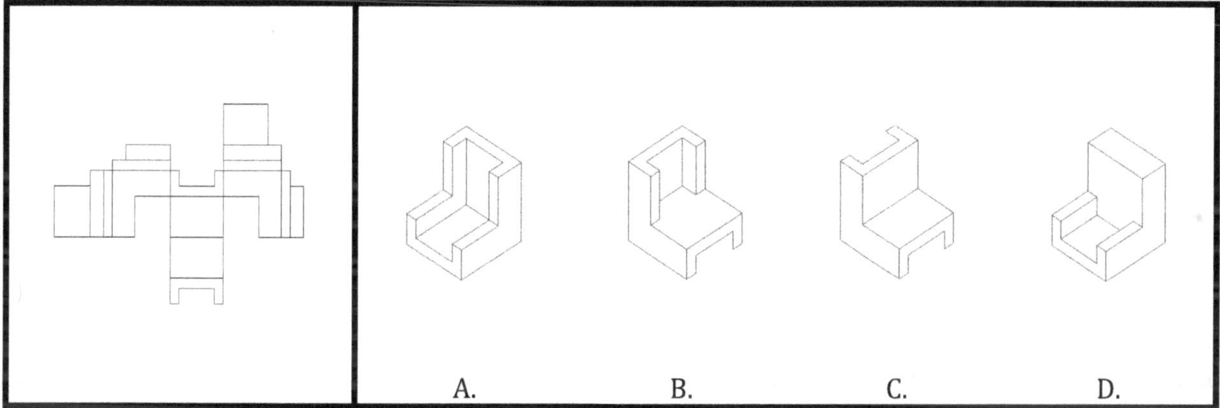

6. Which shape can be formed by folding the given pattern?

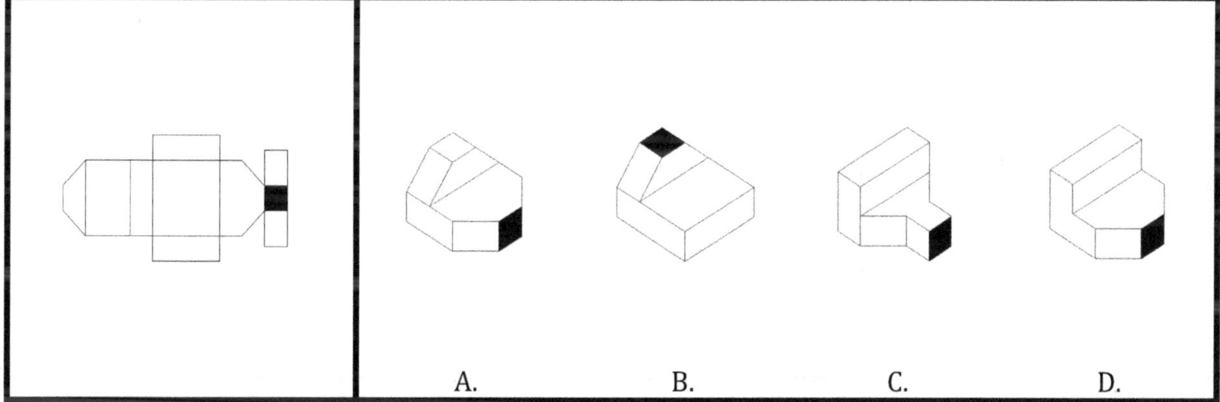

7. Which shape can be formed by folding the given pattern?

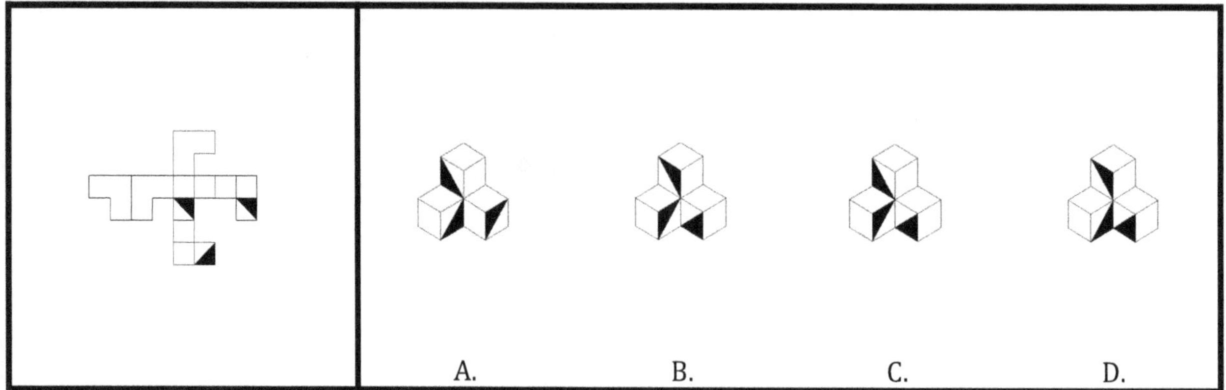

8. Which shape can be formed by folding the given pattern?

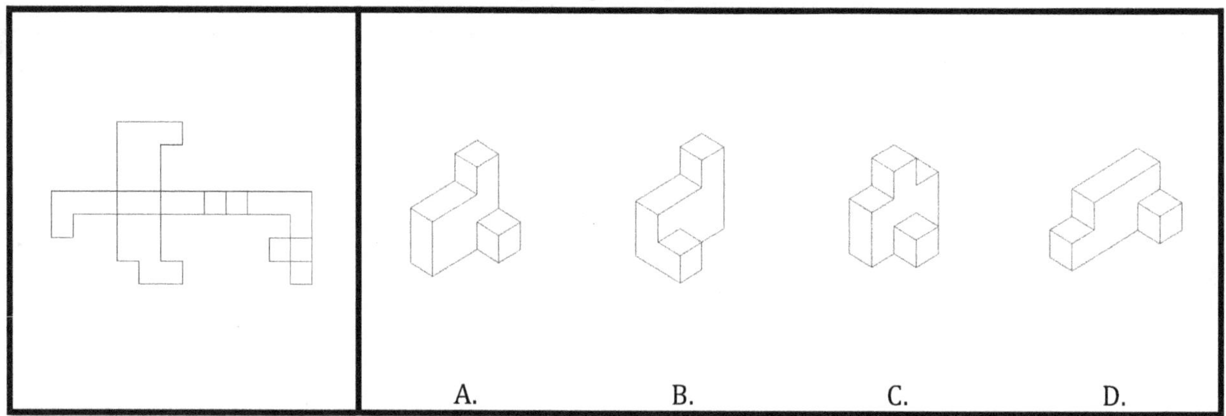

9. Which shape can be formed by folding the given pattern?

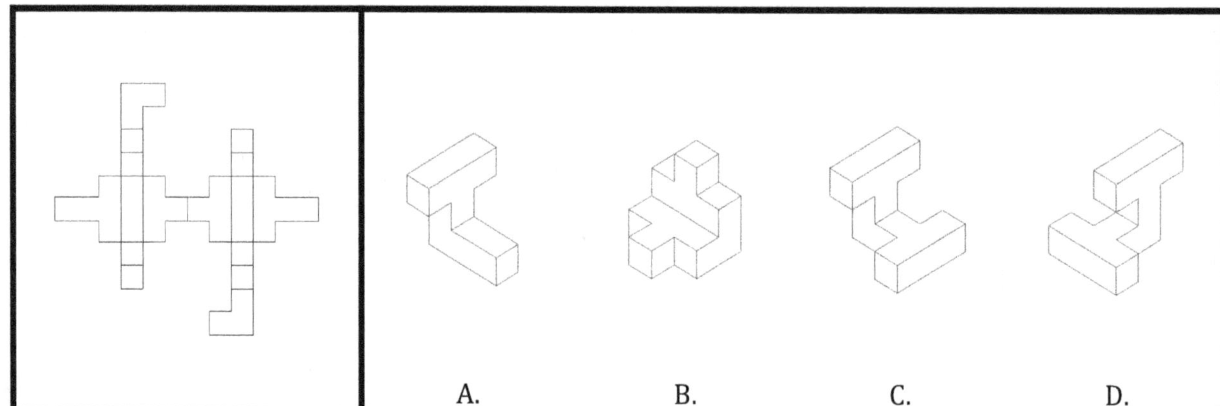

10. Which shape can be formed by folding the given pattern?

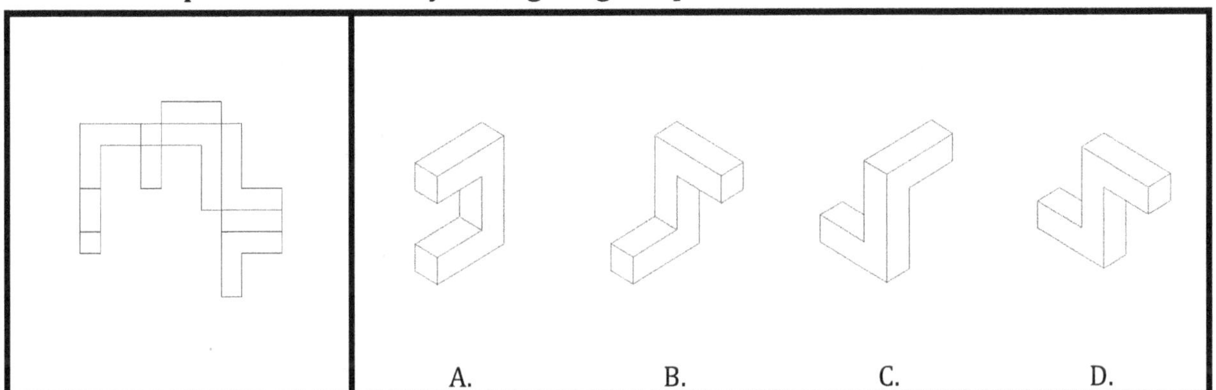

Rotated Blocks

1. Which of the answer choices shows the same block as the original?

A. 

B. 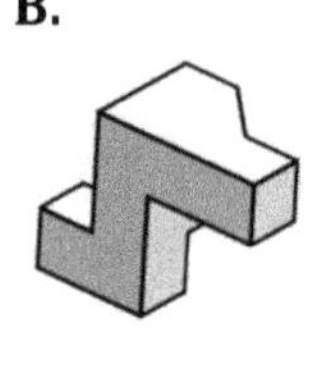

C. 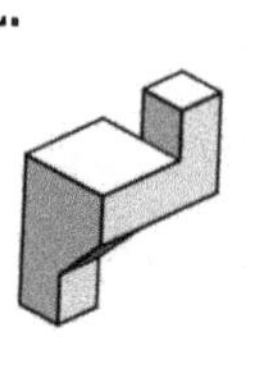

D. 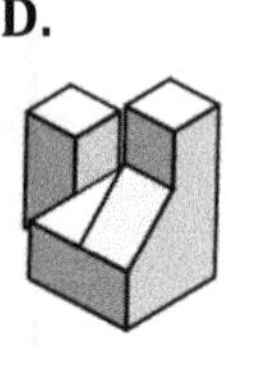

E. 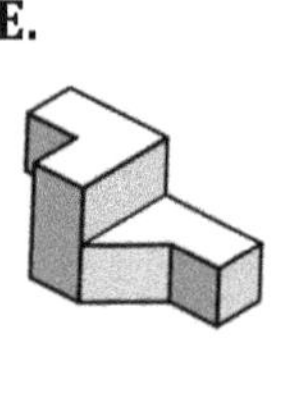

2. Which of the answer choices shows the same block as the original?

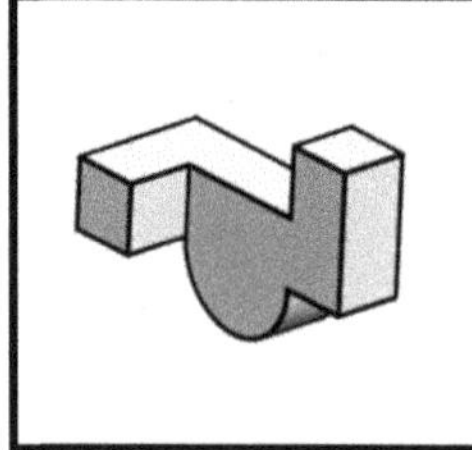

A. 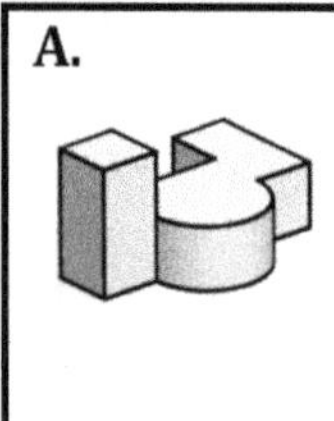

B. 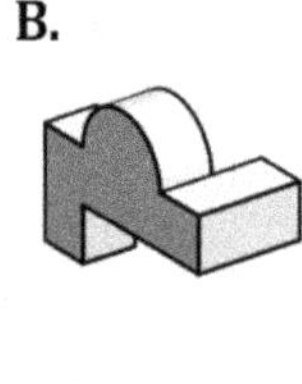

C. 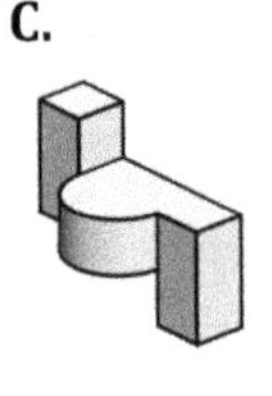

D. 

E. 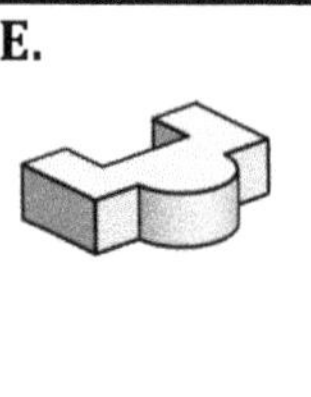

3. Which of the answer choices shows the same block as the original?

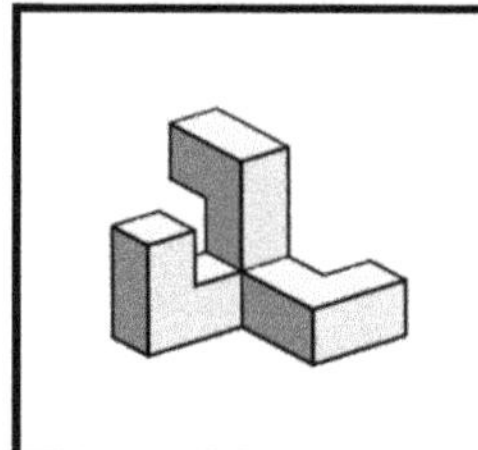

A. 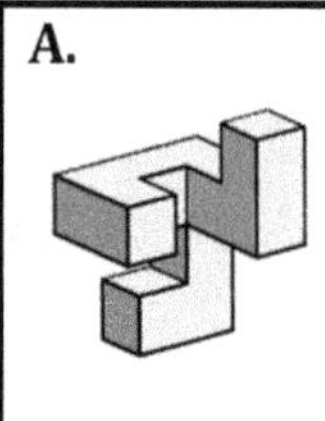

B. 

C. 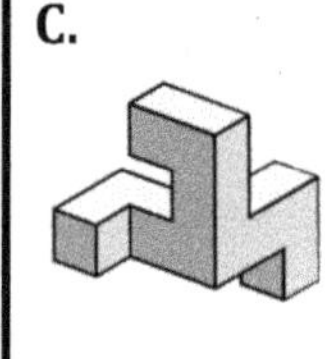

D. 

E. 

4. Which of the answer choices shows the same block as the original?

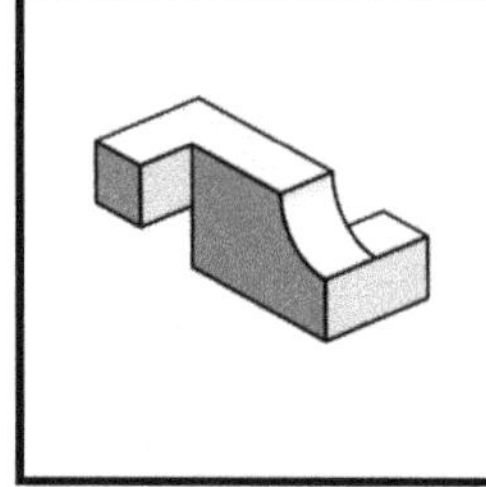

A. 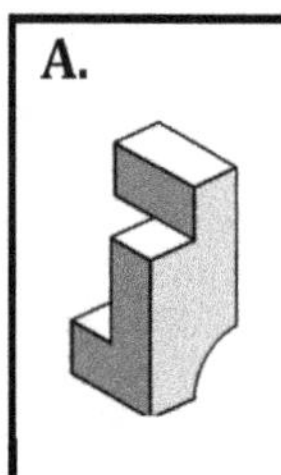

B. 

C. 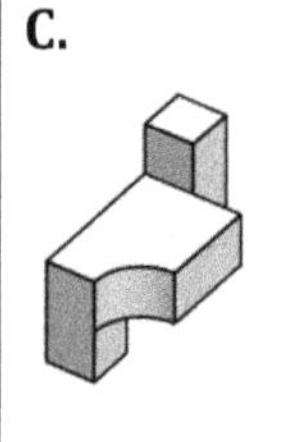

D. 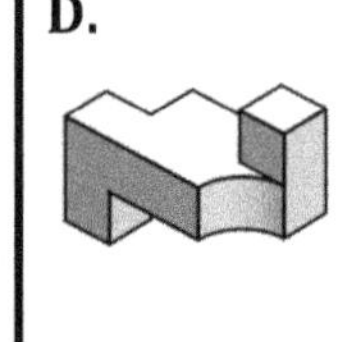

E. 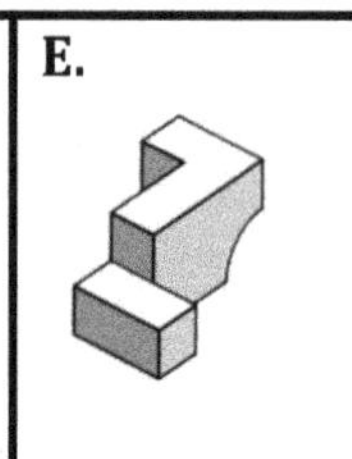

5. Which of the answer choices shows the same block as the original?

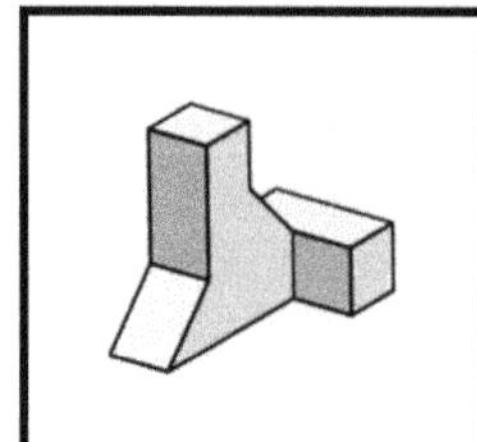

A. 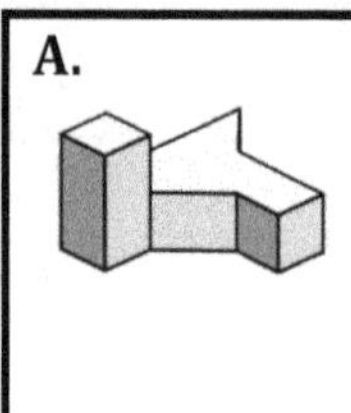

B. 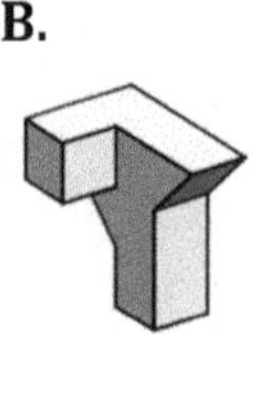

C. 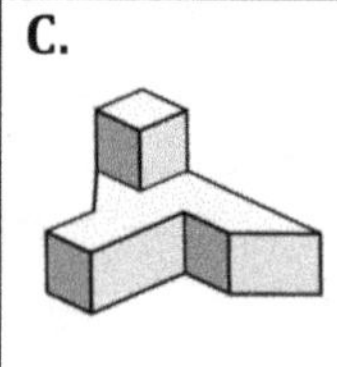

D. 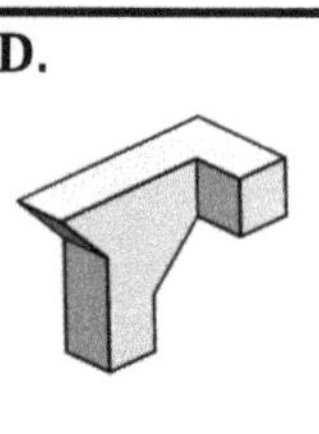

E. 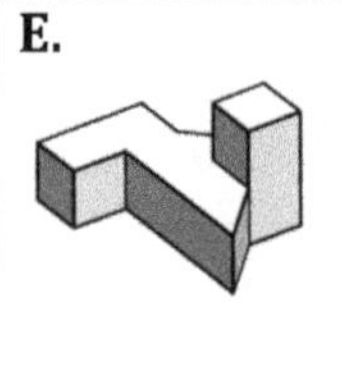

6. Which of the answer choices shows the same block as the original?

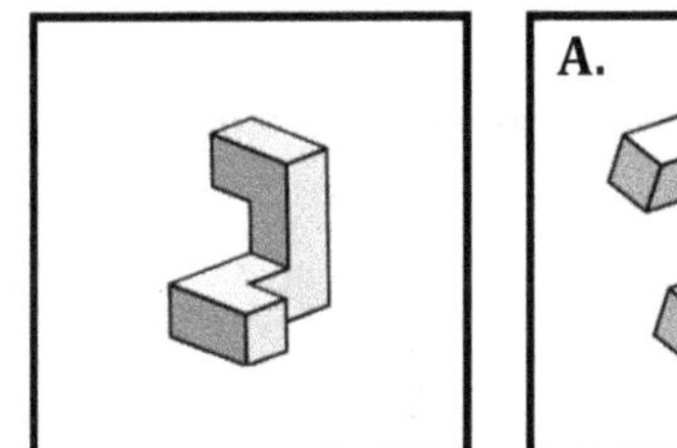

A. 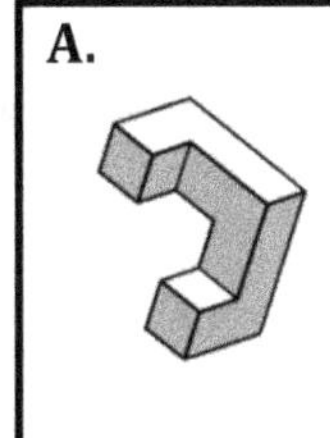

B. 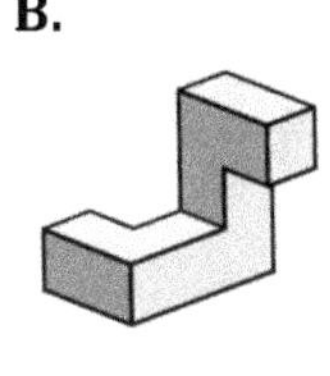

C. 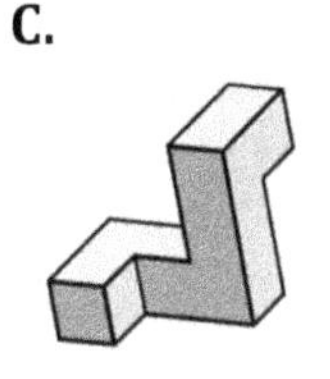

D. 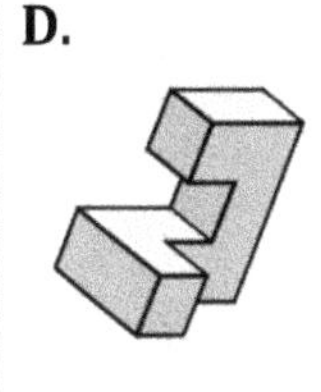

E. 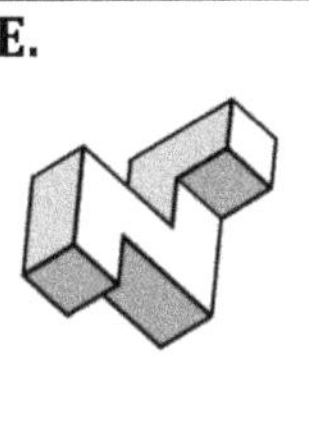

7. Which of the answer choices shows the same block as the original?

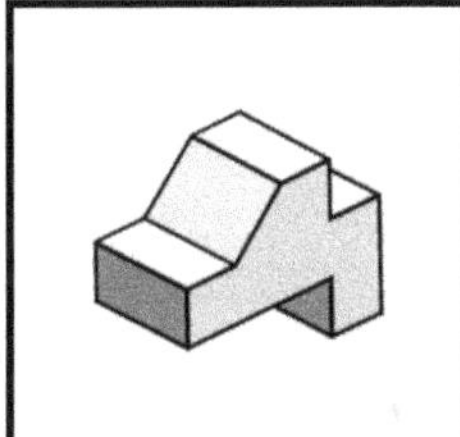

A. 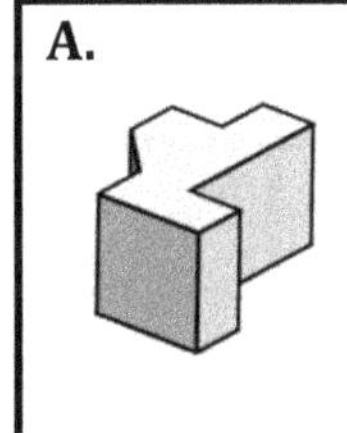

B. 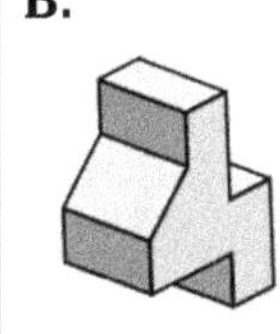

C. 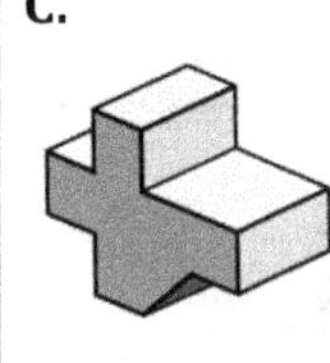

D. 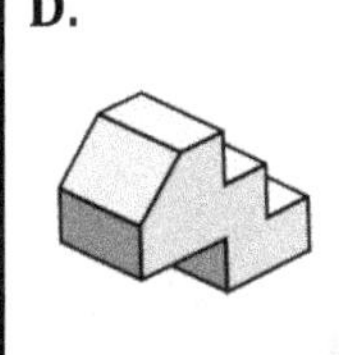

E. 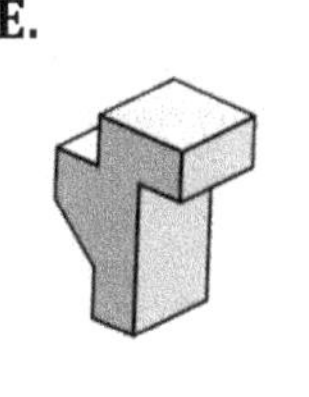

8. Which of the answer choices shows the same block as the original?

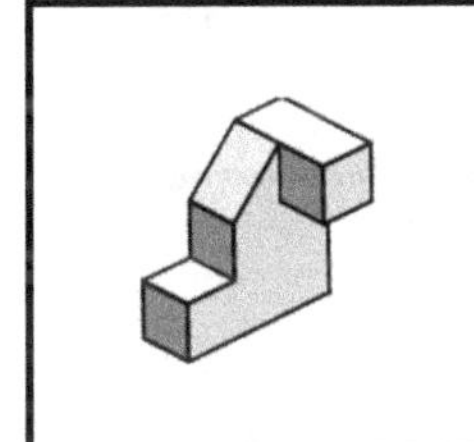

A. 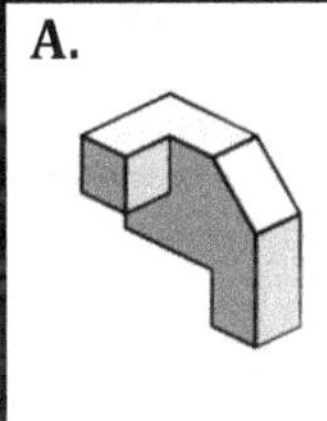

B. 

C. 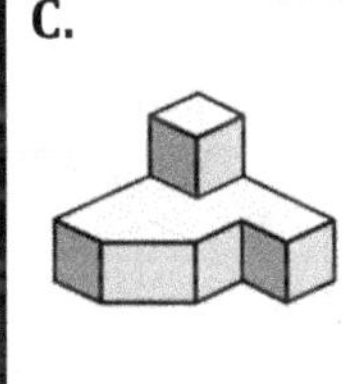

D. 

E. 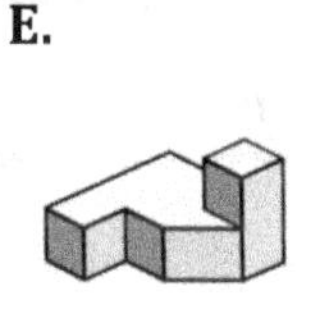

Apertures

1. Which of the following apertures could the object pass through?

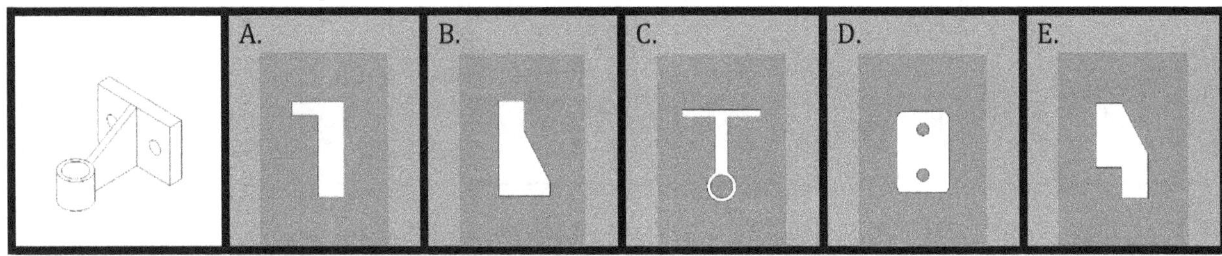

2. Which of the following apertures could the object pass through?

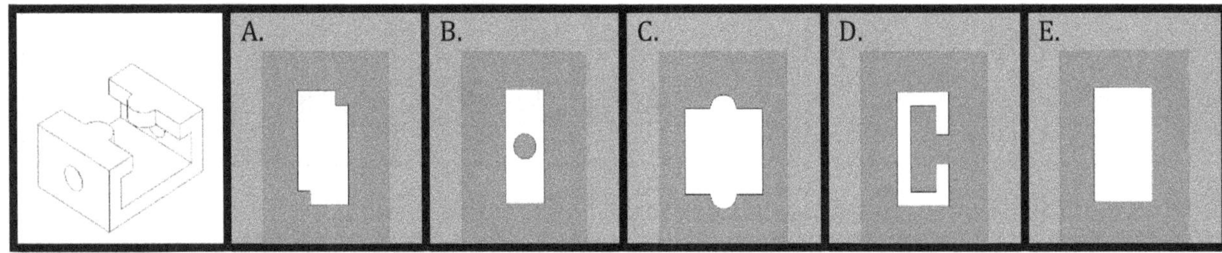

3. Which of the following apertures could the object pass through?

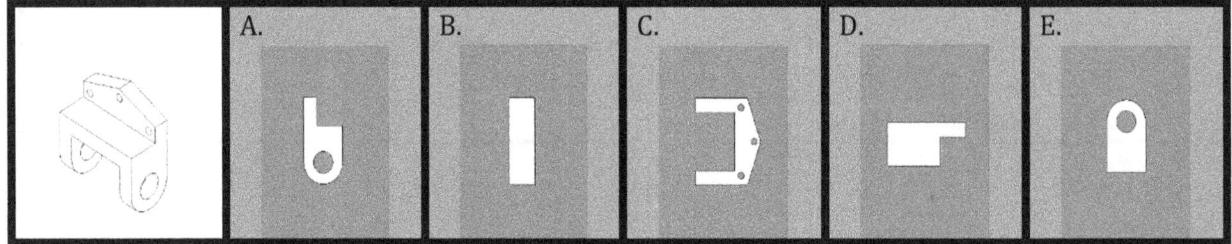

4. Which of the following apertures could the object pass through?

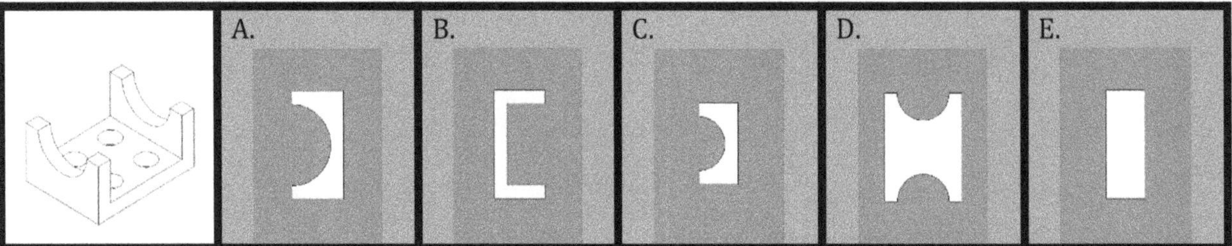

5. Which of the following apertures could the object pass through?

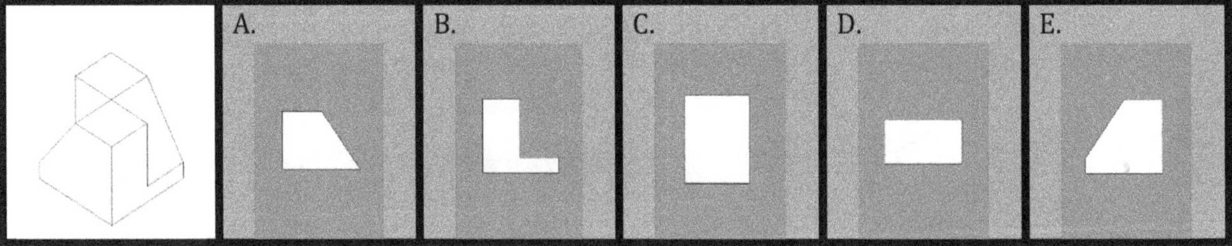

6. Which of the following apertures could the object pass through?

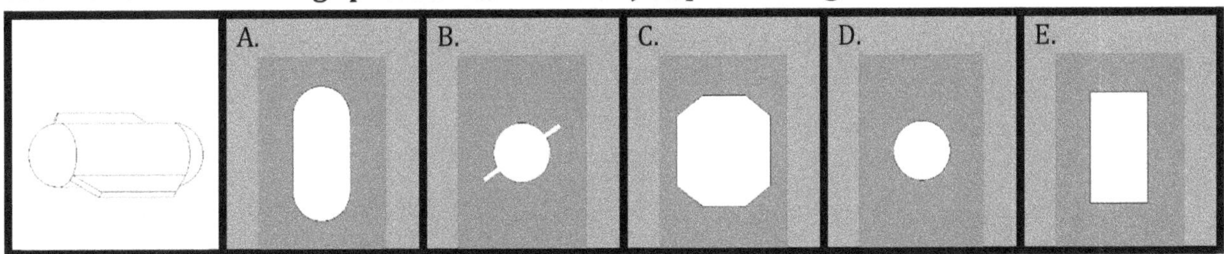

7. Which of the following apertures could the object pass through?

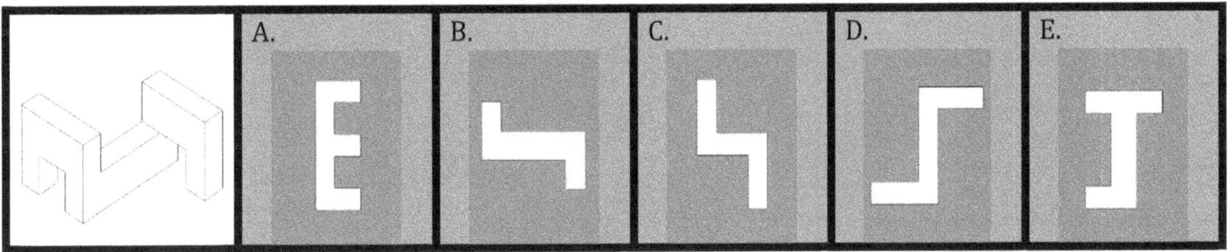

8. Which of the following apertures could the object pass through?

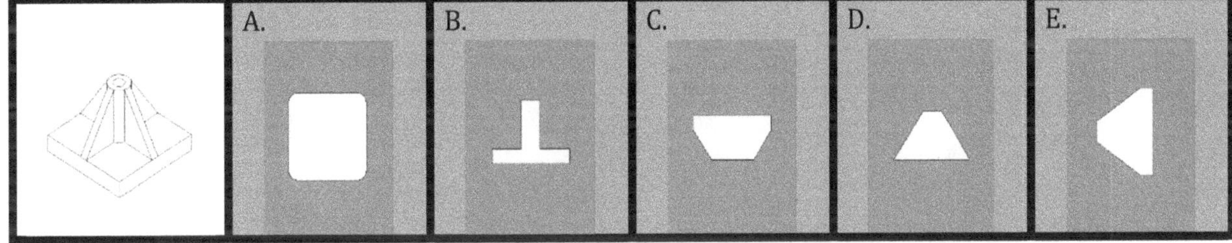

9. Which of the following apertures could the object pass through?

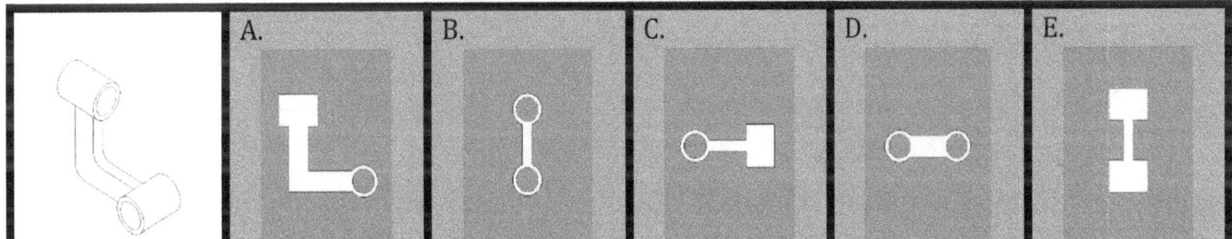

10. Which of the following apertures could the object pass through?

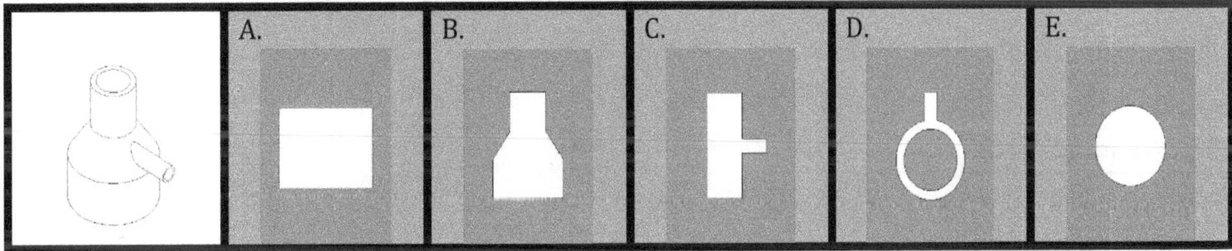

Perspective Visualization

1. Which of the following answer choices shows a front view of the object?

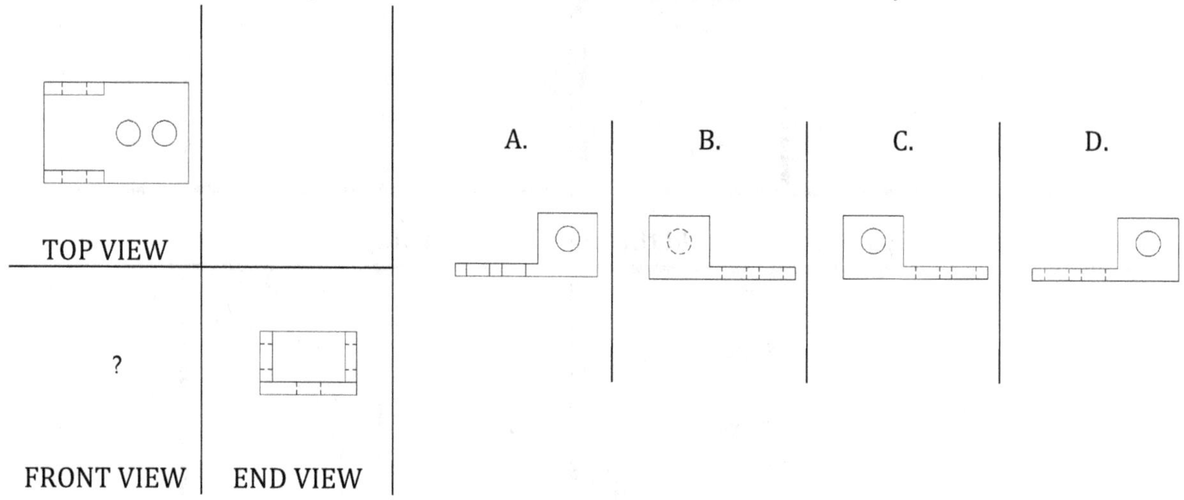

2. Which of the following answer choices shows an end view of the object?

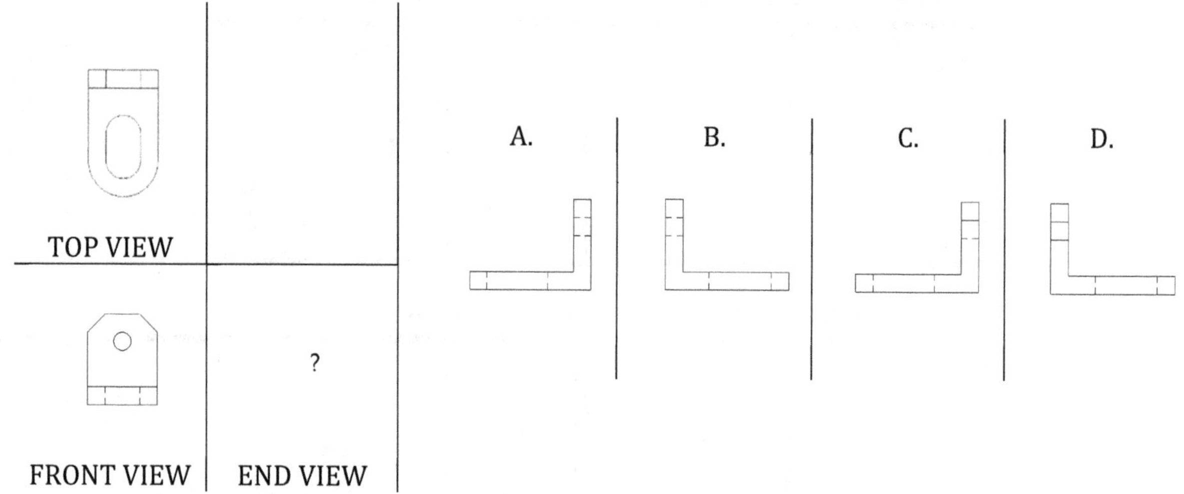

3. Which of the following answer choices shows a top view of the object?

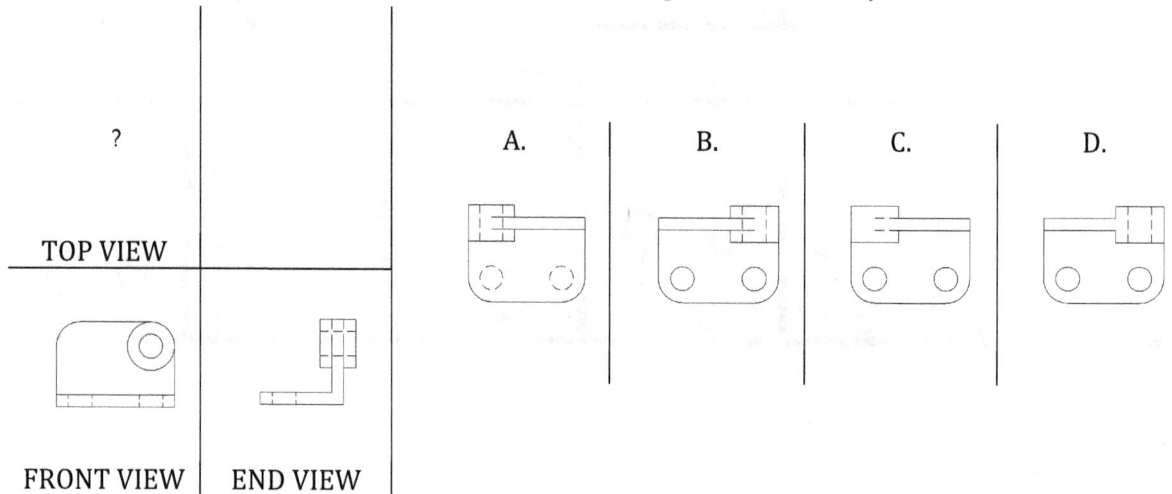

4. **Which of the following answer choices shows a front view of the object?**

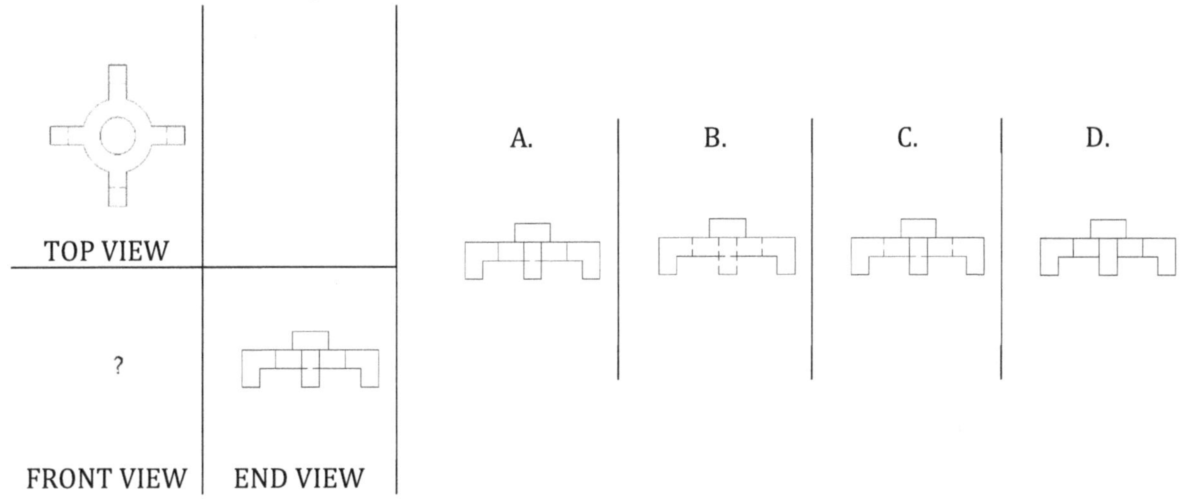

5. **Which of the following answer choices shows an end view of the object?**

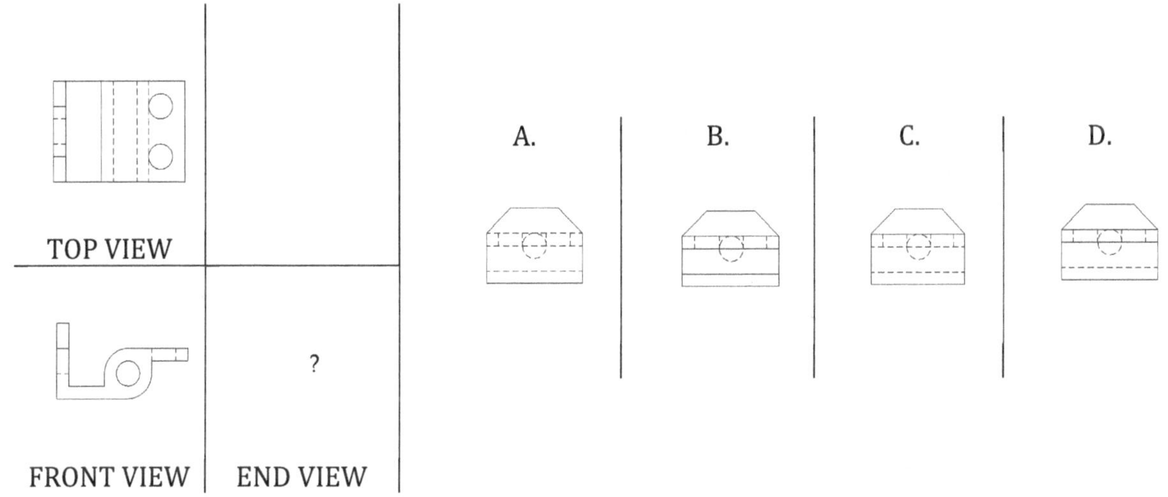

6. **Which of the following answer choices shows a top view of the object?**

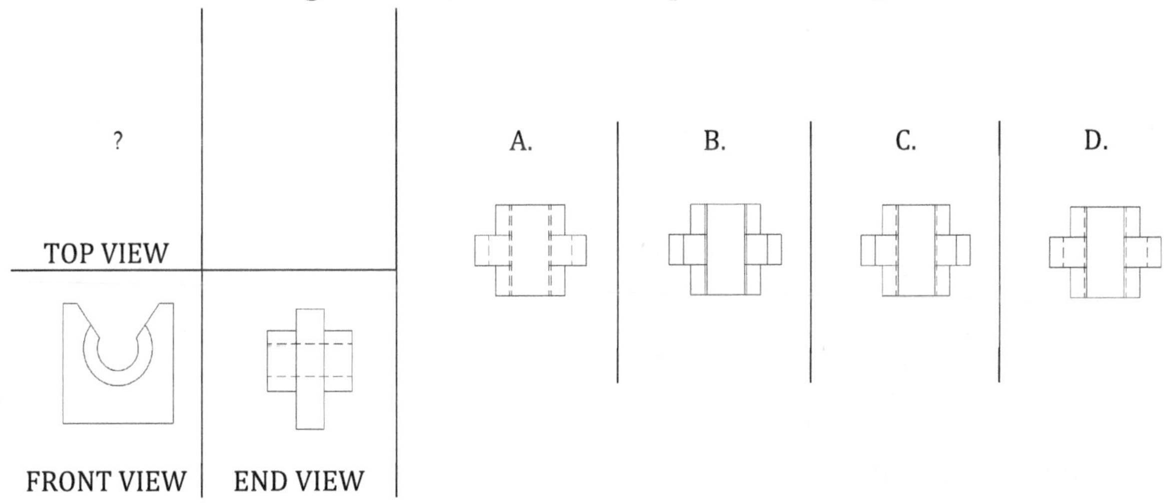

7. Which of the following answer choices shows a front view of the object?

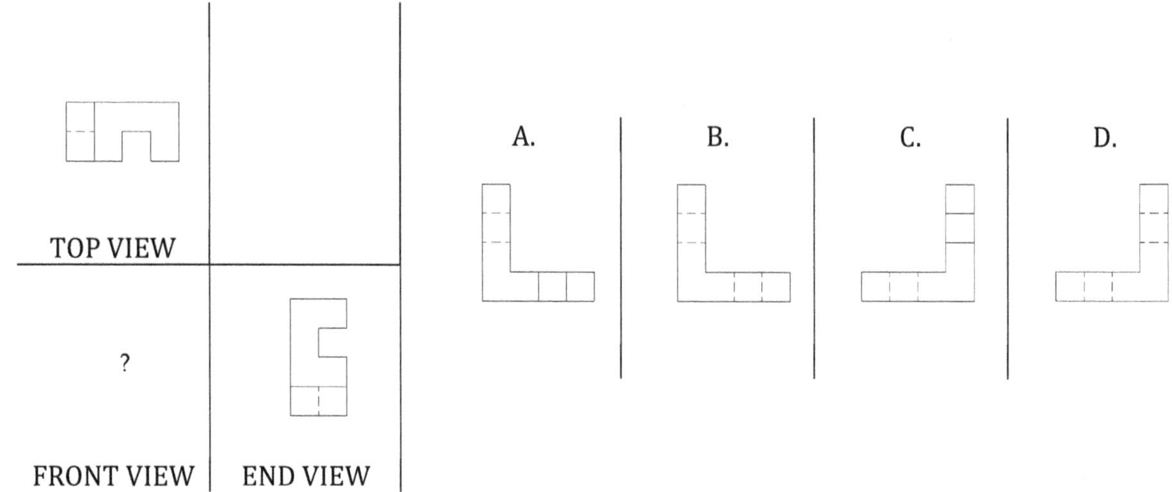

8. Which of the following answer choices shows a top view of the object?

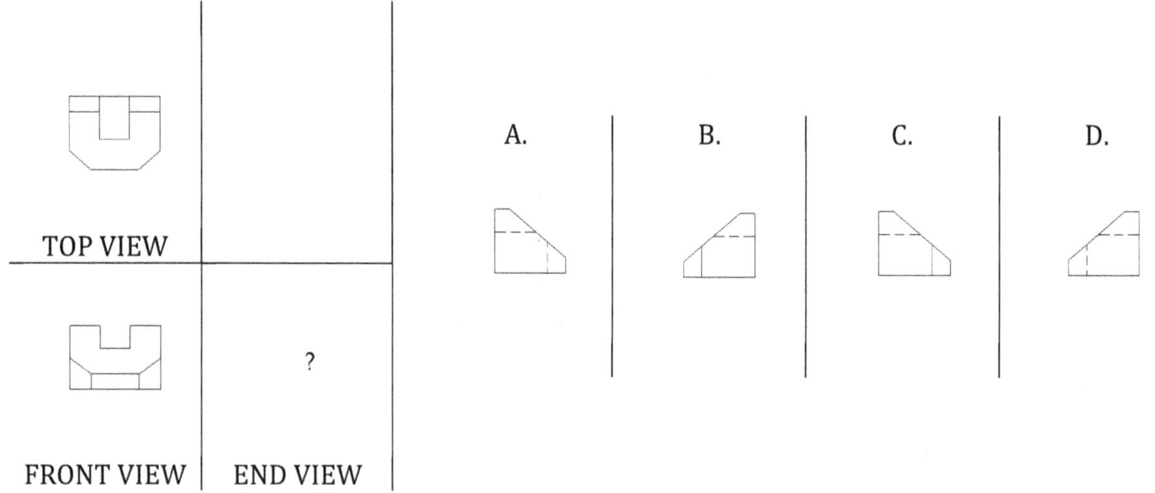

9. Which of the following answer choices shows a top view of the object?

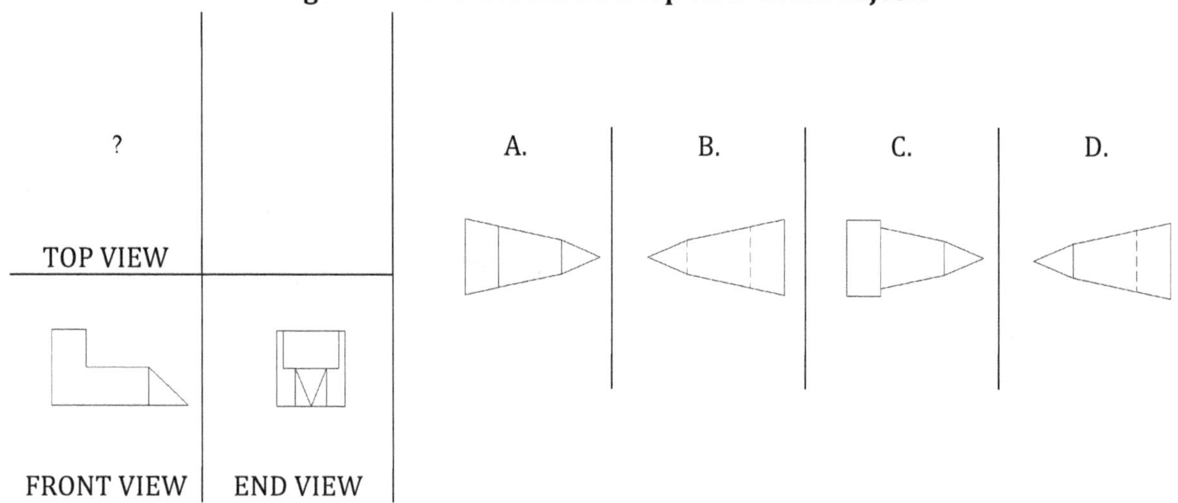

10. Which of the following answer choices shows a top view of the object?

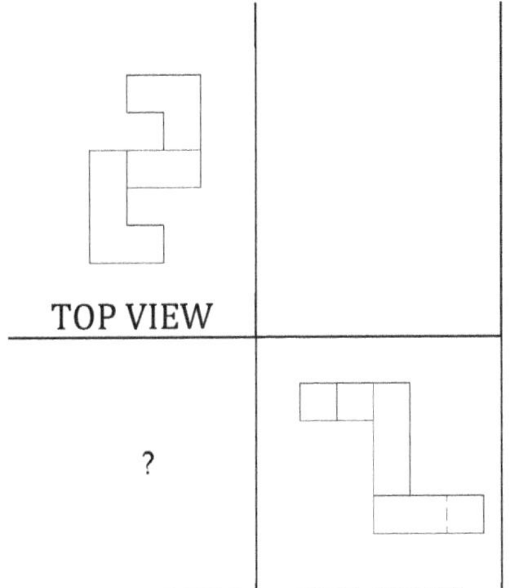

A.

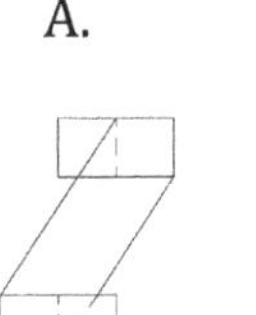

B.

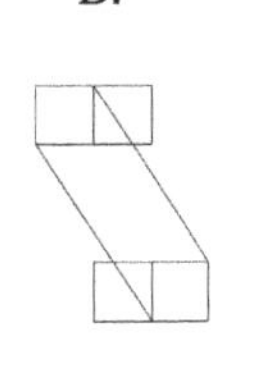

C.

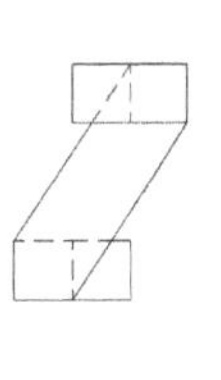

D.

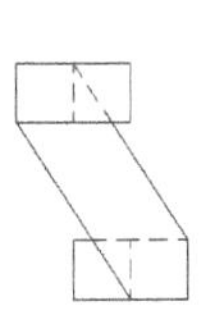

Painted Blocks

The blocks shown below have been glued or cemented together as shown, and each exterior surface of each block has been painted, except the bottom.

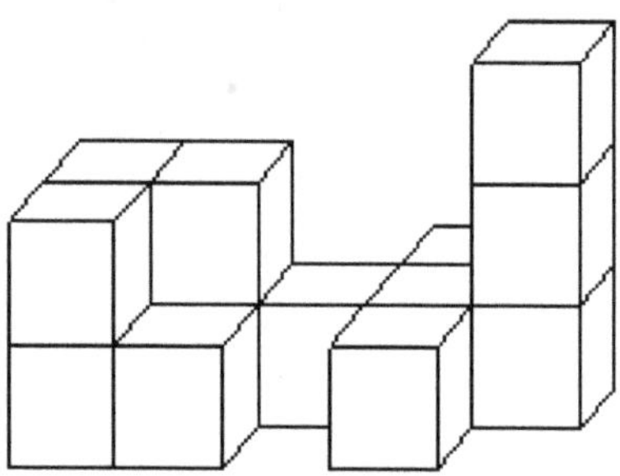

1. In the figure shown above, how many cubes have only one side painted?

2. In the figure shown above, how many cubes have exactly two sides painted?

3. In the figure shown above, how many cubes have exactly three sides painted?

4. In the figure shown above, how many cubes have exactly four sides painted?

5. In the figure shown above, how many cubes have exactly five sides painted?

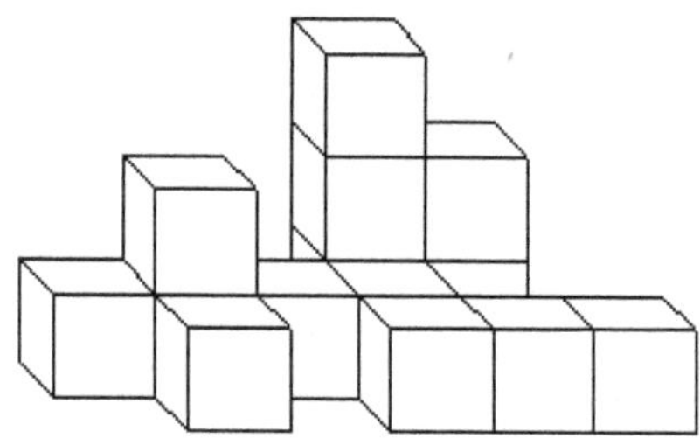

6. In the figure shown above, how many cubes have exactly one side painted?

7. In the figure shown above, how many cubes have exactly two sides painted?

8. In the figure shown above, how many cubes have exactly three sides painted?

9. In the figure shown above, how many cubes have exactly four sides painted?

10. In the figure shown above, how many cubes have exactly five sides painted?

Instrument Comprehension

1. Which of the answer choices represents the orientation of the plane?

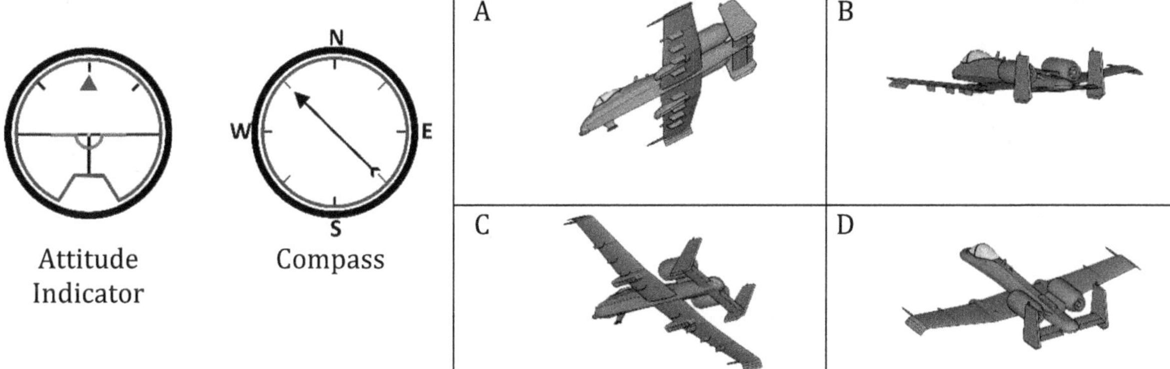

2. Which of the answer choices represents the orientation of the plane?

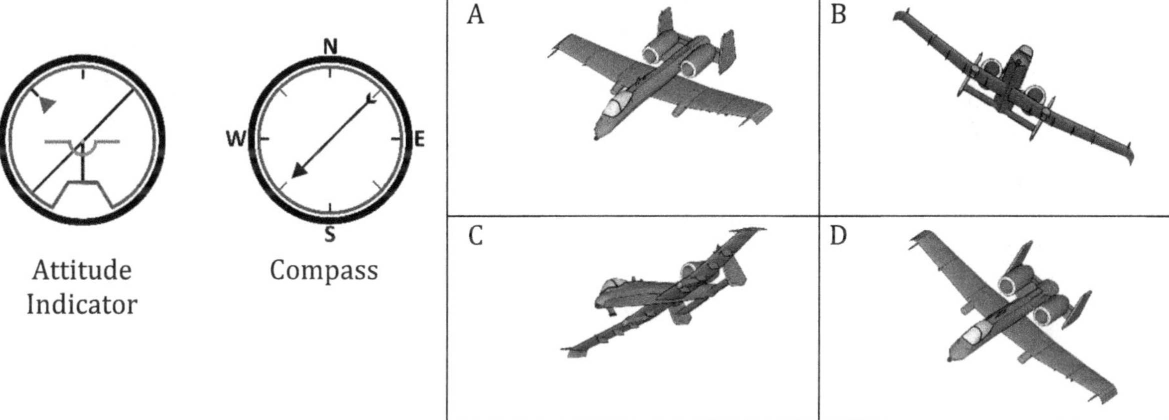

3. Which of the answer choices represents the orientation of the plane?

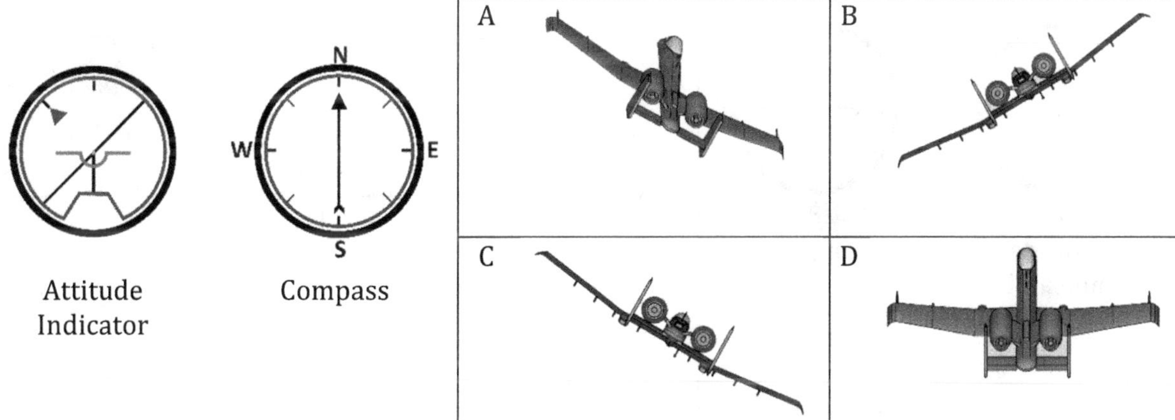

4. Which of the answer choices represents the orientation of the plane?

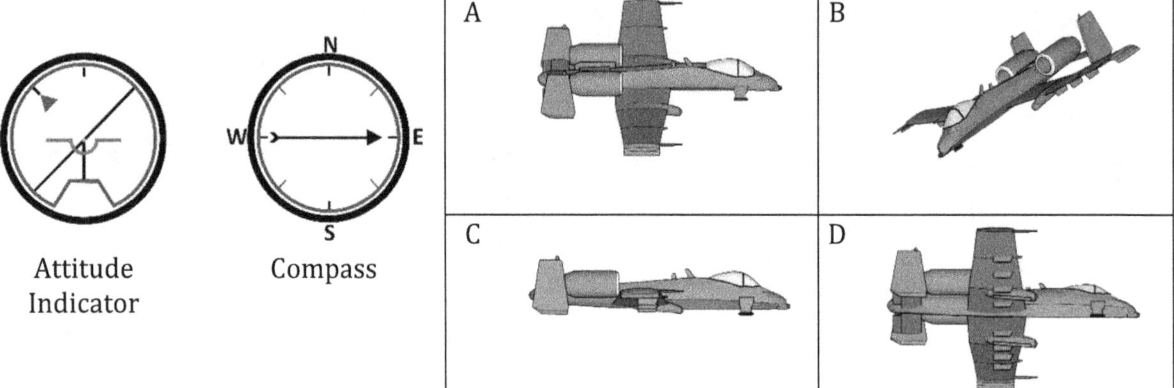

5. Which of the answer choices represents the orientation of the plane?

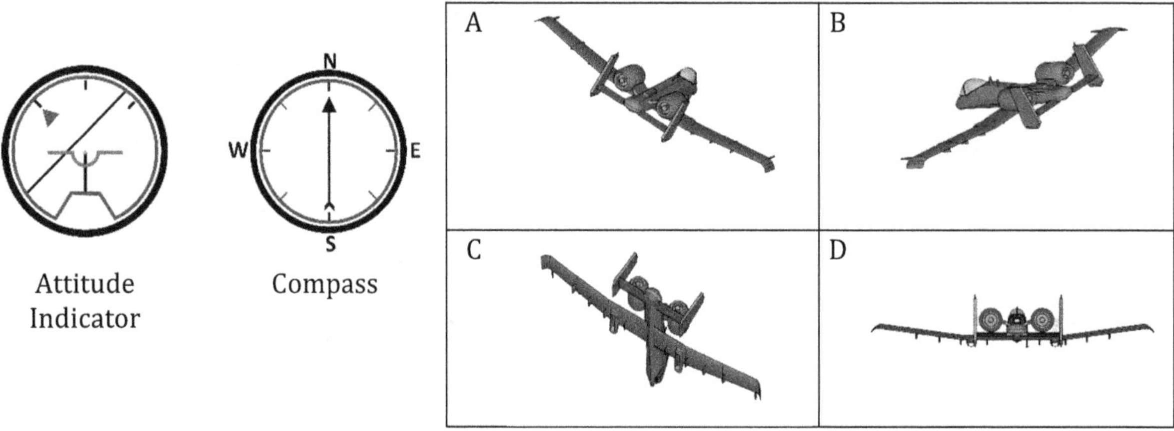

6. Which of the answer choices represents the orientation of the plane?

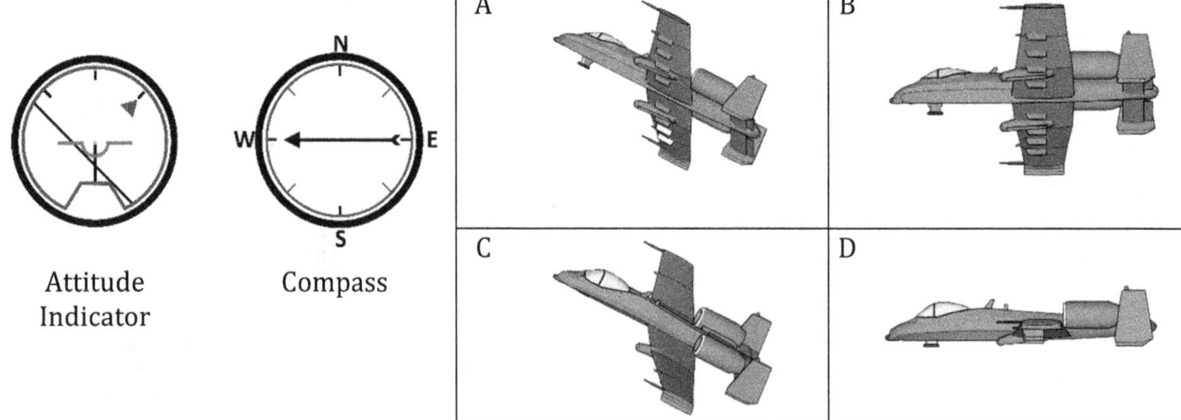

7. Which of the answer choices represents the orientation of the plane?

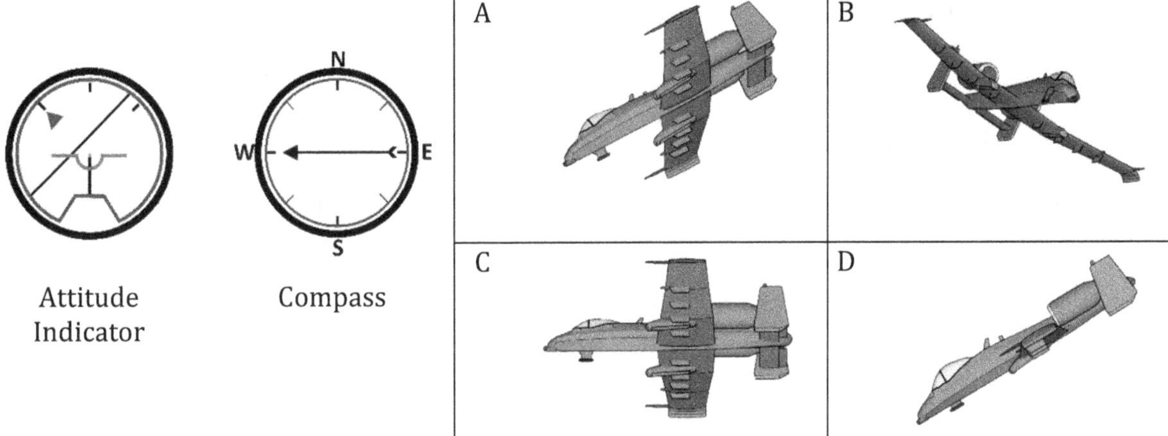

8. Which of the answer choices represents the orientation of the plane?

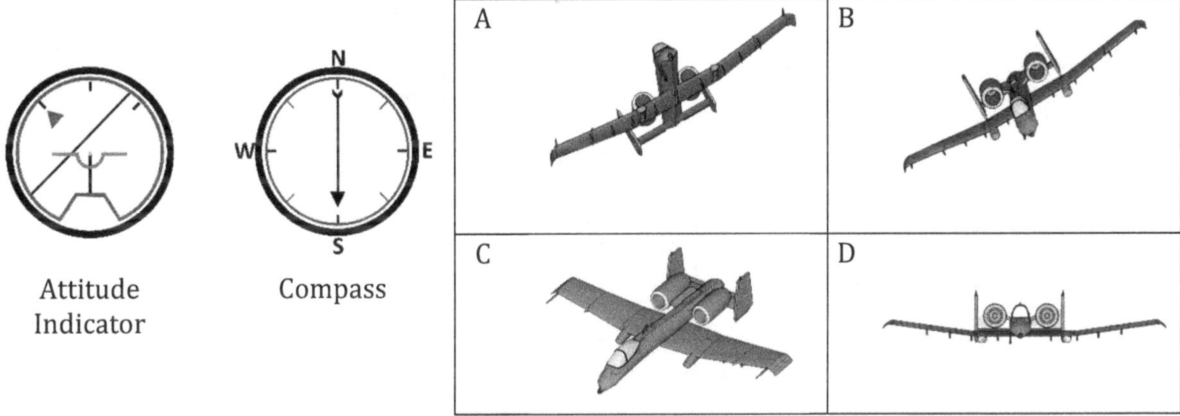

9. Which of the answer choices represents the orientation of the plane?

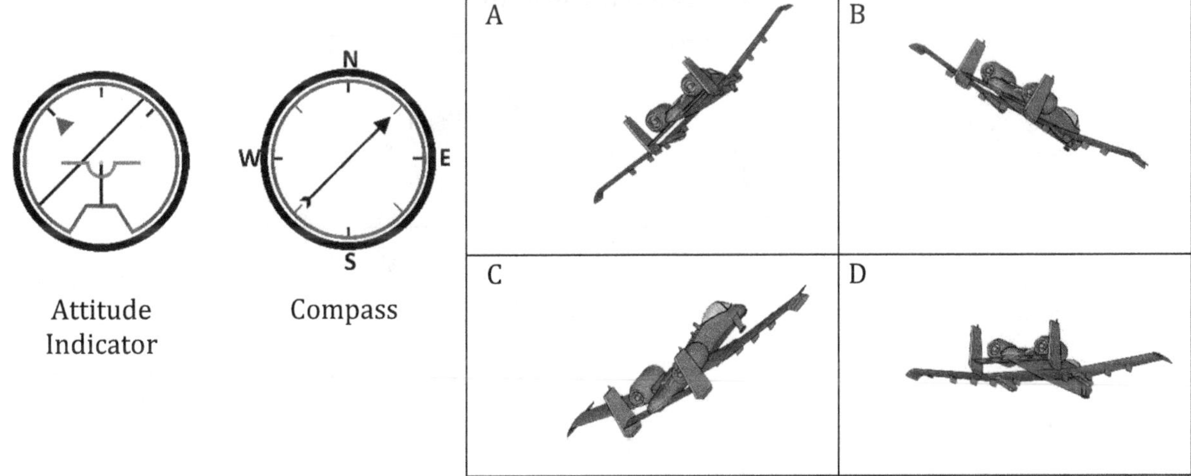

10. **Which of the answer choices represents the orientation of the plane?**

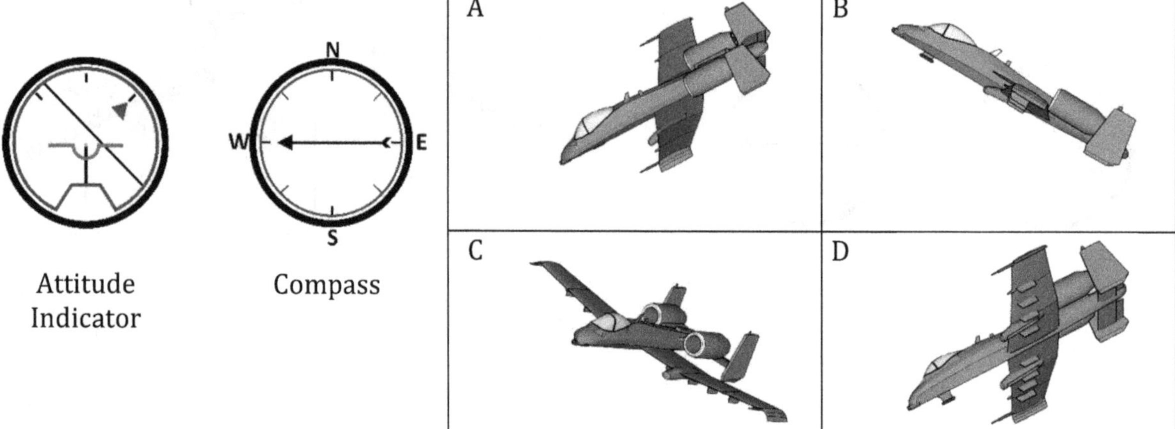

11. **Which of the answer choices represents the orientation of the plane?**

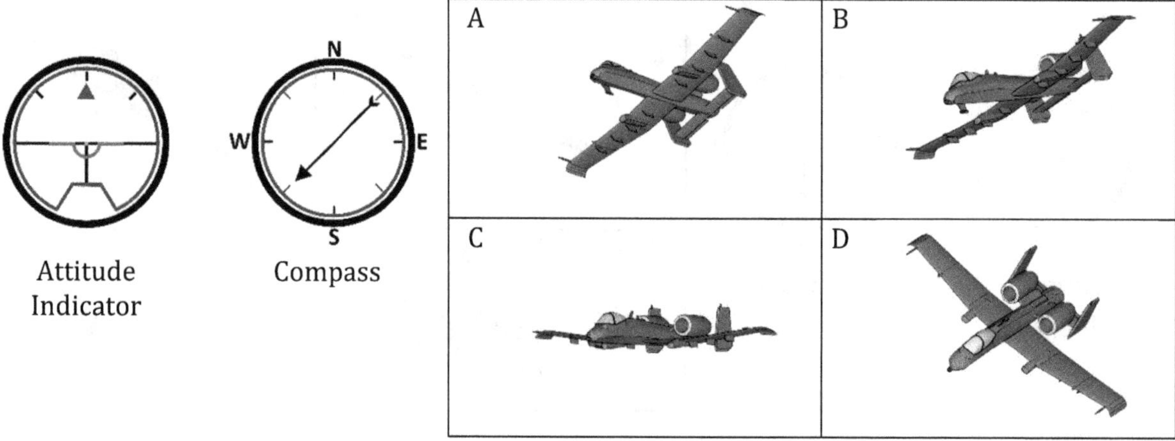

12. **Which of the answer choices represents the orientation of the plane?**

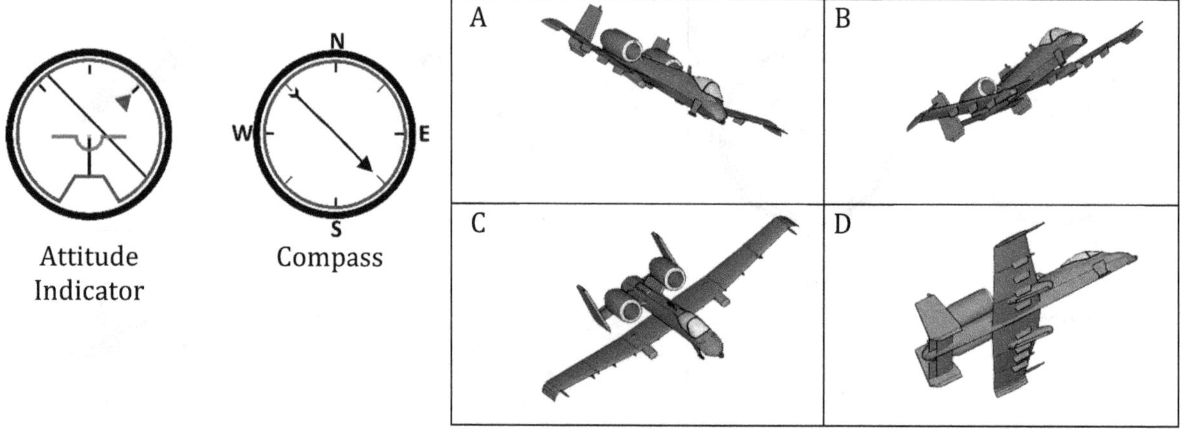

Hole Punching

1. How will the holes appear when the paper is unfolded?

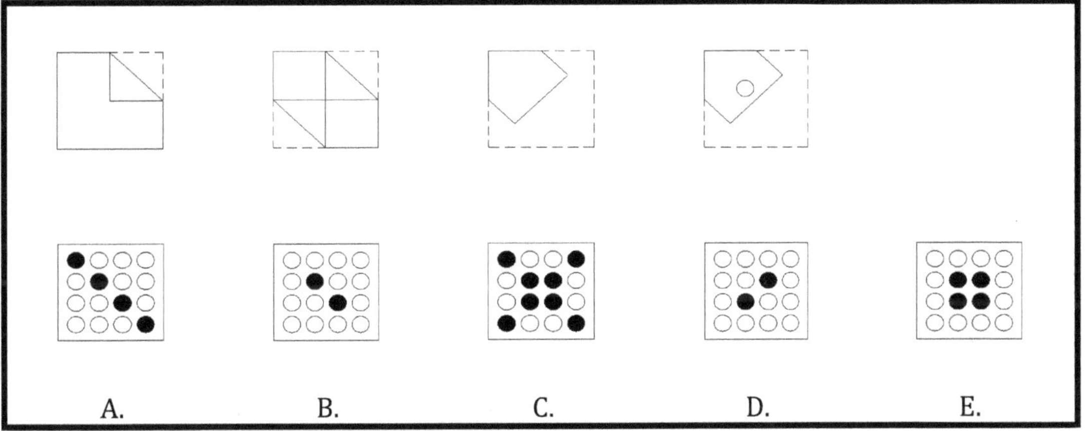

2. How will the holes appear when the paper is unfolded?

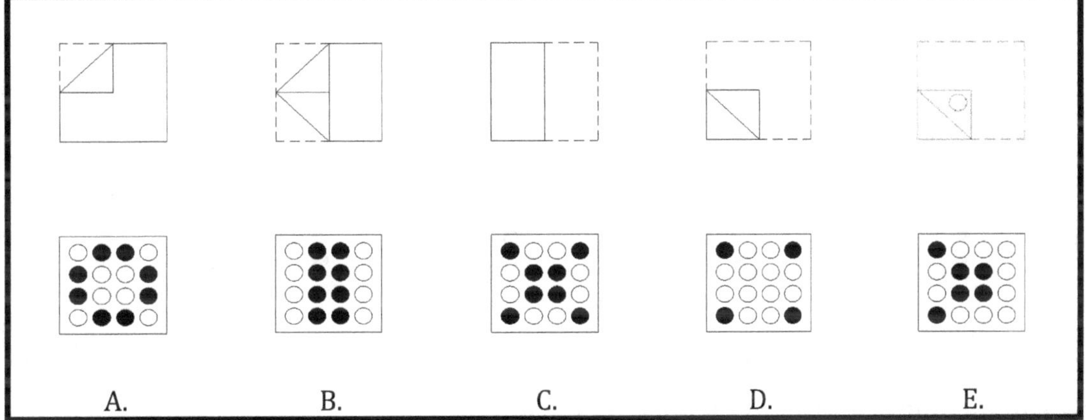

3. How will the holes appear when the paper is unfolded?

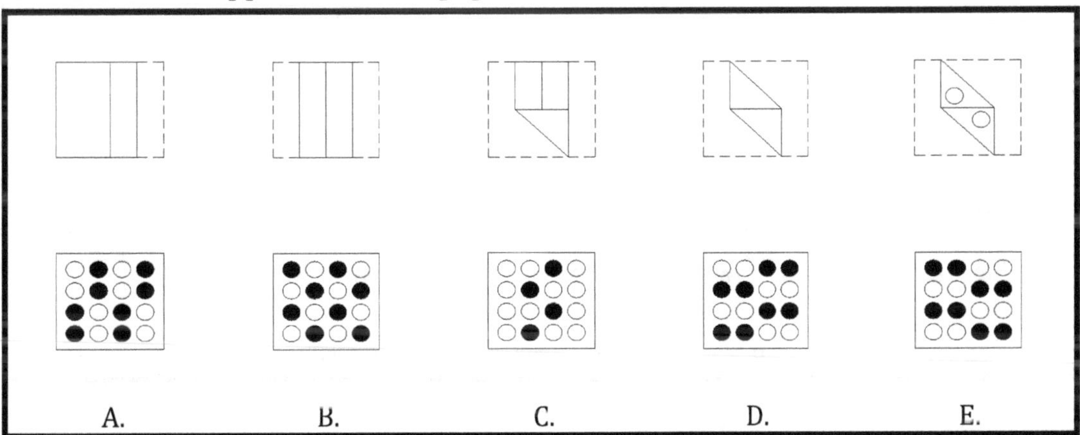

4. How will the holes appear when the paper is unfolded?

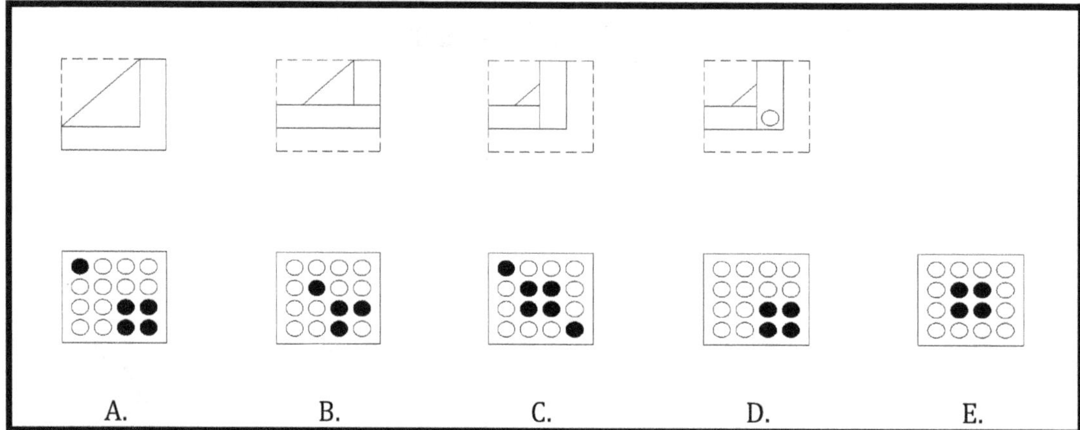

5. How will the holes appear when the paper is unfolded?

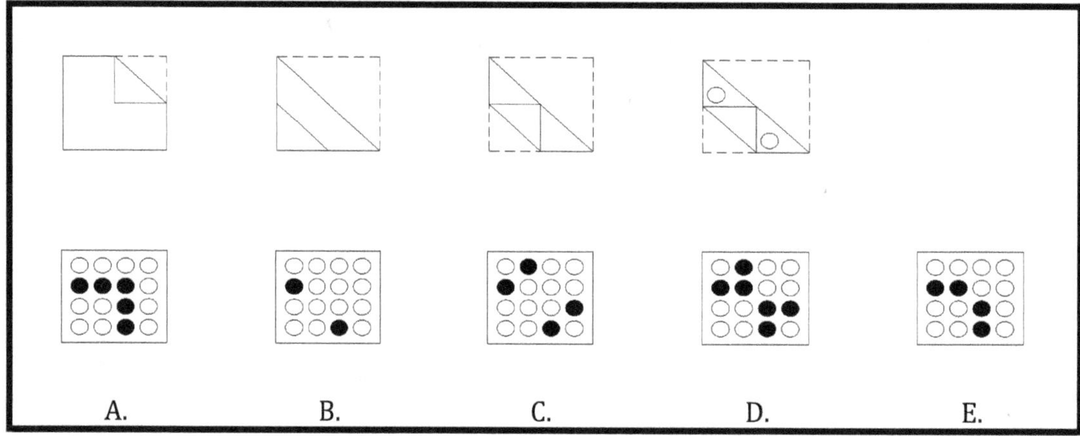

6. How will the holes appear when the paper is unfolded?

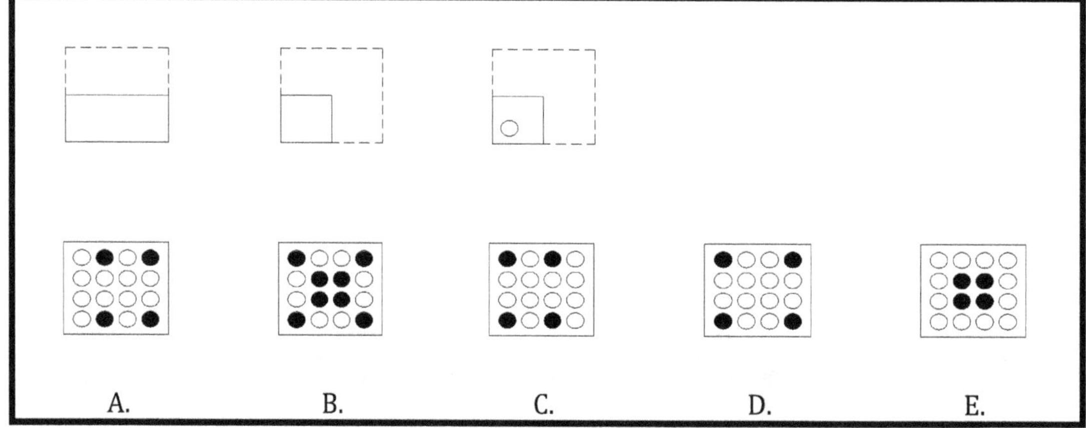

7. How will the holes appear when the paper is unfolded?

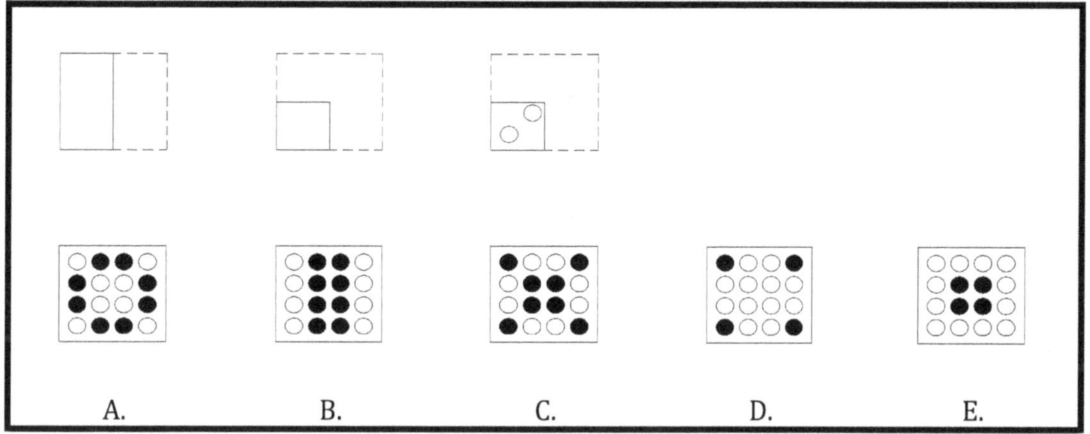

8. How will the holes appear when the paper is unfolded?

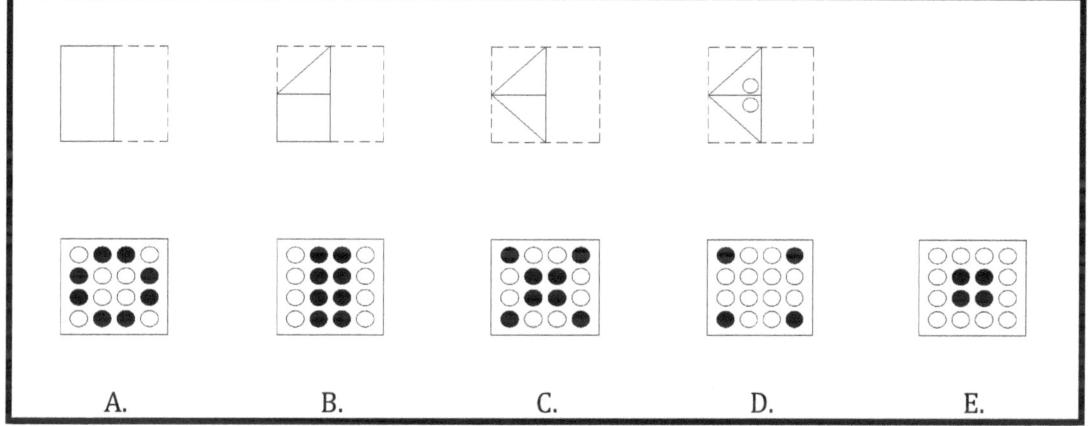

9. How will the holes appear when the paper is unfolded?

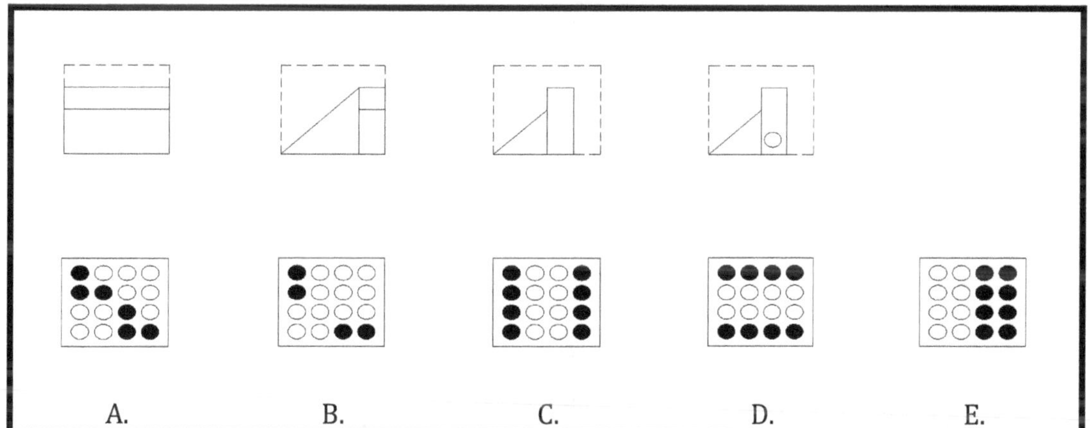

10. How will the holes appear when the paper is unfolded?

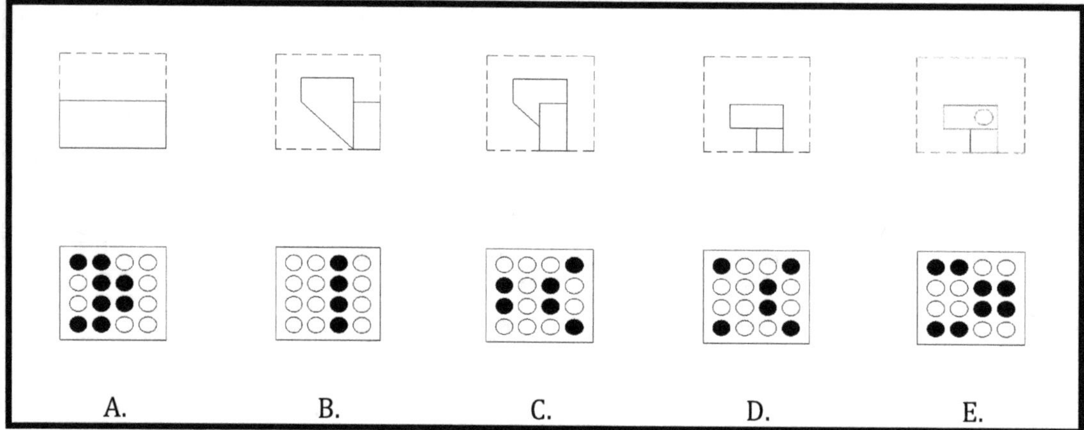

Hidden Blocks

1. How many blocks are in the arrangement below?

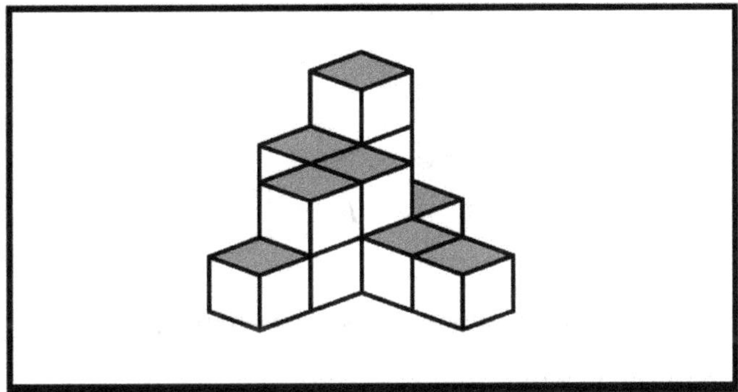

2. How many blocks are in the arrangement below?

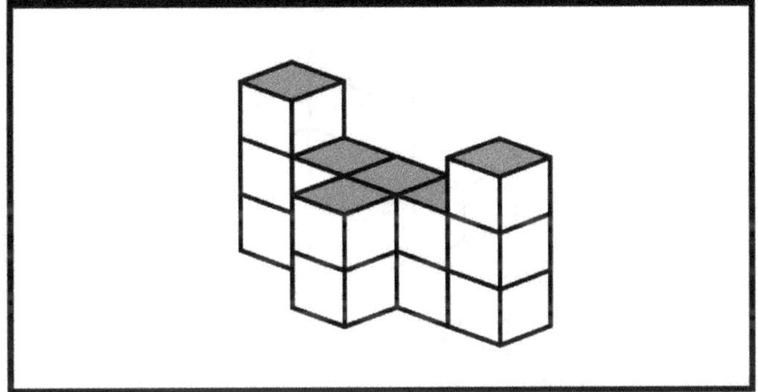

3. How many blocks are in the arrangement below?

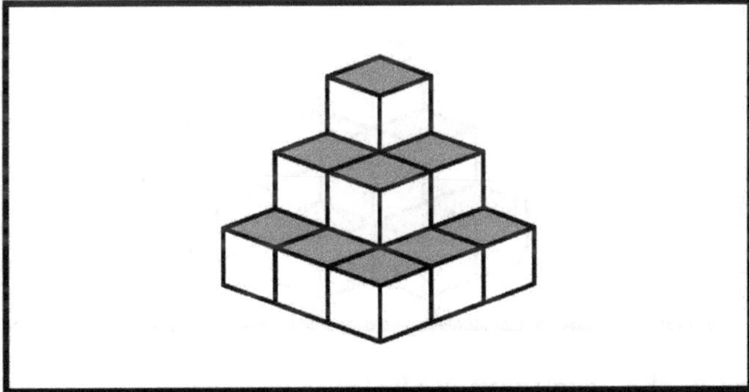

4. How many blocks are in the arrangement below?

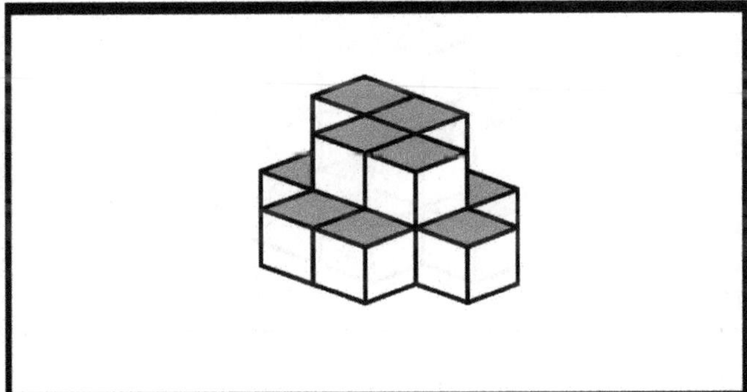

5. How many blocks are in the arrangement below?

6. How many blocks are in the arrangement below?

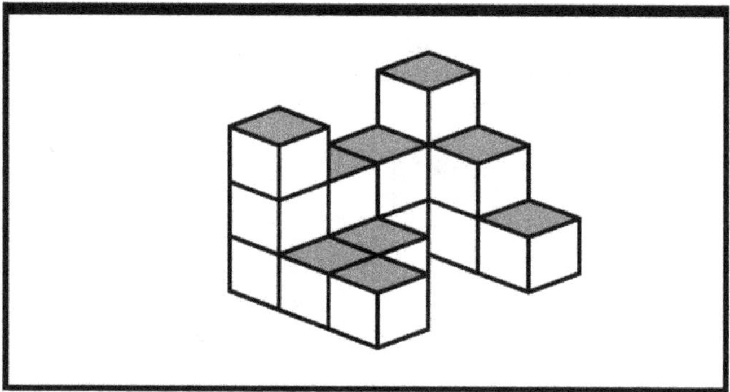

7. How many blocks are in the arrangement below?

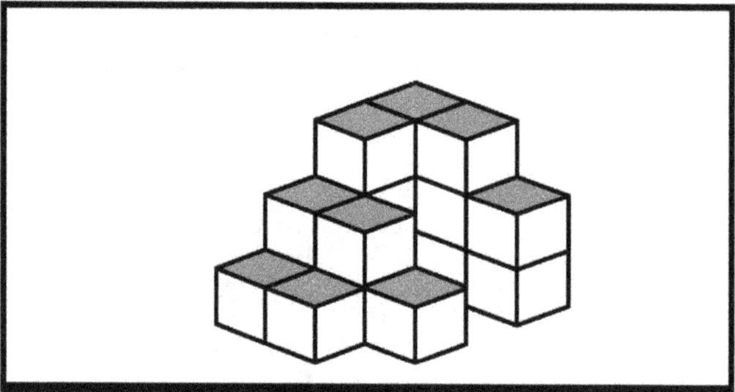

8. How many blocks are in the arrangement below?

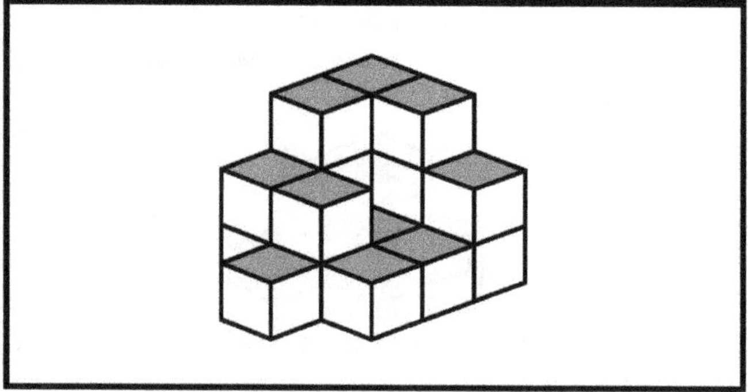

9. **How many blocks are in the arrangement below?**

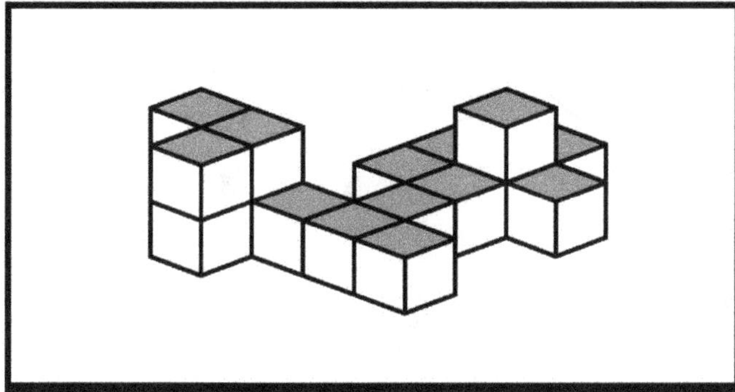

10. **How many blocks are in the arrangement below?**

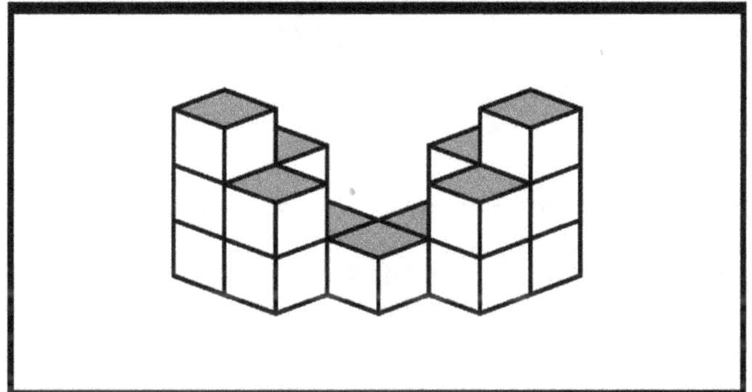

Counting Touching Blocks

1. How many blocks are touching block 5 in the figure above?

2. How many blocks are touching block 1 in the figure above?

3. How many blocks are touching block 3 in the figure above?

4. How many blocks are touching block 6 in the figure above?

5. How many blocks are touching block 7 in the figure above?

6. How many blocks are touching block 9 in the figure above?

7. How many blocks are touching block 15 in the figure above?

8. How many blocks are touching block 11 in the figure above?

9. How many blocks are touching block 13 in the figure above?

10. How many blocks are touching block 16 in the figure above?

11. How many blocks are touching block 19 in the figure above?

12. How many blocks are touching block 20 in the figure above?

Cut-ups

1. Which of the shapes below can be formed from the given pieces?

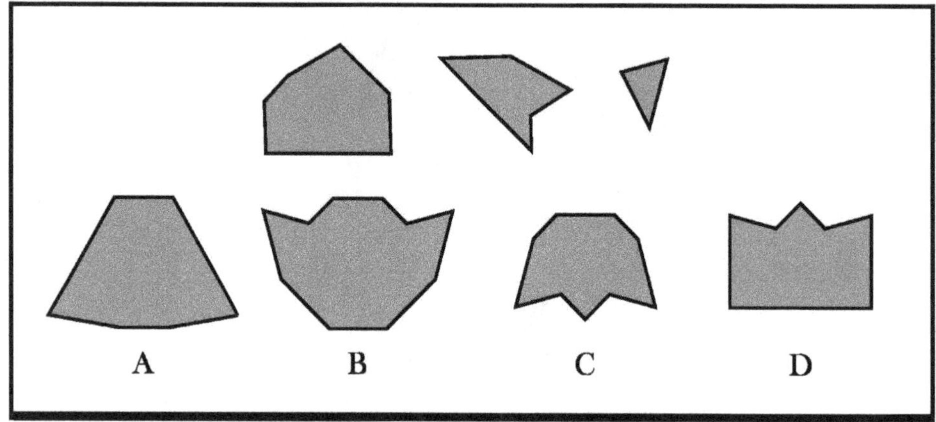

2. Which of the shapes below can be formed from the given pieces?

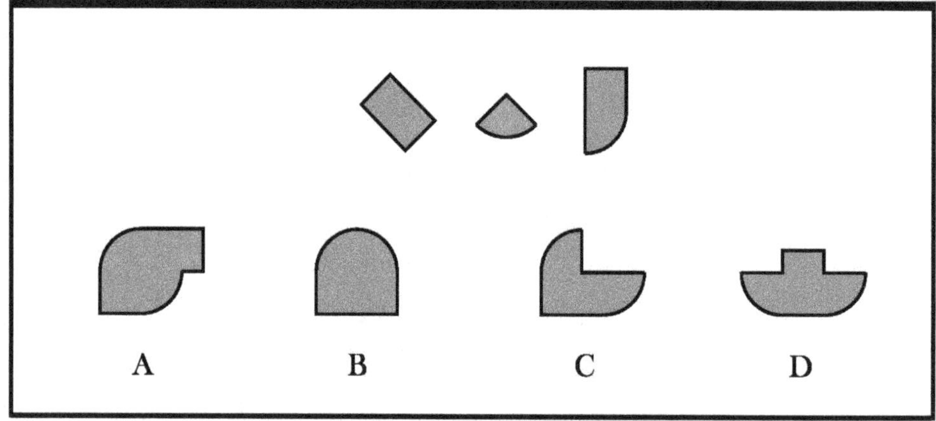

3. Which of the shapes below can be formed from the given pieces?

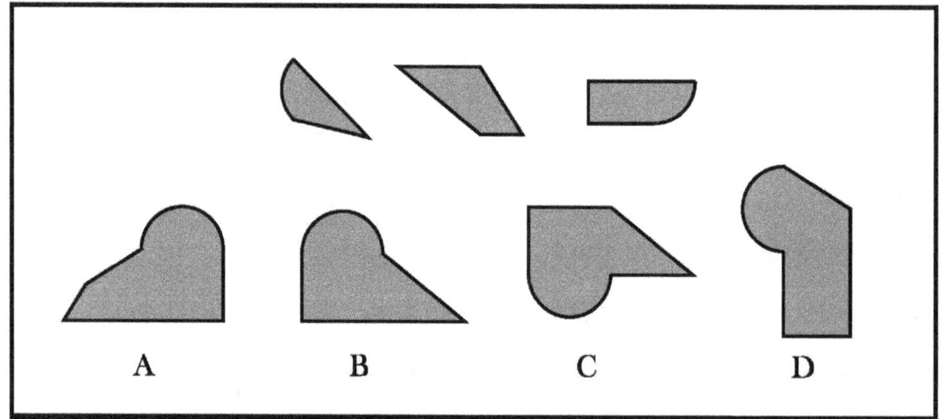

4. Which of the shapes below can be formed from the given pieces?

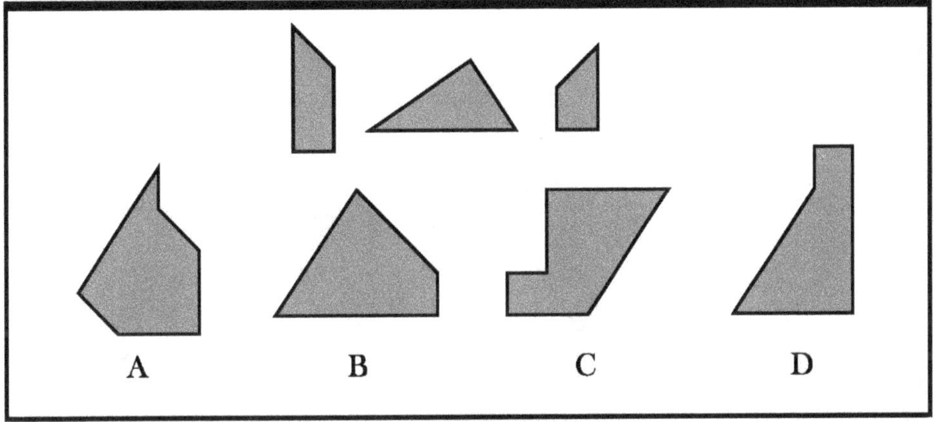

5. Which of the shapes below can be formed from the given pieces?

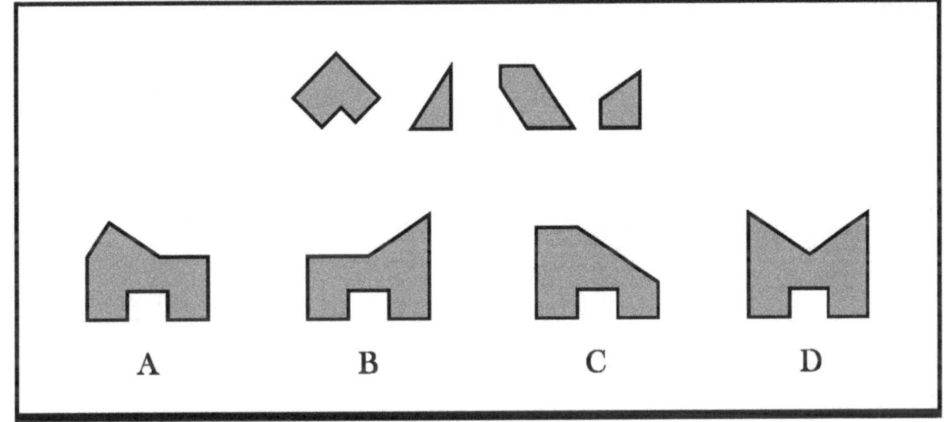

6. Which of the shapes below can be formed from the given pieces?

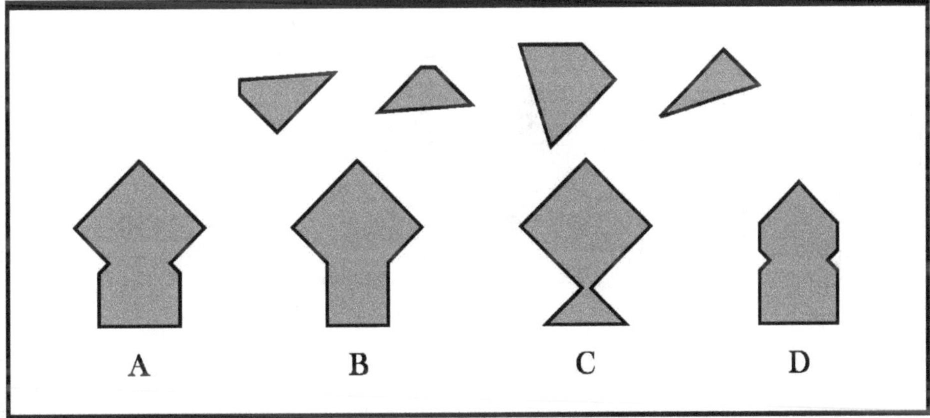

7. **Which of the shapes below can be formed from the given pieces?**

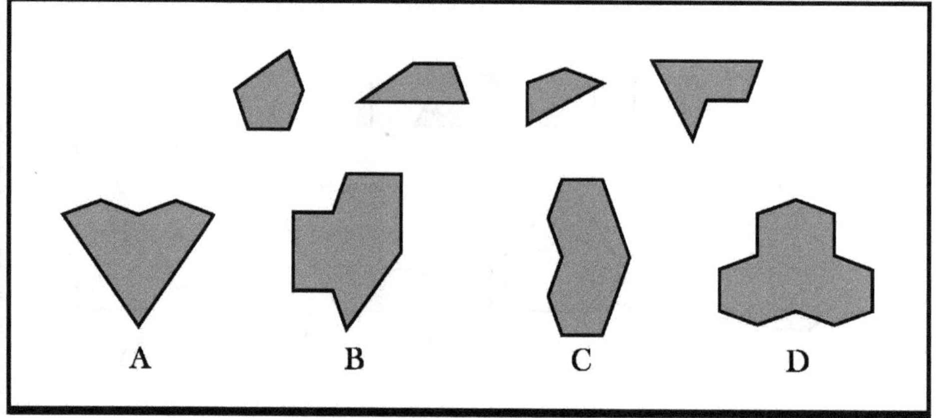

8. **Which of the shapes below can be formed from the given pieces?**

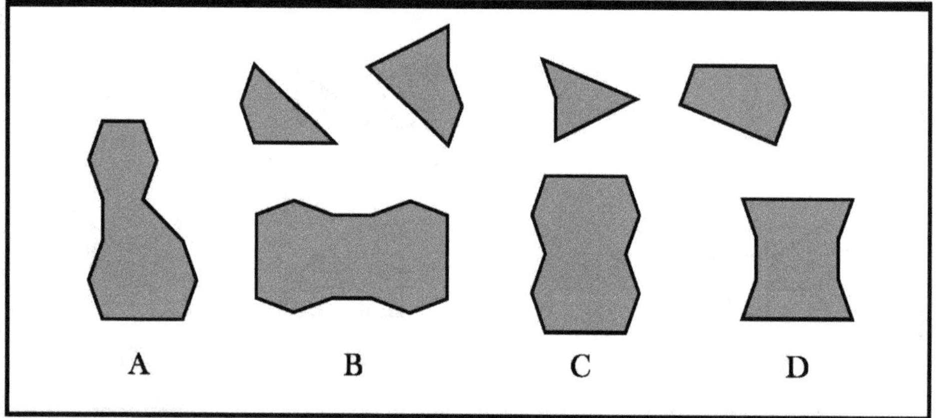

9. **Which of the shapes below can be formed from the given pieces?**

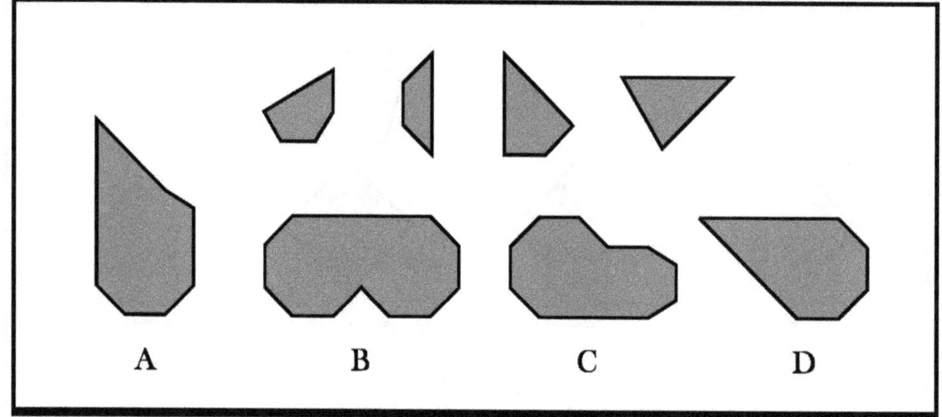

10. Which of the shapes below can be formed from the given pieces? D

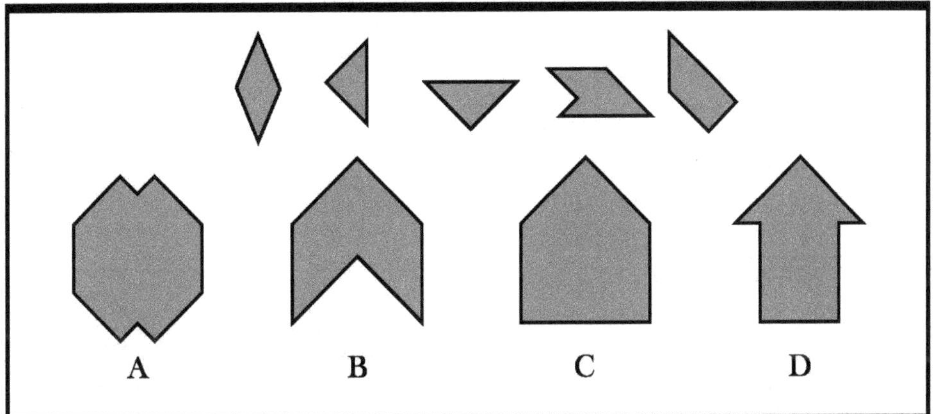

Hidden Figures

Match one of the figures A-E with each of the arrangements numbered 1-5 below.

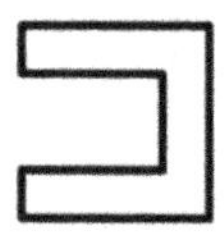
a.

b.

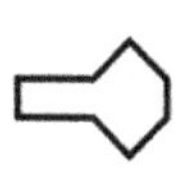
c.

d.

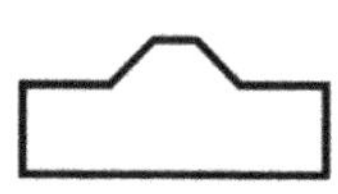
e.

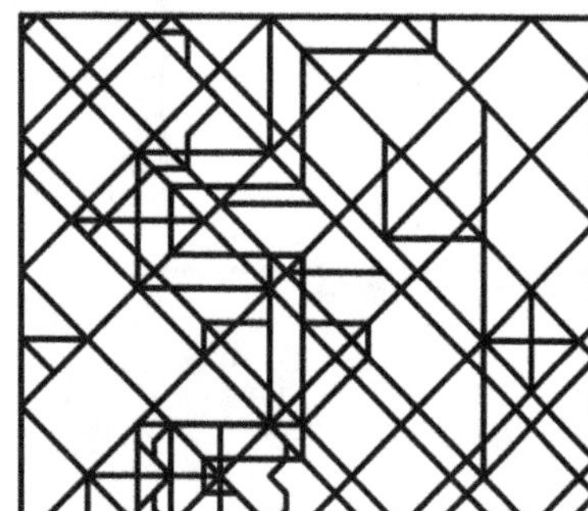
1.

4.

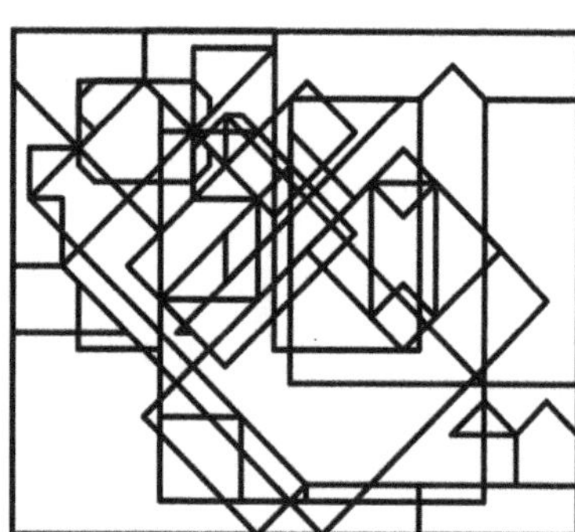
2.

5.

3.

Match one of the figures A-E with each of the arrangements numbered 6-10 below.

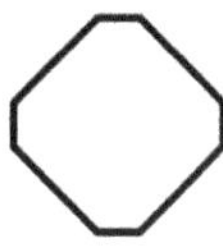
a.

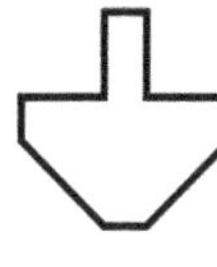
b.

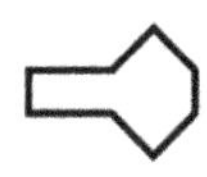
c.

d.

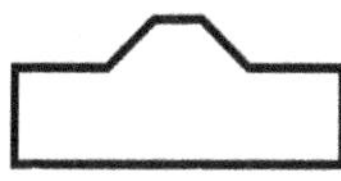
e.

6.
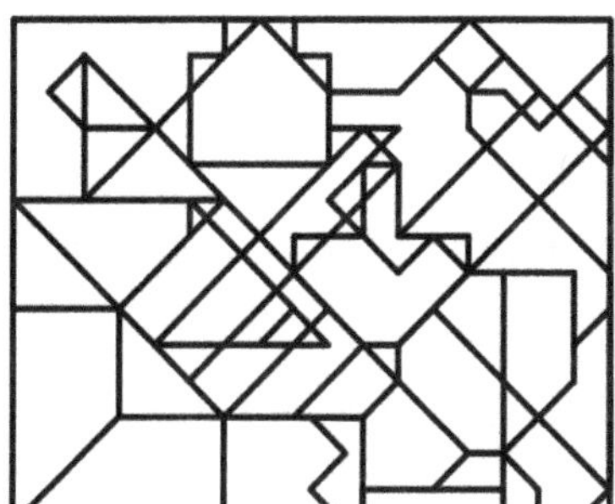

9.

7.
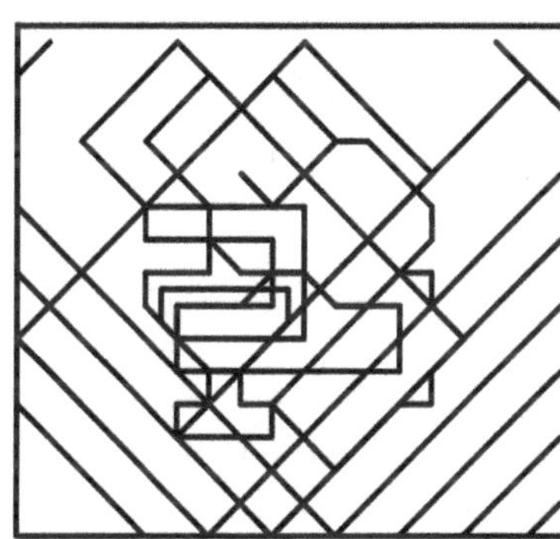

10.
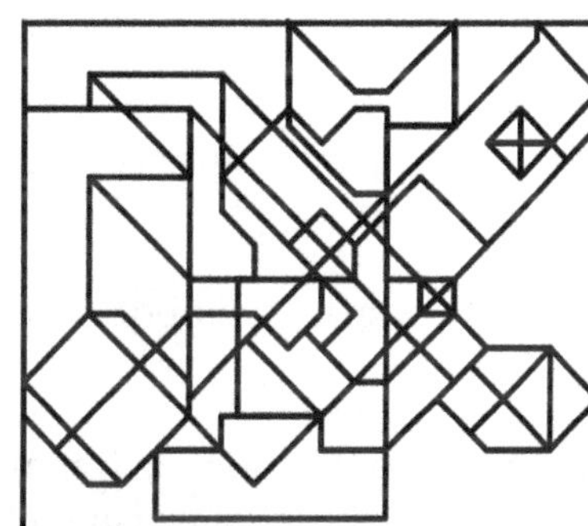

8.
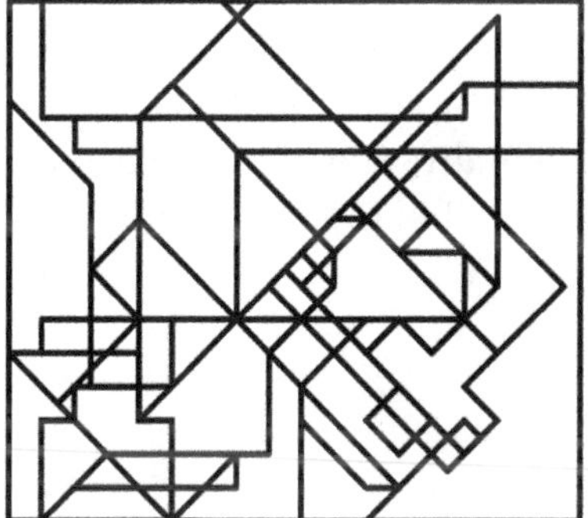

Answer Key

Pulleys

1. C: There are two rope segments supporting the weight in this figure, so the 100 pounds is divided by 2.

2. B: This is only one rope segments supporting the weight in this figure, so the man has to pull with the entire 100 pounds.

3. D: There are four rope segments supporting the weight in this figure, so the 100 pounds is divided by 4.

4. A: Even though the rope passes through five pulleys, it is still just the one segment supporting the 100 pounds.

5. C: There are three rope segments supporting the weight in this figure, so the 100 pounds is divided by 3.

6. C: There are two rope segments supporting the weight in this figure, so the 100 pounds is divided by 2.

7. D: There are four rope segments supporting the weight in this figure, so the 100 pounds is divided by 4.

8. C: There are three rope segments supporting the weight in this figure, so the 100 pounds is divided by 3.

9. A: This pulley system is actually making it more difficult for the man to raise the weight. Instead of the weight being supported by 2 rope segments, the rope the man is pulling on is attached to a pulley that is resisted by two rope segments, each of which carries 100 pounds of tension from the 100-pound weight. Therefore, the man has to pull with 200 pounds of force to lift the 100-pound weight here. As a consolation though, for every foot he pulls, the weight is raised two feet.

10. D: In this system, the 100 pounds of the weight is supported by two rope segments, each of which holds 50 pounds of tension. One of these segments is supported by two more rope segments, each of which holds half of the 50 pounds, or 25 pounds of tension. Finally, one of these segments is supported by yet another pair of rope segments, each of which holds half of the 25 pounds, or 12.5 pounds of tension. This rope is the one the man is pulling on.

Gears

1. B: Adjacent gears turn in opposite directions. The direction alternates 3 times between D and A.

2. D: Gear B is only about half as big as gear C, so it must be turning about twice as fast.

3. B: Gears B and D are adjacent in this figure, so they must be turning opposite directions.

4. C: Gears A and C are the same size, so they will turn at the same rate.

5. A: Adjacent gears turn in opposite directions. The direction alternates twice between B and D.

6. A: Gear A is between three and four times the size of B, so gear A will turn between a third and a quarter as fast as B.

7. C: This statement has two gears that are spaced three apart turning the same direction. All other statements given are possible.

8. D: This statement has two gears that are the same size turning at vastly different speeds. All other statements given are possible.

9. B: This statement has two gears that are spaced two apart turning in opposite directions. All other statements given are possible.

10. A: Although gears C and F are the same size, they are spaced three apart, so they cannot be turning the same direction. All other statements given are possible.

Mechanical Concepts

1. B: When an object is submerged into a container of liquid, it naturally displaces an amount of liquid equivalent to that object's volume. Object 2 is larger than object 1, so it will displace a greater volume of water and cause the level in tank B to be higher than that of tank A.

2. A: Newton's third law is used to understand that momentum is conserved in all collisions, and there is no indication that the balls merge into one upon colliding. Because of this, the balls will conserve momentum but exchange direction with the ball they collide with. In this case, ball 1 will rebound off ball 2 in the direction ball 2 was initially traveling; i.e., toward the upper left pocket (A). Conversely, ball 2 will follow ball 1's initial path toward the upper right pocket.

3. A: Consecutively attached gears alternate rotation direction, which means all even-numbered gears will turn in one corresponding direction, and all odd-numbered gears will turn the opposite corresponding direction. Since gear 1 is spinning counter-clockwise, all other odd-numbered gears will spin counter-clockwise as well (A). Gears 2 and 4 will spin clockwise.

4. B: The spring under object B is compressed noticeably further, and therefore has more elastic potential energy stored up to launch the ball higher into the air.

5. B: Water (along with nearly every other substance) seeks the lowest energy state in which to rest. Functionally, this means that the water level will be equally high in all parts of the watering can.

6. C: Every point on the belt, and consequently every point on the outside of each pulley, is moving at the same linear speed. Therefore, the pulley with the smallest circumference will rotate the fastest.

7. B: A pulley only reduces the amount of force required to lift an object if the weight is distributed across multiple sections of the rope, as is done in A. The force needed to pull the weight is reduced, but the distance the rope must be pulled increases in proportion to the number of pulleys used.

8. C: Only switch C creates a closed loop between the generator and the motor. Closing B creates a short circuit that does not pass through the motor, and closing A does nothing.

9. A: The mechanical advantage of an inclined plane can be determined by dividing the length by the height. Since both ramps are 5 feet tall, the mechanical advantage of ramp A is significantly lower at 4. As mechanical advantage decreases, the amount of force needed increases proportionally, so ramp A will require much more force.

10. B: Because of friction losses within the spring and between the ball and the surface, the ball will not travel as far the second time.

11. A: More force is required to push a boulder up a steeper incline because it has less mechanical advantage.

12. B: In ballistic flight, the horizontal component of velocity is essentially constant. At point B, the vertical component of the cannonball's velocity is zero, making the peak of its arc the slowest point.

13. A: Since the same volume of water that enters the pipe must exit as well, the water must travel significantly faster at point B to move the same volume, since the opening is much smaller. In other words, as the cross-sectional area of a pipe decreases, the speed of the water must increase to maintain the same volume flow rate.

14. A: In figure A, the load is centered much closer to the man and much farther from the wheel (fulcrum) than in figure B. This means that the man will have to bear a larger percentage of the weight of the load.

15. B: On truck A, the load is evenly distributed, while on truck B it is concentrated on one end, making it more likely to tip over.

16. B: The load on the stretcher is concentrated more closely to man B than man A, so man B is bearing more of the load.

17. A: The bracing in A is more solid because it extends higher up on the post.

18. A: Though the force of gravity is the same on both objects, object A will have had more time to build up speed, so it will hit the ground with more force than object B.

19. B: The wagon will roll more easily up the smoother slope because there is less rolling resistance.

20. C: The amount of liquid will be easiest to measure when the angle of the water line matches the lines drawn on the cylinder.

21. A: In figure A, the weight is much closer to the fulcrum, so it will require less force to raise.

22. C: Only switch C creates a closed loop from one terminal of the battery, through the light, and back to the other terminal.

23. A: Since a bowling ball weighs nearly 50 times as much as a baseball, the bowling ball's path will not be significantly affected by its collision with the baseball, so it will maintain its original trajectory.

24. B: Roll B will turn faster, both because it is lighter, thus having a lower moment of inertia, and because it requires less paper to be pulled to undergo a revolution.

25. B: Water in container B will cool more slowly because less of the surface of the water is exposed to the air.

26. A: Adding salt to water increases the density of the solution, making objects more likely to float on it.

27. A: Reflector A is farther from the center of the wheel. Therefore, it will travel more distance when the wheel turns.

28. C: Since air resistance on a javelin is negligible, and its horizontal velocity is effectively constant throughout its flight, the fastest point will be the point that has the greatest vertical velocity. Since point C is the lowest point, it is the point at which the maximum potential energy will have been converted to kinetic energy.

29. C: The child will travel to the approximately equivalent height on the other side of the swing set before returning to the initial side, as this is simple harmonic motion.

30. C: To maintain a constant volume flow rate, all the water must leave at the same rate at which it enters. Since both the entry and exit pipes have the same size, the water must be traveling at the same speed in both locations.

31. C: In the absence of air resistance, the acceleration of an object in freefall is entirely dependent on gravity and independent of the object's size, shape, or mass. Thus, both objects will fall at the same rate.

32. A: When the ball is released, it will continue traveling in whatever linear direction it was traveling at the time of release. The path it takes will be along a line that is tangent to the circle.

33. A: Since wheel A has a larger circumference, it travels farther on each full rotation.

34. B: The same amount of gas will be under greater pressure in the smaller tank since there is less volume for it to occupy.

35. B: Tank B is 100 feet higher than tank A, which means that the water it holds has an additional 100 feet of potential energy contributing to the pressure at the end of the hose.

36. C: Since the boxes are evenly distributed and their center is equal distance from both ropes, the two ropes support equal amounts of the weight.

37. A: Water is significantly more dense than oil, so an object dropped in water is more likely to float than an identical object dropped in oil.

38. B: In figure A, the weight is split between two sections of the rope, while in figure B, it is distributed among three sections. This means that it will only require a third of the effort to lift the weight in figure B, versus half the weight in figure A.

39. C: Potential energy is dependent on the height of an object relative to the ground. Both ramps are 10 feet tall, so the ball has the same amount of potential energy.

40. A: Oil is much more viscous than water, so it will take longer to reach the bottom of the funnel.

Parts Assembly

1. 4

2. 1

3. 2

4. 5

5. 2

6. 3

7. 5

8. 4

9. 1

10. 2

Paper Folding

1. A: When folded, the pattern will form a shape like the bottom half of a pyramid, with a large protrusion extending from the middle of one edge. Only choice A shows such an arrangement.

2. C: This the only choice that shows the correct-sized angled pieces.

3. D: A doesn't have the "notched" face shown in the pattern, and B and C don't have the five-sided face.

4. A: When the pattern is folded, the shape will have a base that flares out lengthwise, but not widthwise.

5. C: The notch at the base of the part will be facing downward, and the notch in the upper part will be facing away from the part.

6. B: The painted square will be at the top of an angled section that is perpendicular to the large rectangular base.

7. D: Begin by identifying which painted segments relate to which square on the final orientation. The correct orientation of the center-most painted triangle appears in B and D, while the correct orientation of the lower painted triangle appears in A and D, making D the correct answer.

8. A: The shapes of the two largest areas on the foldout correspond to the front and back of object A. None of the other objects include these shapes.

9. C: The two T-shaped sections are joined at the small end of the T, and are not rotated as in D.

10. B: The key to choosing between B and C here is noting how the two largest L shapes are joined. The vertex between the two L's is on the back side of B.

Rotated Blocks

1. B

2. A

3. C

4. D

5. A

6. C

7. E

8. D

Apertures

1. B: This corresponds to a side profile of the object. Choice C almost matches the top-view profile of the object, but the thicknesses are wrong. D closely approximates the front view of the object, but the corners are rounded, so the object won't pass through.

2. D: This corresponds to a side view of the object.

3. A: This corresponds to a side view of the object. Aperture C approximates a front view of the object, but is not big enough for the object to pass through.

4. B: This corresponds to a side view of the object.

5. C: Although the part has slanted pieces, it will appear square when viewed from the top, front, or side. The only aperture that could accommodate the part is the large rectangular aperture in C.

6. B: This corresponds to the profile of the object, as you look down the length of it. While the object could fit through a few of the other openings, only B represents an exact fit.

7. D: This opening matches the top view of the object.

8. E: This corresponds to the front or the side view of the object.

9. C: This corresponds to the side view of the object. The aperture in A is nearly accurate, but the corners of the elbow are not rounded.

10. B: This corresponds to a side view of the object.

Perspective Visualization

1. C: There are two ledges that protrude upward from the left side of the main base. Each ledge has a horizontal hole, and the base has two vertical holes. Based on this information, you can eliminate choices A and D, which show the ledge on the right side instead of the left. Of the remaining choices, C is correct because the holes through the ledges are not hidden in the side view, so the holes should not be drawn with dashed lines.

2. C: The part has a large protrusion that juts out toward the front. In an end view, the protrusion will appear to jut out toward the left, so this eliminates choices B and D. Of the remaining choices, only C has a solid line that indicates the slope on the ledge.

3. B: The part has an upper ledge, with a hollow cylinder going through the upper right corner of the ledge. The top view should show hollow lines indicating the hole through the ledge. In addition, the top ledge stops at the midpoint of the cylinder, so the lines indicating the top ledge should stop about halfway through the cylinder.

4. A: The part has radial symmetry, so the front view in this case will be the same as the end view.

5. D: The end view should have a dashed line near the bottom, because this line is hidden in the end view. Further up, there should be two solid parallel lines because the ledge is not hidden in the end view.

6. C: As viewed from the top, the diameter of the hole through the center of the part is slightly wider than the part of the hole that meets the sloped part. Thus, there should be a pair of solid lines that run through the center of the top view, and a pair of dashed lines just outside the solid lines.

7. A: The dashed lines in A correspond to the cutout shown in the end view, while the solid lines correspond to the cutout shown in the top view.

8. B: The correct end view will a horizontal dashed line representing the cutout shown in the front view and a solid vertical line representing the cut front corner.

9. A: The front and end views demonstrate that the pointed end of the shape will be on the right side in the top view. The front view shows that the shape continuously tapers from left to right until it nears the right edge, ruling out C.

10. D: The top view indicates that the diagonal section will run from top left to bottom right in the front view, ruling out A and C. Front view D correctly shows the hidden features with dashed lines.

Painted Blocks

1. The answer is 2. There is one block with only one side painted on the bottom level, next to the three-block high stack of blocks. The other block is hidden on the left side of the arrangement.

2. The answer is 2. There are two blocks with two sides painted in the left part of the arrangement: one in the front row, the other in the back row. The block in the back row is hidden, but is necessary to support the block above it.

3. The answer is 4. There is one block with three sides painted in the front row of the arrangement, and three blocks with three sides painted in the middle row.

4. The answer is 5. There are two blocks with four sides painted in the front row, two blocks in the middle row, and one block in the back row.

5. The answer is 1. The only block with five sides painted is the uppermost block.

6. The answer is 1. The only block with only one side painted is hidden, and it is on the left side of the arrangement.

7. The answer is 2. There is one block in the back row with two sides painted, and one block in the middle row.

8. The answer is 5. There are two blocks in the front row with three sides painted, two in the middle row, and one in the back.

9. The answer is 4. There are two blocks in the front row with four sides painted, one block in the middle, and one in the back.

10. The answer is 2. There is one block in the middle row with five sides painted, and one in the back.

Instrument Comprehension

1. B: The instruments show that the aircraft is flying level with its wings level and is on a NW heading. This is represented by choice B.

2. C: The instruments show that the aircraft is flying level with its wings banked right and is on a SW heading. This is represented by choice C.

3. C: The instruments show that the aircraft is flying level with its wings banked right and is on a N heading. This is represented by choice C.

4. A: The instruments show that the aircraft is flying level with its wings banked right and is on a E heading. This is represented by choice A.

5. C: The instruments show that the aircraft is descending with its wings banked right and is on a N heading. This is represented by choice C.

6. C: The instruments show that the aircraft is ascending with its wings banked left and is on a W heading. This is represented by choice C.

7. A: The instruments show that the aircraft is descending with its wings banked right and is on a W heading. This is represented by choice A.

8. B: The instruments show that the aircraft is descending with its wings banked right and is on a S heading. This is represented by choice B.

9. B: The instruments show that the aircraft is descending with its wings banked right and is on a NE heading. This is represented by choice B.

10. A: The instruments show that the aircraft is descending with its wings banked left and is on a W heading. This is represented by choice A.

11. C: The instruments show that the aircraft is flying level with its wings level and is on a SW heading. This is represented by choice C.

12. A: The instruments show that the aircraft is descending with its wings banked left and is on a SE heading. This is represented by choice A.

Hole Punching

1. B: Although the paper is folded several times, the hole passes through only two layers of paper, so there will be two holes. Based on this information, you can eliminate answer choices A, C, and E. When the paper is unfolded, the two holes will be in the positions shown in choice B.

2. E: The hole is punched through six layers of paper, so there will be six holes when the paper is fully unfolded. Based on this information, you can eliminate every answer choice except E.

3. D: When the triangles in the paper are unfolded, the pattern of holes will match that shown in answer choice C. However, when the paper is further unfolded along the vertical fold lines, four additional holes will appear that match the pattern shown in choice D.

4. A: The hole pierces five layers of paper, so there will be six holes when the paper is fully unfolded. Based on this information, you can eliminate every answer choice except A.

5. C: Although the paper is folded multiple times, each of the holes pierces only two layers of paper. Therefore, there will be four holes, so you can eliminate answer choices A, B, and D. When the paper is fully unfolded, two new holes will appear on the opposite side the diagonal line, as choice C shows.

6. D: With the paper folded in half twice like this, there will be one hole in each corner.

7. C: With the paper folded in half twice like this, there will be two holes in quarter, forming the shape of an *x*.

8. C: Both holes here pierce four layers. When you unfold the diagonal folds, you see that there will be holes in the corners in addition to the ones in the middle.

9. B: If you backtrack the location of the hole across each fold, you will note that four layers of paper were pierced. Since there is only one hole made, there can only be four holes in the correct answer.

10. E: If you backtrack the location of the hole across each fold, you will note that eight layers of paper were pierced, meaning there must be eight holes in the correct answer. Of the two options with eight holes, E matches the correct pattern.

Hidden Blocks

1. 13: Viewing the blocks from the front left side, the back row has columns of 3 and 1. The next row forward has columns of 2, 2, 1, and 1. The remaining columns of 2 and 1 are visible.

2. 14: Viewing the blocks from the front left side, the back row has columns of 3, 2, 2, 2, and 3. The front row has a single column of 2.

3. 14: Viewing the blocks from the front left side, the back row has columns of 3, 2, and 1. The next row forward has columns of 2, 2, and 1. The front row has 3 single blocks.

4. 13: Viewing the blocks from the front left side, the back row has columns of 2, 2, and 1. The next row forward has columns of 1, 2, 2, and 1. The front row has 2 single blocks.

5. 22: Viewing the blocks from the front left side, the back row has columns of 3, 3, 3, 3, 3, and 1. The next row forward has columns of 2 and 2. The front row has 2 single blocks.

6. 16: Viewing the blocks from the front left side, the back row has columns of 3, 2, and 1. The next row forward has a single column of 2. The next row forward has columns of 2 and 1. The front row has columns of 3, 1, and 1.

7. 18: Viewing the blocks from the front left side, the back row has columns of 3, 3, and 2. The next row forward has a single column of 3. The next row forward has a columns of 2, 2, and 1. The front row has 2 single blocks.

8. 19: Viewing the blocks from the front left side, the back row has columns of 3, 3, and 2. The next row forward has columns of 3, 1, and 1. The next row forward has columns of 2, 2, and 1. The front row has 1 single block.

9. 17: Viewing the blocks from the front left side, the back row has 1 single block. The next row forward has columns of 1, 2, and 1. The next row forward has 2 single blocks. The next row forward has 1 single block. The next row forward has columns of 2, 2, 1, 1, and 1. The front row has a single column of 2.

10. 17: Viewing the blocks from the front left side, the back row has columns of 2 and 3. The next row forward has columns of 1 and 2. The next row forward has columns of 2, 1, and 1. The front row has columns of 3 and 2.

Counting Touching Blocks

1. 6: 1 on the front, 2 on the back, 2 on the top, 1 on the bottom.

2. 3: 2 on the right, 1 on the top.

3. 6: 1 on the front, 3 on the left, 2 on the top.

4. 5: 1 on the back, 1 on the right, 3 on the top.

5. 5: 3 on the front, 2 on the top.

6. 9: 1 on the front, 3 on the back, 3 on the top, 2 on the bottom.

7. 4: 1 on the front, 1 on the back, 1 on the right, 1 on the bottom.

8. 3: 1 on the right, 2 on the top.

9. 5: 2 on the front, 1 on the back, 1 on the left, 1 on the bottom.

10. 9: 4 on the front, 4 on the back, 1 on the top.

11. 6: 2 on the back, 3 on the left, 1 on the bottom.

12. 4: 1 on the right, 3 on the top.

Cut-Ups

1. B

2. B

3. C

4. D

5. D

6. A

7. D

8. B

9. C

10. D

Hidden Figures

 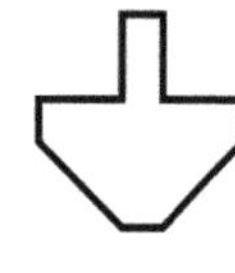 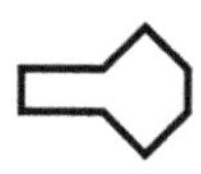  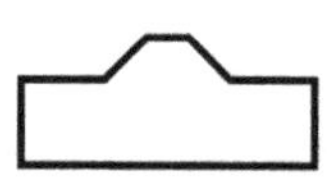

(A) 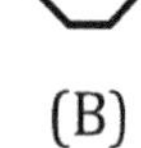 (B) (C) (D) (E)

1. (B)

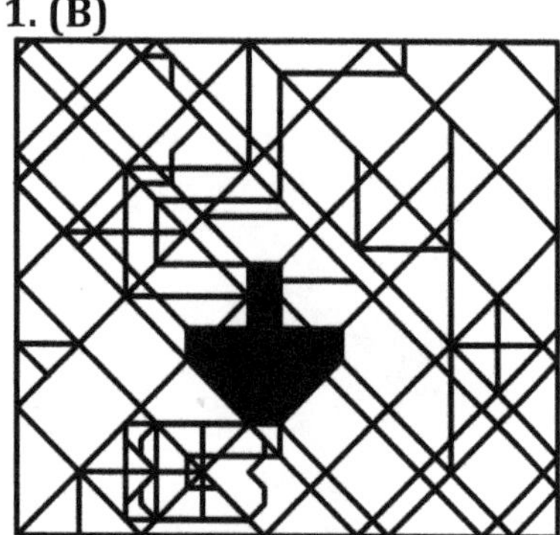

2. (D)

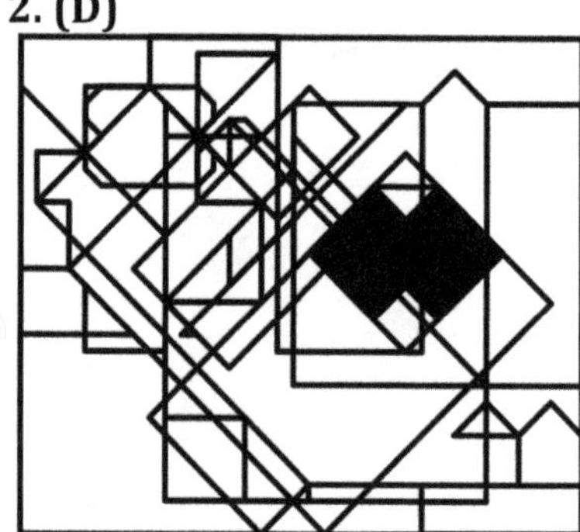

3. (E)

4. (C)

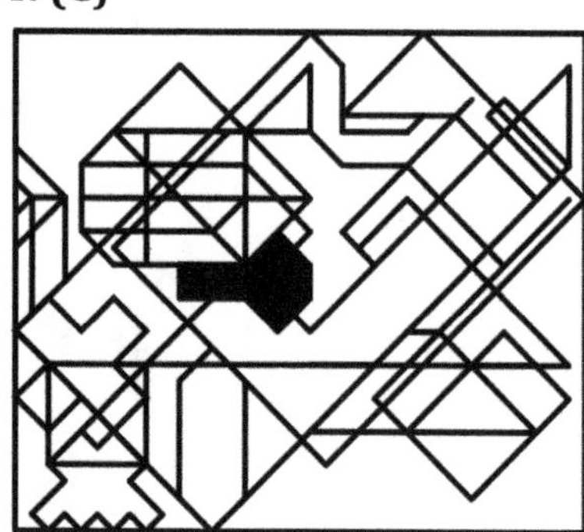

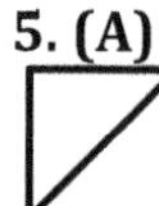

5. (A)

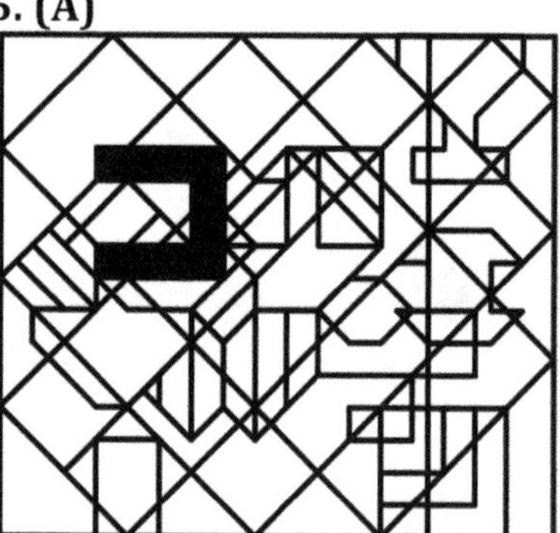

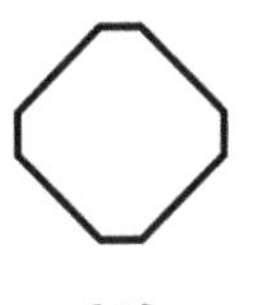
(A)

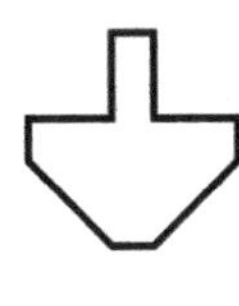
(B)

(C)

(D)

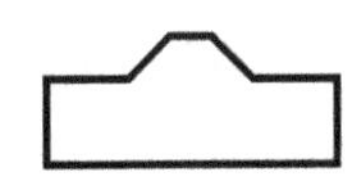
(E)

6. (B)

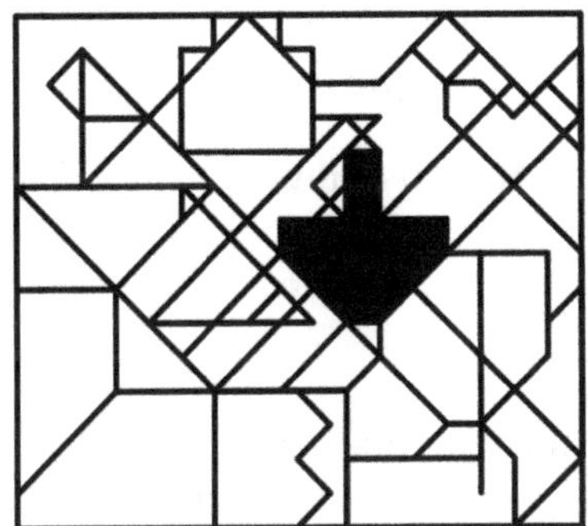

9. (C)

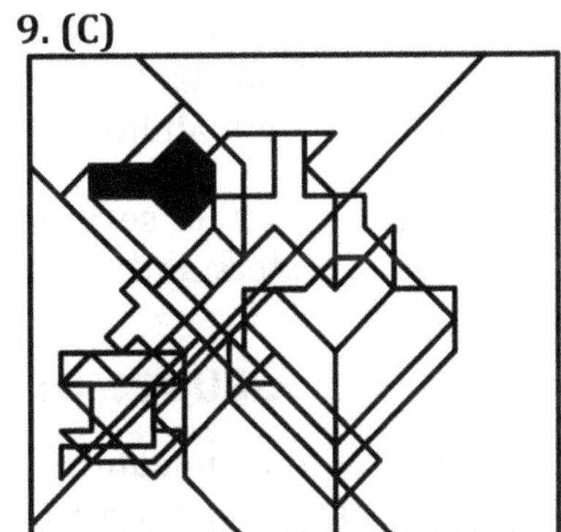

7. (E)

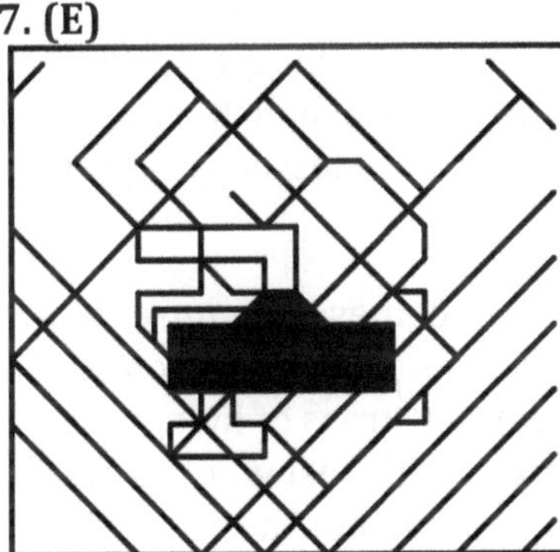

10. (A)

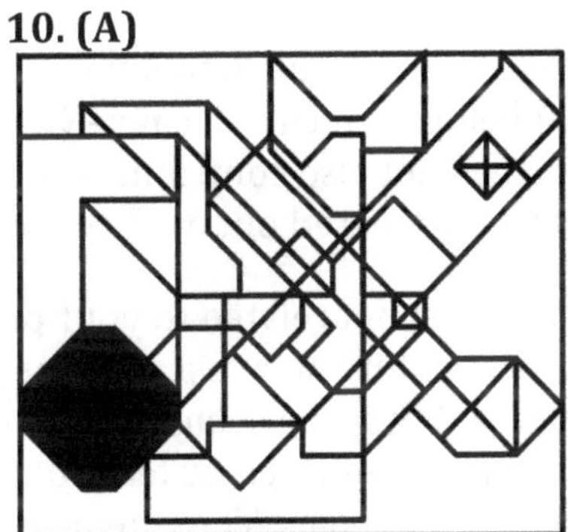

8. (D)

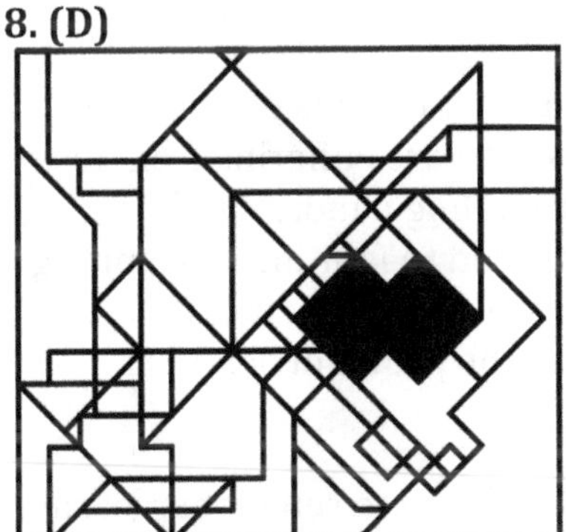

How to Overcome Test Anxiety

Just the thought of taking a test is enough to make most people a little nervous. A test is an important event that can have a long-term impact on your future, so it's important to take it seriously and it's natural to feel anxious about performing well. But just because anxiety is normal, that doesn't mean that it's helpful in test taking, or that you should simply accept it as part of your life. Anxiety can have a variety of effects. These effects can be mild, like making you feel slightly nervous, or severe, like blocking your ability to focus or remember even a simple detail.

If you experience test anxiety—whether severe or mild—it's important to know how to beat it. To discover this, first you need to understand what causes test anxiety.

Causes of Test Anxiety

While we often think of anxiety as an uncontrollable emotional state, it can actually be caused by simple, practical things. One of the most common causes of test anxiety is that a person does not feel adequately prepared for their test. This feeling can be the result of many different issues such as poor study habits or lack of organization, but the most common culprit is time management. Starting to study too late, failing to organize your study time to cover all of the material, or being distracted while you study will mean that you're not well prepared for the test. This may lead to cramming the night before, which will cause you to be physically and mentally exhausted for the test. Poor time management also contributes to feelings of stress, fear, and hopelessness as you realize you are not well prepared but don't know what to do about it.

Other times, test anxiety is not related to your preparation for the test but comes from unresolved fear. This may be a past failure on a test, or poor performance on tests in general. It may come from comparing yourself to others who seem to be performing better or from the stress of living up to expectations. Anxiety may be driven by fears of the future—how failure on this test would affect your educational and career goals. These fears are often completely irrational, but they can still negatively impact your test performance.

Elements of Test Anxiety

As mentioned earlier, test anxiety is considered to be an emotional state, but it has physical and mental components as well. Sometimes you may not even realize that you are suffering from test anxiety until you notice the physical symptoms. These can include trembling hands, rapid heartbeat, sweating, nausea, and tense muscles. Extreme anxiety may lead to fainting or vomiting. Obviously, any of these symptoms can have a negative impact on testing. It is important to recognize them as soon as they begin to occur so that you can address the problem before it damages your performance.

The mental components of test anxiety include trouble focusing and inability to remember learned information. During a test, your mind is on high alert, which can help you recall information and stay focused for an extended period of time. However, anxiety interferes with your mind's natural processes, causing you to blank out, even on the questions you know well. The strain of testing during anxiety makes it difficult to stay focused, especially on a test that may take several hours. Extreme anxiety can take a huge mental toll, making it difficult not only to recall test information but even to understand the test questions or pull your thoughts together.

Effects of Test Anxiety

Test anxiety is like a disease—if left untreated, it will get progressively worse. Anxiety leads to poor performance, and this reinforces the feelings of fear and failure, which in turn lead to poor performances on subsequent tests. It can grow from a mild nervousness to a crippling condition. If allowed to progress, test anxiety can have a big impact on your schooling, and consequently on your future.

Test anxiety can spread to other parts of your life. Anxiety on tests can become anxiety in any stressful situation, and blanking on a test can turn into panicking in a job situation. But fortunately, you don't have to let anxiety rule your testing and determine your grades. There are a number of relatively simple steps you can take to move past anxiety and function normally on a test and in the rest of life.

Physical Steps for Beating Test Anxiety

While test anxiety is a serious problem, the good news is that it can be overcome. It doesn't have to control your ability to think and remember information. While it may take time, you can begin taking steps today to beat anxiety.

Just as your first hint that you may be struggling with anxiety comes from the physical symptoms, the first step to treating it is also physical. Rest is crucial for having a clear, strong mind. If you are tired, it is much easier to give in to anxiety. But if you establish good sleep habits, your body and mind will be ready to perform optimally, without the strain of exhaustion. Additionally, sleeping well helps you to retain information better, so you're more likely to recall the answers when you see the test questions.

Getting good sleep means more than going to bed on time. It's important to allow your brain time to relax. Take study breaks from time to time so it doesn't get overworked, and don't study right before bed. Take time to rest your mind before trying to rest your body, or you may find it difficult to fall asleep.

Along with sleep, other aspects of physical health are important in preparing for a test. Good nutrition is vital for good brain function. Sugary foods and drinks may give a burst of energy but this burst is followed by a crash, both physically and emotionally. Instead, fuel your body with protein and vitamin-rich foods.

Also, drink plenty of water. Dehydration can lead to headaches and exhaustion, especially if your brain is already under stress from the rigors of the test. Particularly if your test is a long one, drink water during the breaks. And if possible, take an energy-boosting snack to eat between sections.

Along with sleep and diet, a third important part of physical health is exercise. Maintaining a steady workout schedule is helpful, but even taking 5-minute study breaks to walk can help get your blood pumping faster and clear your head. Exercise also releases endorphins, which contribute to a positive feeling and can help combat test anxiety.

When you nurture your physical health, you are also contributing to your mental health. If your body is healthy, your mind is much more likely to be healthy as well. So take time to rest, nourish your body with healthy food and water, and get moving as much as possible. Taking these physical steps will make you stronger and more able to take the mental steps necessary to overcome test anxiety.

Mental Steps for Beating Test Anxiety

Working on the mental side of test anxiety can be more challenging, but as with the physical side, there are clear steps you can take to overcome it. As mentioned earlier, test anxiety often stems from lack of preparation, so the obvious solution is to prepare for the test. Effective studying may be the most important weapon you have for beating test anxiety, but you can and should employ several other mental tools to combat fear.

First, boost your confidence by reminding yourself of past success—tests or projects that you aced. If you're putting as much effort into preparing for this test as you did for those, there's no reason you should expect to fail here. Work hard to prepare; then trust your preparation.

Second, surround yourself with encouraging people. It can be helpful to find a study group, but be sure that the people you're around will encourage a positive attitude. If you spend time with others who are anxious or cynical, this will only contribute to your own anxiety. Look for others who are motivated to study hard from a desire to succeed, not from a fear of failure.

Third, reward yourself. A test is physically and mentally tiring, even without anxiety, and it can be helpful to have something to look forward to. Plan an activity following the test, regardless of the outcome, such as going to a movie or getting ice cream.

When you are taking the test, if you find yourself beginning to feel anxious, remind yourself that you know the material. Visualize successfully completing the test. Then take a few deep, relaxing breaths and return to it. Work through the questions carefully but with confidence, knowing that you are capable of succeeding.

Developing a healthy mental approach to test taking will also aid in other areas of life. Test anxiety affects more than just the actual test—it can be damaging to your mental health and even contribute to depression. It's important to beat test anxiety before it becomes a problem for more than testing.

Study Strategy

Being prepared for the test is necessary to combat anxiety, but what does being prepared look like? You may study for hours on end and still not feel prepared. What you need is a strategy for test prep. The next few pages outline our recommended steps to help you plan out and conquer the challenge of preparation.

Step 1: Scope Out the Test

Learn everything you can about the format (multiple choice, essay, etc.) and what will be on the test. Gather any study materials, course outlines, or sample exams that may be available. Not only will this help you to prepare, but knowing what to expect can help to alleviate test anxiety.

Step 2: Map Out the Material

Look through the textbook or study guide and make note of how many chapters or sections it has. Then divide these over the time you have. For example, if a book has 15 chapters and you have five days to study, you need to cover three chapters each day. Even better, if you have the time, leave an extra day at the end for overall review after you have gone through the material in depth.

If time is limited, you may need to prioritize the material. Look through it and make note of which sections you think you already have a good grasp on, and which need review. While you are studying, skim quickly through the familiar sections and take more time on the challenging parts.

Write out your plan so you don't get lost as you go. Having a written plan also helps you feel more in control of the study, so anxiety is less likely to arise from feeling overwhelmed at the amount to cover.

STEP 3: GATHER YOUR TOOLS

Decide what study method works best for you. Do you prefer to highlight in the book as you study and then go back over the highlighted portions? Or do you type out notes of the important information? Or is it helpful to make flashcards that you can carry with you? Assemble the pens, index cards, highlighters, post-it notes, and any other materials you may need so you won't be distracted by getting up to find things while you study.

If you're having a hard time retaining the information or organizing your notes, experiment with different methods. For example, try color-coding by subject with colored pens, highlighters, or post-it notes. If you learn better by hearing, try recording yourself reading your notes so you can listen while in the car, working out, or simply sitting at your desk. Ask a friend to quiz you from your flashcards, or try teaching someone the material to solidify it in your mind.

STEP 4: CREATE YOUR ENVIRONMENT

It's important to avoid distractions while you study. This includes both the obvious distractions like visitors and the subtle distractions like an uncomfortable chair (or a too-comfortable couch that makes you want to fall asleep). Set up the best study environment possible: good lighting and a comfortable work area. If background music helps you focus, you may want to turn it on, but otherwise keep the room quiet. If you are using a computer to take notes, be sure you don't have any other windows open, especially applications like social media, games, or anything else that could distract you. Silence your phone and turn off notifications. Be sure to keep water close by so you stay hydrated while you study (but avoid unhealthy drinks and snacks).

Also, take into account the best time of day to study. Are you freshest first thing in the morning? Try to set aside some time then to work through the material. Is your mind clearer in the afternoon or evening? Schedule your study session then. Another method is to study at the same time of day that you will take the test, so that your brain gets used to working on the material at that time and will be ready to focus at test time.

STEP 5: STUDY!

Once you have done all the study preparation, it's time to settle into the actual studying. Sit down, take a few moments to settle your mind so you can focus, and begin to follow your study plan. Don't give in to distractions or let yourself procrastinate. This is your time to prepare so you'll be ready to fearlessly approach the test. Make the most of the time and stay focused.

Of course, you don't want to burn out. If you study too long you may find that you're not retaining the information very well. Take regular study breaks. For example, taking five minutes out of every hour to walk briskly, breathing deeply and swinging your arms, can help your mind stay fresh.

As you get to the end of each chapter or section, it's a good idea to do a quick review. Remind yourself of what you learned and work on any difficult parts. When you feel that you've mastered the material, move on to the next part. At the end of your study session, briefly skim through your notes again.

But while review is helpful, cramming last minute is NOT. If at all possible, work ahead so that you won't need to fit all your study into the last day. Cramming overloads your brain with more information than it can process and retain, and your tired mind may struggle to recall even previously learned information when it is overwhelmed with last-minute study. Also, the urgent nature of cramming and the stress placed on your brain contribute to anxiety. You'll be more likely to go to the test feeling unprepared and having trouble thinking clearly.

So don't cram, and don't stay up late before the test, even just to review your notes at a leisurely pace. Your brain needs rest more than it needs to go over the information again. In fact, plan to finish your studies by noon or early afternoon the day before the test. Give your brain the rest of the day to relax or focus on other things, and get a good night's sleep. Then you will be fresh for the test and better able to recall what you've studied.

Step 6: Take a Practice Test

Many courses offer sample tests, either online or in the study materials. This is an excellent resource to check whether you have mastered the material, as well as to prepare for the test format and environment.

Check the test format ahead of time: the number of questions, the type (multiple choice, free response, etc.), and the time limit. Then create a plan for working through them. For example, if you have 30 minutes to take a 60-question test, your limit is 30 seconds per question. Spend less time on the questions you know well so that you can take more time on the difficult ones.

If you have time to take several practice tests, take the first one open book, with no time limit. Work through the questions at your own pace and make sure you fully understand them. Gradually work up to taking a test under test conditions: sit at a desk with all study materials put away and set a timer. Pace yourself to make sure you finish the test with time to spare and go back to check your answers if you have time.

After each test, check your answers. On the questions you missed, be sure you understand why you missed them. Did you misread the question (tests can use tricky wording)? Did you forget the information? Or was it something you hadn't learned? Go back and study any shaky areas that the practice tests reveal.

Taking these tests not only helps with your grade, but also aids in combating test anxiety. If you're already used to the test conditions, you're less likely to worry about it, and working through tests until you're scoring well gives you a confidence boost. Go through the practice tests until you feel comfortable, and then you can go into the test knowing that you're ready for it.

Test Tips

On test day, you should be confident, knowing that you've prepared well and are ready to answer the questions. But aside from preparation, there are several test day strategies you can employ to maximize your performance.

First, as stated before, get a good night's sleep the night before the test (and for several nights before that, if possible). Go into the test with a fresh, alert mind rather than staying up late to study.

Try not to change too much about your normal routine on the day of the test. It's important to eat a nutritious breakfast, but if you normally don't eat breakfast at all, consider eating just a protein bar. If you're a coffee drinker, go ahead and have your normal coffee. Just make sure you time it so that the caffeine doesn't wear off right in the middle of your test. Avoid sugary beverages, and drink enough water to stay hydrated but not so much that you need a restroom break 10 minutes into the test. If your test isn't first thing in the morning, consider going for a walk or doing a light workout before the test to get your blood flowing.

Allow yourself enough time to get ready, and leave for the test with plenty of time to spare so you won't have the anxiety of scrambling to arrive in time. Another reason to be early is to select a good seat. It's helpful to sit away from doors and windows, which can be distracting. Find a good seat, get out your supplies, and settle your mind before the test begins.

When the test begins, start by going over the instructions carefully, even if you already know what to expect. Make sure you avoid any careless mistakes by following the directions.

Then begin working through the questions, pacing yourself as you've practiced. If you're not sure on an answer, don't spend too much time on it, and don't let it shake your confidence. Either skip it and come back later, or eliminate as many wrong answers as possible and guess among the remaining ones. Don't dwell on these questions as you continue—put them out of your mind and focus on what lies ahead.

Be sure to read all of the answer choices, even if you're sure the first one is the right answer. Sometimes you'll find a better one if you keep reading. But don't second-guess yourself if you do immediately know the answer. Your gut instinct is usually right. Don't let test anxiety rob you of the information you know.

If you have time at the end of the test (and if the test format allows), go back and review your answers. Be cautious about changing any, since your first instinct tends to be correct, but make sure you didn't misread any of the questions or accidentally mark the wrong answer choice. Look over any you skipped and make an educated guess.

At the end, leave the test feeling confident. You've done your best, so don't waste time worrying about your performance or wishing you could change anything. Instead, celebrate the successful completion of this test. And finally, use this test to learn how to deal with anxiety even better next time.

Review Video: Test Anxiety
Visit mometrix.com/academy and enter code: 100340

Important Qualification

Not all anxiety is created equal. If your test anxiety is causing major issues in your life beyond the classroom or testing center, or if you are experiencing troubling physical symptoms related to your anxiety, it may be a sign of a serious physiological or psychological condition. If this sounds like your situation, we strongly encourage you to seek professional help.

Online Resources

Due to our efforts to try to keep this book to a manageable length, we've created a link that will give you access to all of your online resources:

mometrix.com/resources719/mechapt

It's Your Moment, Let's Celebrate It!

Share your story @mometrixtestpreparation

www.ingramcontent.com/pod-product-compliance
Lightning Source LLC
Chambersburg PA
CBHW082003150426
42814CB00005BA/212

* 9 7 8 1 5 1 6 7 0 5 3 2 0 *